Finding centre P28

Support P.63 ALSO P.39 (feeling support)

Always be aware of your body, breath & voice.
Never vocalize without support. P.45 never speak until you are
completely ready. P.47

Biggest problem we all have as speakers: Lack
of breath and support P.39

"whenever I'm asked for my key tip about speaking
before the public, I always answer, 'Breathe. Take
breath when you speak. Many of us under stress
of speaking publicly, do exactly the opposite and
stop breathing just when we need it the most.
Frequently we try to speak on one long breath
rather than supporting the with frequent and
regular breathing. The truck is to keep breathing
as you speak." P.39

" as you walk on the stage, breathe
" as you wait for action or to respond, breathe.

" Do not push anything from the throat" P.61

" At this stage of my career, I feel that the understanding
and correct use of support is the most important
aspect of good, strong, healthy voice work. P.63

you should use support in your daily speaking P.63
(in every day contexts)
use support at noisy parties

"Many actors support at the performance and forget
at the party. P.64

P71 Tension of the jaw, tongue, throat, etc arise from one
common misconception: that the voice operates from the
neck up and not from the deep breath support system that
comes from below. Until there is a marriage between

Head resonance.! P94

It's silly to take too much breath. a huge breath to say a
casual "no" is a waste of power, but you might need massive
support if the "no" was packed with passion or delivered to
a crowd. The natural breath is when you breathe in,
feel supply, and when ready, breathe out. the moment of
readiness is not a ponderous, held position but it does take
a fraction and when reached makes you feel complete
before you breathe out. The support action should be: I breathe
in, feel ready, & breathe out. This recognition of support
& how much to support seems to me to be the most important
thing in training any speaker" P.48 seems to me it's a
good way to read too.

When you speak without support you build up voice tightness! P.47

"Funnily enough we have to learn to take in a breath when we need it. It is not always a natural reaction. P. 47

"Never speak until you are completely ready. At first you might think this is a laborious process, but in the end you start to feel this ready support position very quickly — in fact faster than a non supported position when the breath system is free the breath falls in, low and full, quite easily.

P. 47-48

Read p. 48 re breath support
When breathing while not planning to speak
I see no reason not to practice deep
breathing. (THROAT)

"Keep the head up and looking out at the world. P.29

"Keep the neck free" P 33

"You must be able to breathe, keep the voice open, and the jaw released in order to make vocal sense"
P. 36

"Keep checking that the throat feels free
always act from the center" P. 38

THROAT CONSTRICTIONS- P.68

Two blinks of the eye is sufficient to get full support.
Humming in the head resonators will relieve throat tension.

Co-ordinating your breath to support your voice is of course
essential. But how much breath does one take (and remember
it must be a deep abdominal breath. But "deep" doesn't
necessarily mean a lot of quantity of breath. Usually, a brief
pause (say two quick flicks of the eye lash) will supply you with

The Actor Speaks

sufficient breath. If you sense a
lot of breath will be needed, take what you need. But usually
we overbreath. A "puff of the stuff" is all you usually need.

Patsy Rodenburg heads the Voice Departments at Britain's
Royal National Theatre and London's Guildhall School of Speech
and Drama where she has worked with and trained some of
Britain's best actors, giving voice workshops and tutorials to
groups and individuals throughout the world. After graduating
from the Central School of Speech and Drama, she worked with
the Royal Shakespeare Company for nine years as well as with
ensembles such as Cheek by Jowl, Shared Experience and Theatre
de Complicite, creating in 1990 the first Voice Department at the
Royal National Theatre In North America she has frequently
worked with actors at the Stratford Festival Theatre in Ontario,
Canada, in the professional actor training programme at Southern
Methodist University, Dallas, Texas, and at the Michael Howard
Studio for actors in New York City. In London she also gives
classes at the Voice and Speech Centre which she helped to found.

Patsy Rodenburg has written two previous best-selling books about
the voice for Methuen: *The Right to Speak* (1992) and *The Need for
Words* (1993). These together with *The Actor Speaks* form a trilogy
of thought and technique about voice and text work. She has also
made a video, *A Voice of Your Own* (1994), available from
Vanguard Productions, Norwich, England. *The Right to Speak* is
also available on audio cassette.

Breathe, take breath when you speak.
Many of us under stress of speaking publicly
do exactly the opposite and stop breathing
just when we need it most" p. 39

See P. 53 - Breathe in and feel the support -
take enough to count out loud
as you feel more confident in the support
and feel the power of the breath settling
in the body, speed up the counting, as long
as you stay free in the body, you'll be surprised
how quickly the breath comes in - - - .

The breath can be either thru the nose or mouth. P. 6

Dryness of mouth - P. 177
Humming in the head resonators immediately
relieves pressure on the throat. P. 289-290

Also by Patsy Rodenburg

The Right to Speak: Working with the Voice
The Need for Words: Voice and the Text

Audio cassette

The Right to Speak (Reed Audio)

Video tape

A Voice of Your Own (Vanguard Productions)

The Actor Speaks
Voice and the Performer

PATSY RODENBURG

First published in paperback by
PALGRAVE MACMILLAN™ in 2002
175 Fifth Avenue, New York, N.Y. 10010 and
Houndmills, Basingstoke, Hampshire, England RG21 6XS.
Companies and representatives throughout the world.

PALGRAVE MACMILLAN is the global academic imprint of the
Palgrave Macmillan division of St. Martin's Press, LLC and of
Palgrave Macmillan Ltd. Macmillan® is a registered trademark in the
United States, United Kingdom and other countries. Palgrave is a
registered trademark in the European Union and other countries.

ISBN 0-312-29514-6

Published in the United States by St. Martin's Press, 2000

First edition published in the United Kingdom by Methuen Drama,
1997.

Library of Congress Cataloguing-in-Publication Data available from
the Library of Congress

First PALGRAVE MACMILLAN edition: August 2002
10 9 8 7 6 5 4 3 2 1

Printed in the United States of America.

To A.F.

with much love

True ease in writing comes from art, not chance,
As those move easiest who have learned to dance.

Alexander Pope

Praise for Patsy Rodenburg

'Patsy was absolutely invaluable to my beginning to take on the awesome task of playing King Lear. Having been away from the stage for so long, it was vital to have someone who really knew what they were talking about and in whom I could put my trust. She is a great teacher – and I think it absolutely fair to say I could not have played the King without her.'

Ian Holm, 1997 Olivier Award for Best Actor

'Working with Patsy is a unique experience. She gives you a wondrously simple way of releasing the voice and the body – which also becomes a way of life.'

Anna Massey, Actress

'Patsy's work has been a source of inspiration to countless actors. This book shares her years of experience in the theatre in an immediately accessible way.'

Joan Washington, Dialect Coach

'Like athletes and dancers, actors need to warm-up before appearing in public. Patsy's classes during a demanding play like *The Madness of King George* were invaluable. And her books are a wonderful top-up.'

Nigel Hawthorne, Actor

'Patsy Rodenburg's work is holistic – a free voice, a free body and a free flow of emotion are intimately connected. She totally reinforces whatever I am trying to achieve and in many cases she is the one who creates breakthroughs for the actors with her perceptive and sympathetic skills.'

Mike Alfreds, Director

'Patsy Rodenburg's work is not merely concerned with connecting actors with their voices, but in connecting their heads to their hearts. This is an indispensable handbook for actors who are serious about their craft. . . . When Patsy speaks actors should listen, so that when actors get to speak, we all listen.'

John Caird, Director

'Patsy doesn't just "teach voice". She has a very free and open approach in guiding you to find your own voice and not one which is remotely imposed. She has the great gift of making it seem easy.'

Geraldine McEwan, Actress

'The great thing about working with Patsy Rodenburg is that she takes the "mystery" out of speaking in the theatre. She makes it simple and that's her great gift.'

Richard Wilson, Actor

'Struggling with a rehearsal of a platform on the Olivier stage, a reassuring voice called out from the daunting auditorium. I was soon reminded why Patsy is such a unique, dynamic guide in getting us back to the vocal pathway of instinctive expression – by undoing all the habitual blockages of our daily conditioning. Patsy and the "way of the voice" are inseparable.'

Joseph Fiennes, Actor

'Patsy Rodenburg's guidance and the clarity and directness of her approach have been invaluable to me.'   Ralph Fiennes, Actor

'What leaves actors tongue-tied for years, Patsy releases in minutes. Not as a result of a mystical process, but through simple, practical actions that can empower anyone – whatever their background or nationality – with the pleasure and ability to possess and communicate through language. And, more importantly, the ability to speak it in their way.'

Simon McBurney, Actor and Director, Theatre de Complicite

Contents

Foreword

When I went to the Central School of Speech and Drama in 1954, I thought I knew the sort of thing I was expecting – lots of work in relaxation, a bit of breathing, some movement, a few voice exercises, and lots and lots of acting. Not many weeks had passed before I realised that the most important thing was first, the relaxation, then the breathing and then the voice. The voice training I received at Central from Cecily Berry and Clifford Turner laid the groundwork for what was to become a way of life.

After many years in this profession, I find that there is a tendency to come to a play thinking, 'this is one that I will be able to manage with comparatively little trouble'. You don't foresee any problems and you hurry confidently into rehearsals. This scenario, in fact, has never proved to be the case for me because always, in every play, there is a different kind of problem that you haven't had to deal with before and, in most instances, it will concern the voice. In Hugh Whitemore's play, *Pack of Lies*, for instance, I was playing a very ordinary Ruislip housewife. I found it difficult to project not only the character's voice, but also her emotions, to the back of the theatre. I found I longed to come walking down the stairs and bellow 'My Lord of Buckingham . . . !' The answer lies in Patsy's book. Back you come each time to your technique and you find that there are ways of projecting your voice in any circumstance.

I have always maintained that the difference between an amateur and a professional is that the amateur only has to sustain a performance for a week during a year. The professional, if he is lucky, has to sustain it for much longer and this relies completely on the voice and the use of the voice.

I never met Patsy Rodenburg at Central because we were there at different times, but I met her later at the National Theatre. I can honestly say that it is thanks to Patsy that, when I have been in trouble with my voice, she has been able to reassure me and give me some exercises which have enabled me to go on that night but, more importantly, for the rest of the run.

I am not a natural singer (!), and when I was cast as Desiree Arnfeldt in *A Little Night Music* at the National Theatre, I told Patsy that I was worried about sustaining my voice during the scene where I sang 'Send In The Clowns'. The scene was set in my bedroom and all I had by way of a 'set' was a rose-covered bed, on which I had to sit to sing the number. This was all I had to 'hang on to'. Patsy explained that if I pushed down on the bed with my hands, it would raise the diaphragm, which would enable me to breathe properly and the voice would take care of itself. This is exactly what happened and, in fact, Patsy arranged for the bed to be made harder so that it was easier for me to push down on it.

It is essential to warm up your voice before a performance and the best thing you can possibly have is a class with Patsy. This is the way I have felt most confident about going on. By doing exercises, it is one way of getting rid of nerves, or at least utilising them, so that you have something really positive to think about and concentrate on while getting ready to go on. If you cannot have Patsy in person, then her book is the next best thing.

All the great performances I have seen have nearly always come down to the actor and his voice. All the training in the world will not help if the basic training on the voice has not been done. Patsy Rodenburg's book is a Bible. Having read it, I would now feel insecure without it. Even opening it and reading at random whets your appetite to read further and learn more about the voice. I intend to keep it by me at all times – a 'security blanket' which I know will never let me down.

Judi Dench

Introduction

The actor speaks in many voices and passes through many stages of work before coming face to face with an audience. This book takes you through a process that will help you speak on-stage in any and every circumstance. My two previous books, *The Right to Speak* and *The Need for Words*, were written for a wide-ranging audience. This volume is wholly for the actor. And I hope performers everywhere will find it a worthwhile and useful manual. I hope, too, it will take away any fear they may have of speaking on a stage.

To rehearse a part all day and perform on-stage each evening is, vocally, an athletic feat. The natural abilities of the inspired amateur and skilful novice performer are simply not enough to get you through a career as a serious actor. To speak a heightened text clearly to hundreds of people requires a huge vocal extension. To express passion and charged ideas takes enormous vocal range and energy whatever the size of the playing space. And to sustain this kind of work again and again over years takes a combination of consummate craft and dedication. To speak and then sing, to sing and then speak, physically to exert yourself on-stage and then go into speaking or singing, are demanding activities that require skill and stamina. A young working professional performer quickly learns that the chameleon-like nature of playing roles also means extending (and even bending) the voice and the body into new and different shapes. This sort of work – the sheer preparation it takes to perform effortlessly – is a side of acting which the public never sees. But the actor must go through the process every day.

These demands have always challenged actors but today the challenges are more intense than ever, especially where the voice and speaking are concerned. Not only must an actor use his or her voice in a theatre and sound real and believable, but he or she must also be able to use the voice successfully on film, television and radio. The most successful careers put actors in constantly changing situations so they can earn a livelihood. You will quickly learn that your voice, even more than your looks, may be your most valuable asset. This is where the work of a voice coach comes into play.

I have been teaching voice for twenty years to all kinds of actors at every stage of their careers. I love doing it because I love actors and admire the extraordinary courage it takes to face an audience night after night. Each day I am either in a classroom at the Guildhall School of Music and Drama or backstage at the Royal National Theatre preparing an actor to meet an audience. And how varied the work with actors can be. It seems the right time now for me to put down, in the most practical and easy to follow manner, the primary principles which I think enable the actor to speak.

What I offer you here is neither new nor radical, though quite a number of the ideas and individual exercises in Stages One, Two and Three are ones which I have developed out of necessity. If anything, I think what I have to say is quite traditional. I am not afraid to cite useful vocal techniques from the past even when they might not be in vogue today. I will use anything to prompt an actor to speak if I think it will help. Many of the exercises and suggested tips in what follows may seem to you repetitious. But proper vocal technique, I believe, needs to be worked on by means of repetition. By the end of this volume, however, I hope the knowledge will be second nature. I hope, too, that what I offer will inspire you in your work. I will be talking about issues and techniques which good actors have always known about and which I teach and reinforce each day in my work with performers. Perhaps by putting the knowledge all together in a stage by stage pattern, actors at all levels will benefit from what ought to be a kind of collective knowledge.

The structure I have chosen to present the work reflects the seven stages of an actor's life. You might be a young acting student learning how to work on your voice for the very first time and just at the start of your training, or a seasoned professional actor looking for tips or that bit of the training you never had or may have forgotten. So you can read this book in different ways for different needs: seven years of development, seven weeks of a workshop or even a seven-hour refresher course in the essentials of voice work. I have laid out the work in the stages I teach it. Stages One through Three mirror the work I would do in a three-year training programme. Stages Four through Seven are based on the work I do as a voice coach with individual performers and ensembles of actors.

In the later stages of work I speak quite a bit just about acting based on work I have seen. As a voice teacher and coach I have held a privileged position. I have been in rehearsal rooms with some of the finest actors and directors of our time. I have seen extraordinary performances come to life before my eyes. I have worked with students who have become major stars and I have watched from the wings as magnificent actors have made theatrical history on-stage in a particular role. And to whatever degree it has been helpful, the voice work I have done with these performers forms the basis of what I know about the actor's voice. My work is never theoretical but always practical.

One of the words you will hear me use again and again throughout this volume is 'craft'. Acting is a craft, and learning to speak, as a performer must, is one the of the fundamental techniques you simply cannot go on-stage without knowing how to do properly. One of the reasons I am writing this book is because I find acting craft is in serious peril. Drama departments all over the West are cutting down on essential training techniques like voice – it is one of the most expensive and time-consuming parts of training. It is also the side of training which yields slow, though steady, results. But cutting back on craft training is a false economy. No one who has prepared actors professionally can honestly put hand on heart and say it is possible to teach an actor thoroughly without engendering technical fluency. And crafting a performer takes time (generally three years). No voice or speech teacher with any genuine knowledge of the demands of theatre could realistically train a voice in just one year without at least seven hours a week of technical work (covering the basic areas of body, breath, voice and speech). If the trend continues and more hours are taken away from this fundamental first year of training, the spoken word in theatre will not only be in serious danger, it will decline.

The word 'technique' has had a rough press over the last twenty years or so. Younger actors tend to believe that technique will hamper their creativity. There was a time when actors, particularly British ones, were famed for their technical performance skills but were thought disconnected from their feelings. The rejection of certain aspects of technique during the 1960s and 1970s was perhaps a necessary stage for actors to go through in order to break the sometimes rigid application of craft work which did make them sound superior but passionless.

I am a firm believer in technique. Technique is not the end of a process but the beginning of one. Well-applied technique can liberate the actor, I think. I know it does because I've seen it work. I am not suggesting that the actor should think always about technique either in rehearsal or performance, but that the technical work is done so well that it can be forgotten as the imaginative life of the character takes over the actor. That is the transformation we in the audience wait for when the actor speaks.

In writing this book I should, in truth, acknowledge every student, actor, director and writer with whom I have worked over the years. There are, however, numerous people who have helped me either practically with the preparation of the manuscript or with whom I discussed ideas at great length as the book came to life. So, my special thanks to Mike Alfreds, Annabel Arden, Cicely Berry, Mary Carter, Annie Castledine, Sharon Clark, Peter Clough, Ghita Cohen, Garfield Davis, Judi Dench, Gregory Doran, Richard Eyre, Andrew Ferguson, Antonia Franceschi, Jane Gibson, Michael Howard, Nicholas Hytner, Brigid Larmour, Sue Lefton, Robert Lepage, Anna Massey, Simon McBurney, Kelly McEvenue, Nancy Meckler, Jeannette Nelson, Trevor Nunn, Tim Pigott-Smith, Bonnie Raphael, John Roberts, Chattie Salaman, Alaknanda Samarth, Fiona Shaw, Antony Sher, Christina Shewell, Ann Skinner, Jane Suffling, Harriet Walter, Deborah Warner, Joan Washington, Richard Wilson, Nicholas Wright, all of my students at the Guildhall School of Music and Drama and my publisher and editor, Michael Earley, and the staff at Methuen and Reed Books.

Patsy Rodenburg
London
December 1996

Stage One
THE ACTOR FIRST SPEAKS

Grey September. I walk into a room at London's Guildhall School of Music and Drama to meet twenty-four new and nervous students. They have all been through a gruelling audition process but this morning is the real beginning: their first steps towards becoming professional actors. They come from all kinds of backgrounds and from around the world. They are all different shapes, sizes and temperaments. But they each share something in common – they all want to be actors. Most have no real idea what that means yet. Each one has talent. Everyone is brimming with energy and passion. But what they all need is technique and the essential tools to develop a voice that is genuinely their own. So we begin to work on how the actor speaks.

I look around the room. I remember each person from his or her audition. Some can speak fluently, others can barely get out a sentence without feeling self-conscious. Some are extremely literate and may have been to university, while others cannot read well at all and have chosen drama school over college. Some have naturally good voices, others will have to labour incessantly to give themselves a vocal chance. After just a few sessions some will quickly pick up the work we'll do, others will take years to know and appreciate the importance of the exercises we will do together.

Year after year I have begun this same process with other groups of students and later that afternoon, when I go to my other job at the Royal National Theatre on the South Bank, I will continue the same kind of work – on a more advanced level – with professional actors: some just starting out in their careers in small parts and others at the very peak of their achievements in big starring roles. The work with these actors will be different and more concentrated than the work with my Guildhall students. I will be preparing actors at the RNT for specific shows with different vocal demands on the National's three stages. But in many fundamental ways my work with fledgeling students and seasoned professionals will be exactly the same. From the first stage to the last stage of an acting career every performer must go through a vocal process which leads to the same result: learning how to speak on-stage with power, clarity and confidence. For me that is what acting is all about. During the course of a working day I encounter actors at every single stage of their lives and careers. The tentative work I start with on this grey autumn morning with students may culminate later that same evening in some actor's greatest triumph on the stage of the National's Olivier Theatre. Every day I see actors make the full circuit of work we will be talking about in what follows.

At the start of their training few young actors realize how fundamentally important their voices will be for them throughout their careers. For them, acting is just about performing roles in plays. They have yet to think of their bodies and their voices as instruments which they must learn to 'play' properly and pitch in different ways to accommodate different sorts of characters and texts. For them acting is not yet an art, not yet about acquiring the kinds of techniques that will allow you to *repeat* a performance night after night with truth and authenticity. They have no way yet of knowing the stages to which their journey through the voice will take them.

Proper voice work, or the lack of it, could make or break a performer. It could enable you to act with greater ease or be the source of an endless struggle. After all, if an audience or another actor on-stage can neither hear nor understand you, your work is irrelevant. So the first step in learning to speak, as an actor, should and must involve trust in and commitment to an area of work that ought to form the pattern of your lifetime as a performer.

The Anatomy of the Voice

On the first day I explain to my students how their voices work. Most have no idea about how the voice functions and usually confuse voice work with speech work. Few realize the importance of the body, the breath and the powerful acting impulses that can be released by a free and open voice.

On first encounter it is always hard to understand something so natural and fundamental as breath and voice. We breathe and speak as natural functions. We just do both without thinking. We neither analyse the processes nor feel self-conscious about them. But when we stop to consider the processes in more detail we become usefully conscious of the fact that breath and voice actually power much of our acting system. An unfettered voice, powered by breath and free of tension, is the ideal we strive for from the first day of class.

I begin by going through the anatomy of the voice, identifying the chain of physical relationships which help us produce sound:

- *Body* Voice work makes use of the whole body from head to toe. The way you stand, the angle of your head, the drop of your shoulders, the position of your spine and pelvis all contribute to the production of a strong voice. Speaking and singing are really the end results of a whole series of reflexive physical actions and body placement which you simply must become aware of in order to gain mastery and control over your vocal instrument.
- *Breath* Voice is powered and carried by the breath. Knowing how to breathe and how to adjust our breathing allows us to

produce sounds and speech of infinite variety and richness of tone. The most active part of the body as we vocalize is the breath system: the rib cage, diaphragm and the deeper support muscles of the abdomen going down as far as the groin. Literally half your body and a number of organs housed in your torso are utilized to manufacture the breath necessary to produce human sound.

- *Larynx*   Vocal sounds are produced when the air from the lungs passes through the larynx, a bony shell-like container located in the throat, which contains the vocal folds or vocal cords. From the larynx the air passes into and through the pharynx, mouth and nose, allowing us to emit a great variety of sounds. Located just behind your Adam's apple, the larynx is the metaphorical 'voice box'. Consciously knowing it is there will help in the work.

- *Speech Muscles*   The jaw, mouth, lips, tongue and soft palate all contribute further to turning sound produced by the breath passing through the larynx into articulate speech as the breathing sound is channelled into literally bite-sized units of notes, words and phrases. Proper manipulation or articulation of the speech muscles will, of course, be essential to speaking.

This very brief anatomy of the voice at work is naturally just a sketch of a complex physiological process. But I want you to understand how sound rises up within us literally from the ground level, gaining a rush of energy as it passes up and out into the air.

The Vocal Process

Now let's look more closely at the process as if it were an action inside your body.

- The breath powers the voice. You breathe in, gathering strength or inspiration, either through the nose or mouth. Each mode of breathing implies something different. The nasal breath is generally a longer breath, connected to longer thoughts, and is more sustained and relaxed. You often breathe this way when you are thoroughly engrossed in something or simply reflecting. When you breathe in through the mouth the breaths are usually shorter. Generally most of us breathe through the mouth if we are under stress or when our thoughts are shorter and more fragmented. We breathe through the mouth when we are in panic, feeling tension or in flight. This is the kind of breath you gulp when you are gasping for air.

- As the breath enters the body and fills the lungs, feeding much needed oxygen into our respiratory system, the rib cage opens all around the centre of the body. This should happen without any force or lift in the shoulders or upper chest.

- As the ribs open, the diaphragm – the divide between the lungs and the stomach – moves down. You cannot actually feel the diaphragm. What you can feel are the stomach muscles connected to it. If you are physically 'centred' and 'released' (two terms I will go into at greater length below), you can feel a release of muscles right down into the groin. You can even feel movement in your buttocks. We'll be doing an exercise later in this chapter to demonstrate this effect (see p. 41). The rib cage and abdominal muscles are now open and you begin to feel physically wider as the breath drops in. The abdominal muscles not only expel air, they work to create a column of air that can support the voice as it produces sound. As you breathe out, these muscles move in, regulating the voice in a number of ways. Vocal control starts with these support muscles. Learning to tune them for any vocal challenge is one of the actor's most important tasks.

- With each outward breath you ought to become aware of the column of air making its way up through the body. This air should pass, without restrictions in the shoulders and throat (two principal areas of tension and troublesome habits), over the vocal folds or cords making them vibrate to produce sound. A simple hum will quickly demonstrate the process. You are now in the act of voicing rather than just breathing. This same pattern is repeated again and again when you vocalize and speak. When the folds move and change shape or density, getting thicker or thinner like an elastic band, you will be sounding different pitches. This changing pitch is what we call the *range* of the voice. A critical part of our work, as you can imagine, will focus on ways of extending range to meet different vocal challenges on-stage.

- Breath has now made a sound – a single note. The sound travels up and out through the mouth. This note can be further reinforced, extended, resonated or amplified in five main areas of the body: chest, throat, mouth, nose and head. The resonators are what give notes their amplification and tonal quality. They enable the performer to make the vocal music to suit any score or text.

What I have described above is a very simple version of the vocal process, focusing just on the features which I think should most concern the beginner actor.

Voice Work is Craft Work

The first stage of work I do with actors requires very little in the way of inspiration, thought or even language. What it does require is perspiration and plenty of physical endeavour. Our whole first year together is about the foundation of proper technique in different parts of the body. Proper voice work is very physical. It involves the use of the entire body. It is not arduous and athletic like, say, dance training. Yet it does require an awareness of the body and how it aids you in producing an ever expanding range of sound.

So what we begin with is the craft work required to learn a whole new range of skills. This is the apprenticeship phase in the life of the actor. Concentration, repetition and diligence will be required if results of real consequence are to be achieved. This is also the phase in which the first set of hurdles is thrown in front of the beginner actor; the kinds of tests which let you know if you should proceed or if the actor's life is not for you.

This initial craft work, if skilfully achieved and, moreover, retained, will make the later inspiration work of acting more easily achievable and actually release it. If the craft is deeply learned, the voice will respond to any sudden acting challenge like a reflex. What is self-conscious at the beginning of the process will become second nature later on. Repetition of craft through a pattern of carefully linked exercises will enable the work to become embedded and more organic as the challenges of the voice take you deeper inside yourself to meet the oncoming challenges of the actor's art.

My aim in the first year of training is to make the voice so fundamentally a part of the actor's physical being that it actually becomes an extension of both yourself and your talent. A properly rooted and balanced voice is, I believe, fundamental to the process of acting, despite whatever method or school of acting your allied training follows. I remain neutral on that point and assume that the work I do will help any actor in any acting situation from the most traditional to experimental, from the Greeks to Grotowski. I have worked with companies like the Royal Shakespeare Company (where the emphasis is heavily on the classical text) and with Theatre de Complicite (where the work is both physical and improvisatory), and I have never found myself altering the basic means by which I teach and work.

Actors who miss out on the initial craft phase of voice work usually find that consistency in their performances and re-creation of their work from performance to performance is difficult to achieve. They always feel detached from their craft. In the deepest sense they will never really own their voices but always feel alienated from them.

Tension

There is tension in the air. As I begin to work with my first-year students I quickly notice that the room is actually filled with it. There is the tense, mental first-day-of-class suspense which naturally comes from taking the initial steps in an unknown process with a group of people you have barely met. Any actor auditioning or attending a first rehearsal knows this feeling too. That kind of tension, not always a bad thing, is part of the competitive atmosphere of an acting class. But there are also powerful waves of *physical* tension which swell up inside everyone in the room. The kind that is locked inside the body and will prevent the voice from doing its proper work. This sort of tension is more fundamentally insidious and damaging. My students will come to learn that tension is their fundamental foe; it must be brought under control and defeated if the voice is to be liberated. We'll soon get to work on unlocking and releasing that tension through a variety of exercises which will start each working day from here on.

The natural voice, free of constricting tension, will work happily and healthily on its own and grow to meet the demands of new acting challenges. However, most of us carry tensions somewhere inside ourselves and these will constrict the breath and the voice. For an actor the con-sequences of tension can be dire. You may find that your voice serves neither your imagination nor the text. Tension can also prevent you from getting through a performance. The voice might falter in places, or you might feel that you cannot sustain a long run. So many of the various work-outs and exercises in this book are about relieving tension and isolating it in various parts of the body.

Habits

I also begin to notice that a number of students have clear physical habits which, along with tension, can limit, block and suppress the voice from doing its work. As soon as the young actor begins to understand the working of the natural voice he begins to isolate where his own individual habits reside. What I do not classify as debilitating habits are native or regional accents or colloquial speech patterns. Gone, fortunately, are the days when all trained actors were expected to speak with one uniform, impeccable accent. At this first stage of training, however, the habits can often be extreme and are always visible:

- Shoulder tension.
- Spine either too rigid or slumped.
- Jaw tight and clenched.
- Breath held too high.
- Voice tight.
- Speech incoherent.

I cannot tell you the number of times I've worked with an ex-student who is still toiling to break a habit first uncovered fifteen years ago. Maybe it is a posture or breathing problem, or just the simple fear of speaking clearly. So you can see how easy it is for habits to plague a performer throughout a career. Letting habits go takes courage and can be uncomfortable, largely because you feel vulnerable without them.

Some actors will willingly address these habits immediately; others will resist, perhaps for years, until a habit worsens and creates a crisis. It must be an individual's choice as to what to do about habits. All of us have habits that affect the voice and unless they are harmful and blocking your way in performance no habit can be judged as wrong. In training, I am never aiming to create homogenous voices which all sound alike and are problem free. Voice work can never be this restrictive. But it may be necessary to break a habit when it becomes inhibiting because it is one's *only* choice. A tight jaw, for instance, could create an interesting vocal or speech effect, but do you have other options besides this one when you need them or has the tight-jaw habit taken control every time you speak?

As an actor matures, habits usually settle and become more subtle, making it more difficult to root them out. At some future point the actor will either have learned to control them or is being controlled by them. But for a young actor in the earliest stages of training the work required to break habits is usually obvious and clear. All habits can be worked on technically and addressed through training. They can be banished, or laid aside in favour of better habits.

When it comes to habits and their effect on voice work I frequently say to my students: 'You aren't training to reinforce what you can already do but to move into new and dramatic areas of change.' So part of my very first task is to help each student begin to recognize her or his own physical habits, acquired over the years, which block the free passage of the natural voice.* Most of these physical habits (e.g. the pushing forward or pulling back of the head, the bunching up of the shoulders, the locking of the knees, the clenching of the jaw) can instantly be relaxed and banished. But if they are the kinds of habits that have a useful function, vocally, you can learn to use them at will. Many experienced and celebrated actors have made a very good living out of their habits: think of some of your favourite film stars. So I feel I should reassure you that you don't necessarily have to lose your habit. You can return to it again and again if you want. But by learning to drop habits and neutralize body, breath and voice you ought to discover more vocal possibilities in a text and be able to release more of its hidden riches when you speak it. This is why I am so concerned about habits; they can be an obstacle in your work.

The text should transform the actor and the actor's habits must never restrict the text. One of the major habits which we all suffer from in the latter part of the twentieth century is a distrust of words and eloquent speech. We are becoming crippled by non-communication. The habits this breeds are then often foisted onto texts with disastrous results. The more vocal choices you can give yourself and the greater your range and transformative skill, the less you will reduce the text to your own limited speaking capacity. I know countless fine actors, each wonderfully committed to his or her art who are transformed and enlarged during a performance to such an extent that after a show, when they have settled back into themselves and leave the theatre, they are hardly recognized when leaving the stage door. That special, expansive skill practised by great actors through their craft is certainly something that each and every actor ought to be able to grasp. A bad habit, you see,

* I go into the problem of vocal habits in detail in *The Right to Speak.*

will prevent you from ever getting that far unless brought under control now.

All these habits, however interesting they are at defining your physical identity, will ultimately limit any vocal transformation. They will almost certainly interfere with any attempt to speak different styles of text. If the habit is severe enough and deeply ingrained it may take months or years to break. But minor habits, once an actor is made aware of them and has made a commitment to change or understand them, can often vanish overnight.

The Key Components of Voice Work

In the first stage of work there are three primary technical areas which the actor must master before any further advanced work on voice (Stage Two) or text (Stage Three) can be achieved. Actors who fail or neglect to do this work are forever wrestling with their voices throughout their careers and have no real solid bedrock on which to build further techniques. They might survive as actors by means of native skill but their struggle and confusion when it comes to their work will be a constant one.

During their first year I ask my student actors to concentrate on three key components:

- THE BODY
- THE BREATH AND SUPPORT
- THE FREE AND PLACED VOICE

Mastery of this technical triumvirate, with which with the bulk of this chapter is concerned, forms the foundation not only of all good vocal habits but also results in good, clear acting. I devote all my attention to these three areas in the actor's first year and return to them again and again over the next two years. In fact, I never stop stressing these components to actors for years to come. In order for text and acting work to grow and remain linked to the voice, work in these three key areas has to be constantly maintained throughout an actor's career.

Generally this kind of work takes a full year before even the best students begin to feel results, providing, that is, the actor is working continually and *every day*. I can tell you at the outset that the eureka moment in voice work will come when the work we do in the first year suddenly becomes so known and second-nature that the whole body is relaxed and centred; the breath is organic to the thought and space around you; the support remains constant and not faltering; and the freed, placed voice is in perfect pitch and harmony with the vocal task before it. But getting to that point of comfort and control requires an enormous amount of craft work.

I   THE BODY

When you speak well every atom of the body should be engaged naturally and without thinking in the act of speaking. Watch a baby cry, a bird sing or a dog bark. In each instance you can see the whole body is fully involved in generating sound. You can see the same sort of involvement of sheer physical energy in speaking whenever great actors perform. Speaking on stage involves full physical commitment. Speaking is never just from the neck up.

Through physical work and special exercises the actor aims:

- to release all useless tensions which trap the breath and the voice;
- to locate the real source of energy in order to support the voice and the word;
- to find the vital 'centre' or the balance of the body which we can define as a state of readiness and a place of maximum physical and vocal freedom;
- to enter into a heightened physical state that will carry and support a heightened dramatic text;
- to transform or characterize the body but still stay free enough to use the voice;

- to acquire status or ownership of the body and the space. We know long before someone speaks whether we will listen to him or her. We know as soon as an actor walks onto the stage whether he will engage us.

Releasing Tension

Tensions and stress throughout the body can stop any speaker – not just an actor – from breathing, thinking, feeling and speaking. So before we can even start the process of voice work we must begin by relaxing those parts of the body where tension most manifests itself. All of us live daily with physical and mental tensions. To some degree it is the invisible glue that holds us together and keeps us alert. At the worst, however, tension can suppress and depress us and even damage the voice. Some tensions might have to be addressed on a daily basis and throughout our lives. There are very few actors (if any at all) who, walking on-stage to perform, do not feel some kind of tension. All major theories of acting use the relaxation of the performer as their starting point.

Any actor working with unnecessary tension will tire herself and the audience. We will watch the actor's work and feel the actor's effort but hear neither the lines nor the play. And that is the biggest reason of all to go about your work properly. An untrained actor might be heard by an audience but it will be hard for us to listen to him or her. The untrained actor, or any untrained speaker, has a natural tendency to push vocally when confronted with an audience instead of connecting to support and emotional truth. The audience is kept outside the actor's experience, prevented from entering his or her creative realm and pushed away rather than embraced. The thought that comes through the words can be fractured and a monotone may be the end result. Young and inexperienced actors sometimes believe this working with tension is the *real* work and that ease is somehow cheating. Nothing could be further from the truth.

Probably, neck tension for me is a major reason for tension (along with the head) that block the flow of breath — hence to slightly lift my shoulders & to lift my neck & head a bit can be very helpful. You can breathe so much easier

Locating Tension

Since the voice is housed in the body and affected by all parts of the body, try this anatomical check-list from top to bottom. Remember each physical area is interconnected, the totality of which has a profound effect on the voice.

1. *Neck and Head* The neck should be free and the muscles flexible so that the voice has open passage through the throat. The head should rest at the top of the spine, neither tucked in, pushed forward nor pulled back. Tension in the head and neck will result in the voice being held and strained. Tension makes the jaw tighten. Your vocal range will diminish and the words you speak will become trapped in the throat. The head weighs the rough equivalent of a Christmas turkey. So all that weight misplaced on the top of your spine will obviously play havoc with your voice. It's a lot of weight to carry wrongly!

2. *Shoulders* Shoulders should hang easily without being lifted, braced or pulled back. These are common problems with most speakers. Stress attacks the shoulders before it does other areas, so awareness here is of vital importance. Tension gathered in the shoulders will stop your breath coming in and going out and will reduce vocal flexibility. Shoulder tension can severely inhibit the freedom of the voice and an actor's real connection to the thought and feeling in a text.

3. *Jaw* The jaw should rest free, neither with the teeth clenched nor the lips pursed. Stress digs in deep around the mouth and you have to really exercise it away once you are made aware of how damaging it can be. A tight jaw means words cannot escape. The throat can become locked and the tongue clamped. Speech, at worst, becomes unintelligible, the vowels particularly distorted. Every sound

you utter will register as aggressive even if you're feeling romantic!

4 *Spine* The spine should be up and free, not rigidly ramrod. The position of the spine is critical to your whole breath system and vocal freedom. It is literally the backbone and centre of the body. Crucially, the spine carries the nervous system. When you tighten or slump the spine it not only affects the breath, voice and speech but also our thinking, feeling and self-esteem. An osteopath once said to me, 'When your spine goes, you age.' So it is no coincidence that actors still working into their eighties have one thing in common: great posture.

5 *Upper Chest* The upper chest should be open and still when breathing, neither lifted nor collapsed. Eventually performers learn to control this part of the body. Tension in the upper chest will hinder the breath from going deeply into the body and after a few minutes of speaking you'll notice that tension will grip the throat, stopping vocal freedom and range.

6 *Back of Rib-cage* Like the spine, this area should not be constrained but open freely and easily to allow a deep breath to enter into the body. Often this area is held, stopping the breath, or pulled in, which tightens the upper chest and stomach areas. Remember what I said about each part of the body being linked to the others.

7 *Stomach and Abdominal Areas* These should remain relaxed, neither pulled in nor forced out but easily responsive to the inspiration that calm respiration produces. Tension here will further stop the breath from reaching the lower body, disconnect the support system and inhibit the real emotional connection to a text. Actors who hold tension here will often push for emotional connection rather than really feeling it. I am not resorting to metaphor when I say this because the deeper the breath sinks, the more vocal power we give to any utterance we produce. Holds anywhere in the abdominal region can be the result

of vanity, which some actors have in abundance and must be willing to shed. One very famous actress said to me once, 'Patsy, I knew when I was beginning to become a great actress when I found myself sitting on-stage in an awful pair of knickers with my stomach hanging over the top and I didn't care.'

8) *Thighs* Our legs, and particularly our thighs, naturally bear the weight of our tension. And because most performers' natural position is to stand and deliver, this becomes a crucial area to keep relaxed. If the thighs are clamped, this too will stop the breath going deeply into the body and can also tighten the lower back and spine.

9) *Knees* Knees should always be unlocked. Knee locking creates serious tension and even shaking in the body, a held breath, tension in the spine, throat and even in the jaw and the tongue. The effects reach that high up the anatomical chain. Structurally this flexibility in the knees, producing unbraced bracing, is similar to the techniques that architects use for constructing high-rise buildings in earthquake zones. The knees, you see, take a lot of punishment and shock.

10) *Feet* Feet should be evenly spaced and placed on the floor; approximately shoulders' length apart. You should feel agile and ready to move off in any direction. Many people make mistakes through natural tendencies, putting more weight on one foot or on their heels or on the sides of their feet. Through your feet you need to feel a clear connection to the floor in order to stay in control of your whole body. Feel the weight on your big toe and pitch yourself slightly forward as though ready to pounce. Without this connection through the feet between body and stage the whole breath system and the voice will be thrown off balance.

11) *Positioning* The position I always teach actors to adopt when they stand on-stage is *centre* or 'a state of readiness', a heightened sense of being that is responsive to all stimuli

around them: a piece of text, another actor, lights, music, audience, etc. When we are naturally in need – physically, emotionally or intellectually – we will often resort to the right physical position in order to survive. In genuine survival situations, as when we reach out to help or pull back to defend ourselves, our body rejects useless tension in order to spring into action. The cliché headline, 85-YEAR-OLD WOMAN LIFTS CAR OFF HUSBAND, demonstrates need overcoming physical limitations. When most in need we access our real physical power and breath. An actor entering the universe of a heightened text – like the men and women in the opening scenes of *King Lear* – must start precisely at a high point of physical readiness, need, confrontation or freedom. Any actor coming on-stage lives in a current state of readiness akin to an animal state of survival. In time, the trained actor will lose the consciousness of these physical high points and naturally adapt to them.

The Essential Warm-up

My aim in the first weeks of training is to address all these areas of physical tension and pinpoint where in the body they reside. I follow no particular order but simply tackle the bits I need to, when tension surfaces in an actor's work. The source of tension can come from anywhere.

What I like to start the actor on immediately is a series of warm-up exercises designed to reduce tension in all these areas, so that he or she has the best starting position from which to work every day.

During all physical exercises which follow, remember to breathe regularly. Breathing is the key to all voice work. All exercises should be gently worked through. You should experience no stress, discomfort or effort in the exercises. These are not calisthenics. After each exercise release naturally, never controlling that release. You have nothing to prove or punish yourself over. Always do the work for *yourself* and in your own time. I find that everyone must work at their own level and rhythm. You are not out to measure yourself against another person. As you work regularly through these exercises you will gradually master and free yourself from a particular area of tension. You will eventually learn to produce any physical or vocal state on-stage freely.

Throughout the first year of training the actor is trying to test herself or himself against tensions of all kinds and identify reference points of physical freedom through actual experience. Gradually, through experiencing a correct way of working again and again, both you and your body will naturally be able to create any shape or sound on-stage.

Exercise 1: General Stretches

Arms

- Standing with feet comfortably apart, stretch your arms out to the sides. Generally stretch the body, arms above head. Shake out the body, shoulders, hips, legs and feet.
- With arms down to your side, lift and drop the shoulders. Now circle them in the same direction.
- Circle the right arm clockwise, as if you are throwing a ball underarm. When you allow the arm to return to its resting place don't place the shoulder but let it find its own natural position. Repeat with the left arm. Try this release with both arms. Let the swing go through the whole body. (Remember always to take the whole body into account with each part of the exercise.) This should feel liberating as the tension to keep the arms and shoulders stiffly in place relaxes and as the arms find their natural position.
- Standing straight, hold your hands behind your back. Gently lift the arms away from your back and release. Again allow the shoulders to drop naturally and find their own position. One fine actress I regularly work with at the National Theatre swears by this release. It helps her get on-stage from the wings without tension.

Spine

- Stand with your feet close together. Snake or undulate the spine; slowly at first. When you do this even for a few seconds you begin actually to feel your spine for the first time. It is like a coiled spring rather than a rigid pole. You will also feel tension unlocking as you gently do this movement.
- Now, with feet wider apart and under your hips, let the spine slump, then gently, from the centre of the stomach, lift up through the spine. Try this sitting cross-legged on the floor. In this sitting position you will feel the spine better. You will feel as you move from a slumped position into the very rigid pulled-up position of the spine how difficult it is to breathe. You might also experience the spine's central position – a position of ease and balance. What you're aiming for is this balance between a slump and a rigid place.
- Down on your hands and knees, 'hollow' (drop) and 'hump' (raise) through the spine. The more you keep your spine active and warm the more you will stay connected to your whole body.

Back of Rib-cage and Upper Chest

This is a favourite exercise of many actors. They do this in the wings to calm themselves before going on to perform. This important exercise stretches the back open and in doing so, stills the upper chest:

- Hug yourself with arms criss-crossed and reaching for the shoulder blades, but tenderly, not with a rough grip. Keep the shoulders released in this hold; neither tense nor bunch them. Keep your feet apart beneath the hips and parallel with one another.
- Bend the knees gradually and, still hugging yourself, flop over from the waist. Breathe in deeply. You should feel the back open.
- Still in this position, take several unrushed breaths. Let the arms drop down and slowly come up through the spine. Once again, do not place the shoulders but let them find their natural position.
- As you come up, be aware not to hoist yourself into place by lifting the upper chest. If this happens, place your hand there to still it.

- Stand centred and open your arms out in a welcoming embrace. Feel the energy flow through your arms. In this position, drop the shoulders. Then allow the arms to return to your side. The upper chest should feel very open and there should be a sensation of breath going into the back.

Neck and Head Position

- Let the head drop down until your chin touches your chest. Keep the jaw free. Using your hands, massage the back of your neck. As you do this don't tighten your shoulders.
- Swing the head gently across the chest from one shoulder to the other.
- Lift your head until you feel it balanced on top of your spine, neither tucked in nor pushed forward. A good check is, if you put your hand on your throat it will feel open and free of tension. To check for this, pull your head off balance and you will feel tension in your throat.
- Let your head gently fall back, jaw free. Then lift it until you feel it balanced at the top of the spine. Then let it drop from one side to the other.
- Gently rotate your head and circle the shoulders simultaneously.

Jaw

- Always treat the jaw gently. It is the physical mechanism which you can most easily damage. Keep the jaw movement circular, moving the whole facial area in a chewing action rather than swinging the jaw from side to side. Bunch the face up and release. When you release the face, let the muscles find their own position. Don't replace them. Do this several times.
- Massage the face and the jaw hinges by the ears.
- Smile and open the jaw with the smile in place to a drop that will accommodate the width of two fingers.
- Chew around for ten seconds.
- With the jaw open, stretch out the tongue and flatten it against your chin. Let the tongue then slide back into your mouth. Repeat several times.

Feet

- Work barefoot or with light shoes that enable you to feel the floor. Never work with heavy workboots or high heels.
- Place the ball of the foot on the floor and rotate first one ankle and then the other.

● Plant both feet firmly on the floor. Pitch yourself a bit forward and feel slightly more weight on the balls of the feet and the big toe, not on the heels or the side of the foot.

Knees

● Stand in place and gently bounce the knees. When you return to stillness don't lock them or freeze them in tension. The feet and knees are vital to feel a state-of-readiness position. In stillness you should feel ready literally to spring into action from the knees.

Stomach and Thighs

● Here is one very simple exercise. I call it the 'Kabuki'. Stand with your feet wide apart for good support and parallel with one another. Keeping your spine up, bend your knees. Place your hand just above the groin and breathe in enough to move your hand. Stay there for at least five breaths. When you stand up, don't lock the stomach or clamp the thighs.

Once you have done this general stretch warm-up a few times and it becomes a familiar routine, it should take only about five minutes to complete. I will return to many of these basic exercises in a more specific way later. This general preparation should begin every voice session you do.

A Note on Fitness

How did you feel, going through this sequence? Was it hard? Easy? Now that we have done just this one exercise I think it is relevant to say that to speak with vigour you do need to be fit and strong. The energy required to fill a large theatrical space, to speak a heightened text, requires an almost athletic understanding of physical energy. Experienced actors make it look easy, but they are working with very concentrated amounts of energy and make every effort to keep themselves fit while performing.

What separates a theatre actor from a film actor is that the former must, by necessity, sustain speaking energy for long periods of time. Many actors fear moving away from television or films back to the stage. This fear, on a pragmatic level, is justified. Muscles needed by the actor to move and speak, unless regularly worked out in theatrical space, lose their flexibility and strength. Younger actors have very little understanding of how much sustained energy theatre acting requires and the amount of fuel needed, by way of a good diet, to keep that energy fired. Lots of young actresses, for instance, often don't eat enough, thinking it will lead to weight problems. You need fuel to act on stage. Put your physical vanity aside. Acting is not modelling!

Some muscles in voice and speech work, like those around the rib-cage and around the mouth, get flabby very quickly. Without continual work and stretching, the breath and its support lose power within days of inactivity. This is a very important point to remember. Speech also gets sloppy very quickly. I suppose if we all spoke or sang in a committed way every day these muscles would naturally stay fit. Actors lucky enough to work regularly and often, in repertory for instance, have a distinct advantage over the actor who performs irregularly. Actors at rest simply have to keep exercised. Even four days off can mean that by the fifth day the basic vocal instrument is under-powered and will need greater effort from you in order to get back up to performance level. A lazy actor never seems to understand this until he finds himself struggling through the first few scenes. In actual fact that actor is preparing himself in front of a paying audience, rather than working assiduously off-stage to reach and maintain peak form before coming on.

Floor Work

Most of the work I do with actors is done from a standing position. There are many voice teachers who like to get actors lying on the floor to do their exercises. In fact, this kind of floor work was the basis of my own training as a voice teacher. But I now see the pros and cons of floor work. So let me share these with you. Since I both train young actors and work with seasoned professionals, I can see that standing work and floor work have to be combined in the correct proportions and done at the right time and in the right place. Two weeks into my work with student actors I will introduce some floor work where I think it is beneficial.

Advantages of Floor Work

- Release of tension in neck, jaw, shoulders, upper chest and abdominal area.
- Opens rib-cage all around the body.
- Introduces breath to the lowest regions of support.
- A restful and protected means of alleviating stress.

Disadvantages of Floor Work

- It can drain energy, so I don't ever recommend using it as the basis for warm-ups unless the actor is very experienced and understands performance energy. I've seen less experienced actors walk onto the stage like zombies after too much floor work.
- The abdominal support muscles fall in with gravity, so it's harder to support your voice and recover the breath quickly working on the floor.
- It is much harder to place the voice forward on the floor. You have to stand in order to do this.

Deep relaxation and breath work can be very emotional, which for many performers may be either a benefit or a disadvantage. And to release profound physical tension, floor work is essential. I would never use floor work before a performance, but only as an exercise in its own right, far away from a performance situation.

If you do any exercises on the floor, repeat them in a standing position so that the exercise becomes usable and vital in a performance mode. Otherwise the work has no real practical application to the moving and speaking the performer does on-stage.

Exercise 2: Floor Work

I use three different positions for work on the floor. Always work in a comfortable, warm and safe place with plenty of room to stretch out. Never, for instance, near a door that could open on you or in a passageway where there is foot traffic. Some people will need a small cushion or thin book to support the head so that it doesn't fall back and tighten the throat. The head should be resting comfortably. You will know whether you need this prop if your throat feels inhibited without it. Once settled on the floor, feel the throat to make sure it is not tightened.

A. First Floor Position

- Lie on your back, knees up, soles of your feet parallel on the ground.
- Keep the thighs unclamped and relaxed.
- You can move the head gently from side to side.
- Lift and drop the shoulders.
- Push the spine gently into the floor and release it.
- Place your hands on your rib-cage and gently help ease the breath out. Release the hand and feel the rib-cage open. Repeat.
- Check that you are not holding your stomach as you breathe in.
- Unclench your jaw, feel the face release.
- Stretch the tongue.

You can do gentle voice exercises on the floor. Breath capacity exercises on the sounds of 's' or 'z' are ideal. Warm up your range and the resonators. Your speech muscles – consonants and vowels – can be activated, though, as I said above, a distinct disadvantage of floor work is that it is harder to place the voice. Different aspects of speech work will be dealt with later.

However, the main purpose of the floor position is relaxation. Treat yourself. Try doing nothing except taking deep breaths and letting tension fall away from you. By all means do exercises in this position but I usually prefer

Thus, it could be done in bed

just to lie and breathe regularly in and out. In the very pressurized, result-driven world of the theatre it seems a good policy to give yourself permission to do nothing but relax and enjoy free breathing. God knows, this never happens in a rehearsal room or in the midst of a performance.

B. Second Floor Position

This next position is one I prescribe for deeper relaxation and release. This is a great one to do before going to bed or *after* a hard technical rehearsal or performance. It seems to clear away profound physical tension. It also aids sleep.

- Lie comfortably on the floor, but this time rest the calves of your legs on a chair that is at a comfortable height for you. Your thighs should be at right angles to your body and unclamped.
- The extra weight of your thighs releases the lower back very effectively and can really open up the lower breath. Ten to twenty minutes in this position will release you fully.
  One word of warning. This position does open the lower breath and consequently the deeper emotions. You might suddenly become very connected to feelings. I know that people can break down into tears or gales of laughter simply through the relaxation from tension that this exercise affords.

C. Third Floor Position

This is the one I use to connect you to strong support while on the floor. I call it the baby scream position.

- If you've ever watched a baby ready to give one of those powerful, ear-piercing screams that always startle, you will notice the infant's legs go up and the knees flop over the torso. Try it! It will help you feel how the breath strongly connects inside the body.
- You can help this exercise by gently pulling your knees towards your chest with your arms. Then let them go so they can dangle. Try some breath capacity and control exercises there (see pp. 38–63). You will be aware immediately of all your support muscles. This is great for strength and control.

It is extremely important to remember that after any floor work you must come up very slowly. Jolt neither your head nor your body violently. Also never spring up. You will feel very dizzy and even nauseous if you do. Get up by rolling over onto your side, waiting a few seconds, then onto your hands and knees and coming up gradually from all fours through the spine.

Finding Centre

Many experienced actors centre their body throughout the day as if returning to some essential point of reference in the same way that you might see a deer centring itself alertly in the wood. The 'centre' is always a place or position of complete physical balance and, if felt correctly, a position of complete readiness. Often after centring actors can feel drained of their energy and wilt. This is not the purpose of centring. It should help you move from strength to strength like the beats of a play.

Let me tell you why centring is so important. It is the state of being physically balanced in which the body stands upright with the minimum of tension. But there has to be some element of tension in the physique, otherwise you would be unable to stand. One of the purposes of achieving centre is to experience the correct balance of tension, relaxation and power in the right places (i.e. in the breath and the lower support).

Anatomically, the centre position permits the breath and voice to work at their most free and efficient levels with a firm foundation of natural support helping the act of speaking. So the centre is a great reference point of freedom for the performer, not a shackle.

If an actor understands this reference of freedom, he or she can transform physically and vocally into any further position or role, safely retaining a sense of ease and purpose even if the body and voice are held, constricted or

disturbed by the acting challenge. For example, you might be playing a character with your head jutting forward. If you don't understand the freedom of being centred you could all too easily block your throat and damage your voice. If, however, you retain a sense of the centre, you can achieve the wanted effect simply by moving the head back a fraction to the point of freedom and relaxing the throat.

Knowing how to feel centred means knowing how to make the slightest physical adjustment that will lead to vocal ease. The voice might not have the same range, but it will be protected and safe. Centring is a vital acting principle and can be applied throughout the body and voice. Actors grasp this idea by striving to become comfortably centred, finding freedom in their own being first, then making that the source from which they live and speak. Being centred is not something mystical. It is about taking the practical steps to shape yourself and your voice to each and every acting challenge.

Becoming Centred

- You start from the feet up. The feet are parallel, apart and placed underneath the hips as though supporting them. Your energy is pitched slightly forward onto the balls of your feet so that you feel the big toe.
- The knees should be unlocked.
- The weight of the hips is directly over the feet, not pushed forward or pulled back but sitting comfortably.
- Spine up, neither slumped nor rigidly pulled up.
- Shoulders released, finding their own position, neither braced nor pulled back or bunched up.
- Do not distort the throat but keep the head comfortably up and looking out at the world.
- Head balanced on top of the spine and jaw unclenched.

Now you are centred. In centre position, if you were to look down you would not see all of your feet, just the tips of your toes, and your hands fall easily at your sides and just towards the front of your thighs. You should feel

Keep the head up and comfortbly looking out at the world

entirely three-dimensional with energy surrounding your body. The breath you breathe should be opening you all around the middle torso without the slightest restriction. The abdominal area feels released as you breathe in and gently moves in on the outward breath. No shoulder or upper chest lift is required in the centre. The actor is now in the ideal position to begin work.

Centre is also the ideal position of absolute power for the body. You see weight-lifters and martial artists go into this position before they spring into action. In the centre position you can gather your energy together before you set out to perform a task. Again and again during your work you will return to this centre position.

Exercise 3: Basic Centring Exercise

- Stand feet parallel under hips.
- Energy slightly on the balls of the feet.
- Knees unlocked but not too bent.
- Spine up but not rigid.
- Shoulders released.
- Drop head onto chest, feel the weight.
- Let the weight of your head take the upper body over so that you flop over from the waist.
- Shake your shoulders out while bent over.
- Check that the knees remain unlocked and the back of the neck released.
- Come up slowly from the base of the spine.
- Let the shoulders fall easily into place. Avoid the temptation to place them.
- The head is the last thing that should come up.
- Keep breathing and the jaw should remain free.

This exercise is great, but many actors complain of feeling limp or under-energized when they finally feel centred. So let's now go a step further to address this complaint because the centre position should be very active and make you feel alert and alive.

Denial and Bluff – Two Positions Opposing Centre

There are two positions I ask young actors to explore in order to feel the opposite of centre. They are fun to play with for the physical contrast they help you discover.

A. Denial

This is a common stance you see most people take regularly. It speaks of lack of interest, boredom and non-communication. Perhaps what we see, as we see denial, is a victim.

- Weight unevenly distributed throughout the body.
- Feet shuffled and off balance.
- Hips off-centre.
- Spine slumped.
- Shoulders hunched.
- Head looking down at the floor.
- Arms folded.
- Thighs and knees clamped.

What's wrong with this position? All these physical attitudes make it anatomically difficult to power the voice. The vocal characterization of denial usually includes mumbling, tossing words away, not finishing words, falling off or away from thoughts or pulling sound back into the body. In fact, most of the energy contained in denial is shackled and limited; it is not being released but held or returned into ourselves. All the aspects of denial make it impossible to hear a voice in space. Even a microphone will have difficulty in picking up any words spoken.

B. Bluff

This is the puffed-up stance which goes to the other extreme from denial. A lot of us take this position when we have to produce stature or energy artificially in order to sound convincing, to fool the listener into believing that we are strong and in control. Many untrained actors who do not work from the principle of being centred falsely adopt this pose when they enter the realm of a heightened text. We use bluff to hide behind and give ourselves a false sense of confidence.

- The spine is pulled up too rigidly.
- The shoulders are pulled back.
- The upper chest is pigeoned up, which will pull the back of the rib-cage in.
- Tight buttocks.
- The feet are too set, usually one in front of the other and off balance.
- The groin is pushed forward (common for both men and women).
- The head is pulled back and the jaw clenched. Bluffers look down on the world but have a limited field of vision or point of view.

How our attitudes do hurt us!

What's wrong with this position? All these physical attitudes are in some way rigid and restrictive to the breath and voice. Vocal characteristics include the voice being too loud. You can always hear the sound of the bluffer's voice but never listen to the words. The breath is too obvious and marked; it is overly trapped and held in the throat and chest. There is no subtlety in any statement; words are spoken for their power without sense. The message is often, 'I don't know what I'm saying, what I'm feeling or why I'm saying it but I will try to kid you.' Nothing kids us though. We all know vocal truth when we hear it. Bluff just silences listener interest with raw power. If you ever see film footage of dictators like Hitler or Mussolini you'll notice that each spoke from this bluff position. The bluffed voice will bulldoze listeners into their seats. There is no grace in the sound and certainly no room for vulnerability or naturalness.

Just by playing around with these two very different physical attitudes (frequently the attitudes taken by young and inexperienced actors), you begin to see why centre is the more desirable and efficient position. Now try going from denial to bluff and then back to centre. Do you feel more alert and alive? Try speaking a line of text or a short monologue in the different physical positions and feel how lines change not only vocally but emotionally and intellectually, and in terms of the physical status the position has given you.

Exercise 4: States of Readiness (The Centre in Motion)

So many actors when they centre look half dead, not really there but in a trance. As I'll say again and again, centre should equate with a state of readiness. It is the position the voice and body work well within, but it should also be a 'switched-on' position from which we can spring into action and speak easily.

Remember those times you felt you were followed late at night, or any time the adrenalin flows, like being attracted to someone across a crowded room or the alertness after a near accident in a car? You feel switched on. This is the ideal place for an actor to start his or her work – being alert – and it is directly linked to centre and the breath. Although I haven't worked on the breath yet during any of these first several exercises, you should none the less feel your breath working to support you low in the body and be experiencing less physical tension, particularly in the shoulders, legs and arms. With that thought in mind and all I've said above about being centred, let's see if the next set of exercises bring you any closer to feeling centred:

A. The Walk

- Walk around the room, not aimlessly drifting but with real purpose as though you have somewhere important to go.
- As you walk, really feel the floor, look out, not down and keep the neck free. Don't clamp the thighs.

- Now stop. Keep the energy of the walk moving in you imaginatively. And with that energy, centre. You will feel very alert.

You might have to try this a few times, or even stop after trotting or running, but you will eventually achieve centre and a state of readiness.

B. The Push

- Push against a wall as though you need to push it down. Look into the wall, don't look into the ground.
- As you push, release the shoulders and breathe. Now you will feel the lower breath. You are touching your real physical and vocal power.
- When you come away from the wall don't physically pull away from that power. Keep that power and the centre you've created.
- To vary this exercise you can also push against the weight of another actor.

You will use this exercise again and again in your training.

C. The Lift

- Lift a chair (the weight according to your capacity) over your head as though you might throw it.
- With the chair above you, release the shoulders and breathe. Again feel the power.
- Put the chair down and centre. The sense of weight should give you an enlarged sense of your capacity.

D. The Throw

- Throw a real or imaginary ball against a wall. Establish a rhythm.
- After a few catches stop and centre. You should feel the action continuing even though you are now motionless.

All four of these exercises, which I've asked you to do silently here, can also be done while speaking a text. In fact, when I see that an actor has lost the vocal path of a text and the value of centre I will frequently ask him or her to connect the words to centre by speaking through one of these exercises. You can mix and match all the exercises and use them in a variety of ways – in an improvisation, for instance, where you might be trying to make a focused connection with a piece of text or with another actor. In essence these are playful tricks to help you stay alert and centred.

If you think about it, most of our great classical plays come from ages when people walked vast distances daily on rough ground, rode horses or worked very hard. Acting was a physical thing and the voice was an essential part of that physicality. All these activities were best achieved from a physical centre of readiness. This feeling would not have been alien to Shakespeare's actors. One of my pet theories is that we lost a feeling for being centred when we came to expect the ground on which we walk to be smooth and even. When we walk on rougher terrain the body feels wonderfully centred, because it has to take charge of its own balance. So when an actor treads the boards as though they too were still rough-hewn and liable to trip him up at any moment, the body should be allowed to discover the equilibrium of being centred.

Physical Transformation

Of course no actor wants to stand and act from the centre position only. That is just a starting and a return point. It is, after all, only a point of reference to freedom and relaxation. But the notion I want a performer to learn at a very early stage of training is that one should be able to transform and even contort oneself into any physical shape while still remaining free, supported and switched on. Extreme physical positions will certainly take added work and fitness (and the assistance of a good movement coach), but I can assure you, from having worked with scores of actors pushed by directors to their physical limits, that as long as certain key physical areas have some freedom it is possible to speak standing on your head or abseiling down the upstage wall of the stage.

I've learned most of this kind of 'off-balance' voice work through experimentation with very physical companies like Britain's Theatre de Complicite. In other words, I've learned by trouble-shooting voice problems actors encounter through extreme physical daring, like walking up a vertical wall. Let's always be safe, however. When you do this extreme kind of work you must always be aware of your body, breath and voice – all of which must have the freedom to return to centre during and after exertion. It is very possible that your body, breath and voice won't always have maximum freedom, but you must be able to breathe, keep the throat open and the jaw released in order to make vocal sense.

In extreme physical situations you might have to compensate by working harder to provide breath in another part of the body. If, for instance, you have to play a hunched beggar you may have to breathe harder from the abdominal area. Try all the centring exercises above in Exercise 4 and after you are feeling closer to centre, transform physically, retaining the feeling of support and alertness. You might try sitting, hunching up or lying down. As you do this, keep checking that the throat feels free and that you can get the same amount of breath into the system. When you hunch up you might need to breathe more into the back of your rib-cage. If you poke your head forward for an effect, you might have to release it a fraction to keep the throat open. Play with these different physical attitudes. In the end you should be able to play Goneril sitting hunched in a chair, drinking a gin and tonic and smoking, yet still feeling dynamic and switched on. Throughout the first year of training my actors are challenged to do this.

These physical transformations apply to costume as well –
corsets, layers of gowns, shoes, uniforms, collars, hats,
wigs, etc. You will be able to cope with all these trappings
and more if you can still feel centre and support. Again,
you might have to adjust certain aspects of your voice and
physical work, but you will be safe if you can connect to
your centre and keep the throat free.

I love the turn-of-the-century photograph of Oscar Wilde
lounging on a couch. He looks so passive and dreamy, but
so lithe and alert that you can tell he is switched on and
ready to pounce at any moment with a witticism. He looks
off-balance but is actually very balanced. I often equate a
good, switched-on actor with a tiger. As the tiger lies there
with those huge, apparently soft paws, you always know
that this animal could pounce and snatch your life with one
well-aimed swipe. A good stage actor must have this same
air of danger. But a sense of danger cannot be achieved
unless you are switched on, alert and really alive. The
audience should feel that an actor is so charged that she or
he can shift in any direction and at an moment. This kind
of danger is one I like to develop in a performer, especially
once artificial bluff has been replaced by the feeling of
being perfectly centred.

Subliminal Communication

A whole unspoken area of communication between an
actor and the audience starts long before the actor speaks.
A lot has been written about body language and its power,
but many actors seem to neglect this area of physical
power. They do not know what all politicians have learned:
that we all know whom we are going to listen to before they
speak just through sheer presence.

Obviously the state of readiness encourages actors to be
alert, so that when they do speak they are connected to their
power, but this attitude should be in place long before they

speak. If you walk into a room, onto a stage, in front of a camera fully alert and ready, you will already be communicating powerfully. You can multiply the effect once you speak.

Young actors, for many reasons, invest a great deal of energy in being laid-back and 'cool'. They shuffle onto the stage and worry or complain afterwards that it was a bloody battle to capture an audience's attention. You can capture an audience subliminally before you speak just by being ready and alive. Of course, it might be a choice to be under-powered, but make it a conscious choice.

The martial arts are physically based on this presence and studies conducted with muggers also suggest that the centred, switched-on body is too dangerous to tackle and mug easily. Victims are victims because they cave in from the centre.

So if you sense the audiences not noticing you before you speak, or if you are lost in space, fighting for focus, think on it! Always act from the centre.

II   THE BREATH

Breath and Support

Voice work for the stage operates from a simple equation: the bigger the feeling, the longer the thought, the larger the acting space, the more breath you will need to fill all three. In some ways breath is the key factor and the one area we all neglect.

Another simple yet profound acting truth is that every performer breathes differently. We each have different capacities. Until you have a flexible enough breath system to accommodate different breath rhythms you cannot begin to characterize on a wide scale. Good writers consciously or unconsciously hear and write each character with a different breath rhythm in mind. I shall go into this key notion at greater length in Stage Three.

So, to speak passionately, fill a space, serve a character, think at different rates, speeds and length, an actor needs to have a strong, flexible, extended and yet organic breath and support system. All technique – like the capacity to centre yourself – must grow from organic roots. But proper breath and support control take long and concentrated work. In fact, all three years of an actor's training – plus her or his entire career – must be devoted to this side of voice work.

If I analyse an actor's primary fear of switching from television or film back to the theatre it will be based on the lack of breath. In fact, the more I work with the voice the more essential I think breath and support are. As I've said before, but must continue to stress, the breath muscles get lazy within days of not working. They need constant attention.

Breath is the most fundamental lifeline we have but few of us breathe fully. I went into this topic in great detail in *The Right to Speak* and will touch on it again here. Support is the natural, muscular means of controlling breath and powering the voice, yet many actors deny themselves this natural means of power. Here in isolation is the biggest problem we all have as speakers: lack of breath and support. Actors cannot function without breath and support, some try but all continually suffer the consequences.

Whenever I'm asked for my key tip about speaking on stage or before the public, I always answer, 'Breathe. Take breath when you speak.' Many of us under stress of speaking publicly do exactly the opposite and stop breathing just when we need it most. Frequently we try to speak on one long breath, rather than supporting with frequent and regular breathing. The trick is to keep breathing as you speak.

The Breathing Actor

As you sit waiting to go into rehearsal or audition – *breathe.*
As the nerves surge through you – *breathe.*

As you walk onto the stage – *breathe.*
As you wait for 'action' or to respond – *breathe.*

Breathing sustains the actor's life in more ways than one. There is now mounting evidence that if we don't take sufficient breath we cannot efficiently feel, think, hear or respond to activity or conversation around us. That sounds right because we are starving ourselves of the central life force – oxygen. So the breath is the most powerful force in life. I am sure we all accept that. So now let's begin to do pragmatic and physical exercises to prepare your breath system for all acting tasks at all levels of your work. Remember to work though this phase of the training by staying centred.

Feeding Physical Support !

Exercise 5: Breath Stretches   *in breath*

The aim of this next sequence of exercises is to prepare abdominal muscles, making them more responsive and flexible; to free certain breath holds and locate the breath low in the body; and to feel the first experiences of physical support. Earlier in your work you should have felt support when you pushed the wall and walked with purpose and vigour in the centring exercises.

A. Side Rib Stretches

- Stand centred and alert. Take the time needed to place yourself securely.
- Carefully flop over to one side, staying straight, not leaning forwards or backwards.
- Keep the shoulders, neck and jaw free.
- In this position breathe gently several times. You should feel a pull around the rib cage, indicating that it is being stretched.
- Come up and breathe a few times in the upright position. You should feel the stretched side opening more and swinging freely. It feels wider.
- Repeat the same sequence on the other side. Do each side three times.

If you feel you need a stronger stretch and want to test a greater sensation of free breathing, as you flop over to the side, arc your arm over your head and gently pull the arm on the stretched side with your other hand. This will exaggerate the stretch and give it added support. Remember not to exert yourself too roughly. Pull until you feel the breath rush in.

B. The Back Rib Stretch

Here is one of most actors' favourite stretches! It really brings in the breath. This exercise opens the rib-cage at the back and begins to pass energy low into the body down to your bottom and groin. This stretch activates the widest opening of the rib-cage and can remove upper-chest tension.

- Stand centred and alert. Take the time you need to place yourself securely.
- Criss-cross your arms and hug yourself but not too tightly.
- Flop over, still hugging, from your waist.
- Keep the knees unlocked and the back and neck released.
- Breathe.

  You will feel the back stretch open. Perhaps you will feel movement right down into the abdominal and groin areas. Be careful as you come up; don't rush, but come up by dropping your arms and standing up through the spine, then centre. You won't feel the back open as dramatically when you are upright, but you should still notice a widening. This exercise will also calm you.

For a bigger stretch, which releases breath into the lower body, repeat as above, but this time squatting. You will feel the energy really enter the body from this position. Before you come up, let your hands press against the floor as you breathe in. This will activate the lower support muscles.

After this, it might be a good time to go and push against a wall or lift a chair so that you feel the breath power more vividly. Start to notice that the inward breath gathers power as the ribs open wider and the stomach area releases, and

that as you breathe out, those muscles move in to release
energy and eventually sound.

C. *Abdominal Stretch and Release*

Let me make a key point here: when you breathe in you do
not need to push your stomach out. You are allowing the
breath to release your abdominal area, if it needs to. The
muscles should not stop the breath going down if that is
what you need. Equally true, you don't need to force or
pump the breath when you breathe out. Very extended
voice work, like shouting, wailing or screaming (see pp.
139–50) will require some strong muscular contact from
this area, but you don't need to contort yourself or double
over to source this power. The pumping action applied by
some actors who believe they are supporting their voices is
the action the body uses for vomiting! It is an unnecessary
and counter-productive action for good voice work.

Many actors access their lower support by moving the
stomach but not shifting the ribs. Both should be active.
The ribs are connected to the abdomen, the abdomen to
the ribs. As you breathe in and out both are opening and
moving in a natural rhythm which you do not need to
force. All the layers can open and close together, which is
the trick of performance breathing.

D. *Kabuki: Release of Lower Breath*

We've done this above in our basic stretch exercise (1) but
here's a new context that concentrates on the breath.

- Feet apart, parallel and shoulder width.
- Bend knees, but keep spine up and free shoulders.
- Place a hand just above the groin. The hand isn't going to
  manipulate the muscles but simply monitor their movement.
- As you breathe in, make sure that the ribs swing open, so your
  other hand might be on one side of the rib-cage.

- Check whether the abdominal muscles are releasing; you will feel any holds.
- After a few breaths these lower muscles will release.
- When you stand, the breath should be lower and easier. Avoid any tightening of the abdomen when you stand.

E. Hand Stretch of the Rib-cage

This is a quick way of getting the rib-cage released and swinging freely. As you do this exercise, remember to keep your shoulders free and your spine placed and up. Don't at any point of the exercise allow your spine to slump.

- Place the palms of your hands on each side of the rib-cage. Your thumbs will feel your ribs.
- As you breathe out silently, use your hands to help the rib-cage contract but without forcing or squeezing it.
- When all the air is out, release your hands and the rib-cage will swing open freely. Note the sensation through touch.
- Keep the abdominal muscles free. On the outward breath you can gently draw them in.

A few repetitions of these stretches will get the rib-cage swinging easily and quickly.

F. Prayer Position

This stretch is in three parts. If you do the whole sequence it will open and release all the breath muscles. However, you can just do the sections you need. It is important that you get up after each of these floor exercises so that you can test the felt effects of the exercise in the standing position.

Part 1

- Get onto your hands and knees. You should be making a square with the floor.
- Keep your back flat, neck free and thighs unclamped. In this position breathe in and out and you will feel any abdominal holds.
- As you continue breathing, try to release muscles more and more.

- On the outward breath you can draw the abdominal muscles in to begin strengthening them.
- Pant on a gentle 'ha'. See if you can feel the support as the sound starts to connect to these muscles.

Part 2

This is a great exercise to open all the breath muscles but can hurt your feet, so you might want to place some padding, such as a towel or mat, underneath them.

- Keep your thighs open and ready to squat.
- Move from the first exercise by collapsing your bottom onto your feet or as close as you can get.
- Your upper body hunches over towards the floor.
- Your arms can be either out in front or along your sides but the shoulders and neck must be free.
- As you breathe in gently, you should feel the back of the rib-cage open. The sides should be swinging.
- The front of the abdomen will feel restricted because it is squashed against your knees. This restriction will prove useful later.
- Now here is the bit that can hurt your feet: come up through the spine and sit back on your feet.
- As you now breathe in and you are upright, the breath will rush down to the lower abdominal area.
- This might be a good point to try and feel the power of breath support. When you feel this breath settle in your body, vocalize a sigh or speak a line of text.
- After you have felt this, just be perverse and feel what tension can do. Lift your shoulders a fraction, vocalize a sigh or line of text. Your voice will feel and sound very different – thinner and tighter.
- Return the energy of the breath to the lower position.

You can either stand up slowly and try the vocalization again or do the next exercise, which will strengthen the lower support system.

Part 3

- This time, get on the floor and roll over onto your back.
- Lift and pull up the legs so that the thighs are released and resting against your torso.

- The knees should be bent and the calf muscles relaxed. The sort of position babies adopt – the baby dangle position. It's not by accident that babies adopt this position before a good scream or cry. They do it to activate the lower support muscles.
- You might need to hug your legs to you in order to feel this position. As you do this, breathe in and out, then let the legs flop but keep them up.
- This exercise will give you a strong sense of the abdominal muscles which give support. So try to vocalize, sigh or speak, so you can actually feel these muscles underneath the voice.
- Return the feet to the floor.
- Roll over and get up slowly and feel those muscles once standing.
- Maybe return to pushing against a wall, lifting a chair or walking with energy.
- You are now touching your real physical and vocal power.

Exercise 6: Feeling Support

Actually becoming aware of the feeling of support is one of the most important sensations in voice work. Once discovered, it is never forgotten, because all of a sudden the physical sensation explains so much about the value of support. You would have been feeling it already in the above exercises. So I want to you to spend some time understanding this sensation and its relation to a readiness to speak and the gathering of power to vocalize. Once you have really felt support you will never speak or act without it.

- Stand centred and alert. Take the time needed to place yourself securely.
- Breathe in and out silently. Spend a few minutes aiming to feel a readiness to speak. It's the same as the switched-on feeling in the centred position.
- Now you will feel a moment when you are ready to speak. The moment you would jump or hit or throw a ball. When you feel this, try releasing on a light 's' sound. Breathe in, feel ready and release on 's'. Concentrate on controlling the sound from the support muscles.

Never vocalize without support! Here is the next vital sensation.

> ● As you *release* on 's' you will feel a moment when you can carry on making the sound, but you have lost contact with the support muscles. You have gone off support!

Most vocal abuse is caused by not supporting the voice. It is natural to use support. As you go off support you will feel that the whole vocal system constricts to preserve air. Habitual vocal tension will snap into place in order to ration air. The throat will close, spine collapse, jaw tighten, shoulders brace and we are back to the first day of training: speaking without support.

The lungs, unless you are in serious trouble, never empty of air, but there is a point when you cannot contact or retrieve that air with the support muscles. The actor translates this into 'I'll get to the end of the line whatever it takes'. This is a useless and worrying state, but one which so many actors, who never learn how to support, live through line after line. But you can damage your voice and the audience won't hear the words because they are being bellowed out without support and control.

My passionate note to every actor is never speak without support. Directors might bully you. You might feel you have to achieve so many lines on a breath, but please don't suffocate yourself. You'll only damage yourself and your art if you do.

Let's put support into perspective in terms of our work. For a brief moment above in Exercise 6 you probably began to feel support after years of never even knowing it existed. We will now be stretching the breath, making it more flexible, fuller and each of your breath recoveries free and fast. In other words, learning to make support do the voice work for us. Of course breath must be organic with thought and feeling. So we need to learn to take what breath is needed to complete a thought and how to vary the support of both short and long thoughts. For an actor this does mean stretching your breath system beyond its current boundaries, so that you can fill large spaces and communicate long thoughts and immense passion. But the stretching does not mean you will need to learn to contort yourself and go off support. In the end there is always a place to breathe within a thought without losing the power which breath support gives you. Now I aim to show you how to build in the direction of this greater capacity.

Exercise 7: Building Support Capacity

- Stand centred and alert. Take the time needed to plant yourself securely.
- Breathe in, release on 'z' until you lose support. Do this several times until you acquaint yourself with this loss of power and the vocal tightness which follows. Particularly note how tempting it is to collapse or pull your spine down, which will close off the support and tighten the voice. Imagine suffering those tensions when you are using your voice in an extended way. It is enough to hurt it or tire it. Singing or speaking with volume is a good example of extended positions that require this clear notion of not working without support.
- Now repeat the release on 'z' but recover (i.e. breathe in) the breath before you lose support. It is a very clear and wonderfully freeing sensation. Funnily enough, we have to learn to take a breath when we need it. It is not always a natural reaction.
- Now tighten the shoulders. Notice how hard it is to find support.
- Return to releasing sound with support.
- Again try pushing a wall or lifting a chair, this will heighten the feeling of support.

Learning to Control Support

Never speak until you are completely ready. At first you might feel this is a laborious process, but in the end you start to feel this ready support position very quickly –

Note: you can feel the support very quickly

in fact, faster than a non-supported position. When the breath system is free the breath falls in, low and full, quite easily.

A misconception is that this support position is huge. Not so. You will learn to take the support required naturally. It can be small or large depending on need. Young actors are frightened that using support will make them sound like '*actors*' – loud and boorish. But that is only because they find themselves using too much support for normal conversation. Your experience with support in the first year of training will naturally lead to momentary imbalances.

It is important that the support system stays free, so that it can respond to needs, but it is equally silly to take too much breath. A huge breath to say a casual 'no' is a waste of power, but you might need massive support if the 'no' were packed with passion or delivered to a crowd.

The natural breath is where you breathe in, feel support and, when ready, breathe out. The moment of readiness isn't a ponderous, held position, but it does take a fraction of time and when reached makes you feel complete before you breathe out. The support action should be: I breathe in, feel ready, I speak out. A good way of covering this action is to make the 'feel ready' link part of the thought process of the character.

This recognition of support, and how much to support, seems to me to be the most important thing to understand in training any speaker. In my current work I give it supreme importance.

Common Habits Which Affect Support

Try out these habits and see if one applies to you. Not only do they cut off your vocal power, but they have serious consequences in acting terms. *Speaking without breath support takes you out of the acting moment.*

Actors who are not obeying support will frequently say to me in rehearsal, 'When I know *what* I'm saying or *why* I'm saying it I'll be all right.' The physical manifestation of that statement is that when an actor is happy and in control of character, scene and text he or she will be breathing and supporting the voice organically and in tune with the text.

My response to actors on this point is that if you can isolate when support isn't happening you can use your physical technique to allow it to happen. That is, make sure you are on support and ready to speak the text that isn't quite working for you. Owning words technically can actually lead to owning the words organically.

Exercise 8: Non-support Habits

Use counting (1–2–3, etc.) or a line of text for these next exercises:

- Breathe in, feel ready, stop or hold yourself and the breath, then speak. A classic form of hesitation. You will instantly feel the vocal tension in the voice and the inability to power the voice or register much sense in the words. In acting terms you are behind the text and not with it. The experience of the words has been locked off, they have become irrelevant. Too much attention is being paid to misplaced support.
- Breathe in and instantly start speaking before you feel ready. You are now rushing yourself and getting ahead of the words. In this instance the actor always feels he or she has to catch the text. It's like trying to jump on board a rapidly accelerating bus. You are simply not giving yourself the right to take your time to speak and feel that crucial beat which sparks you to speak. Actors will often do this when they feel a director wants them to speak quickly before they are connected to the text.
- This third habit is what I call 'I'm so cool' acting. Breathe in, feel that power, deflate like a full balloon losing air, then speak with only minimum power. The deflation is often accompanied by a sigh and maybe physical gestures which read like sign language. The actor is effectively underneath the text and suppressed by it. It weighs on him to the point of collapse. With this you cannot power or propel anything forward. You are sitting back on the text and it keeps you weighted in place.

By understanding these three particular habits you can continually monitor yourself. If a scene is going wrong and you recognize that you are off the text because you haven't made full support connection to the words, you can shift the balance with breathing and supporting on the text. Support technique can get you back on the road – the whole scene doesn't have to go down the plug hole. Rescue, with breath and support, is at hand.

Interestingly, I have learned to read, only after breath & then waiting for support. But I have had trouble

Feeling Supported and On the Text *speaking with Support.*

There is an image I often use to explain what it is like being in the acting moment, supported and on the text. If you've ever crossed a stream on stepping stones, you will quickly realize that you have to breathe and deal with each stone as you step on it. If you worry about three stones ahead, or the one behind, or the bank you are travelling towards, you will wobble or fall in! The same applies to words. One step at a time with breath and support. Harmony and symmetry working together to form balance.

Now take the exercises above and work out one for yourself where numbers or words stay together. Stay on each word or number with the breath, do not skid over them, or ponder the last word you've spoken, or try too desperately to get to the end of the thought. You will fall off the text. You will not be crossing the stream effortlessly or in balance.

Owning Words

I talk a lot to actors about owning a word and this topic will come up later when we begin applying voice to text work in Stage Three. It seems to me that when an actor organically owns a word the word is touched and held by his or her lower support. The more a word is needed and taken into your possession, the lower the breath and support will naturally become.

Watching rehearsals over the years, I've often noticed that with great actors the word drops low into the body until it nestles in this low support position. This process is probably unconscious and the result of years of work, but for a younger actor can be made conscious with support work. When the word burrows down from the head to the groin, a genuine kind of ownership and truer experience of the word is experienced.

Speak, for instance, the sound 'o' on a low position of the breath and support. Now take the breath higher up in the body or tighten the shoulders which will lift the support. Reposition the breath a few times, low and then high. You will notice that not only does the lower support feel freer and sound richer, but your connection to the sound, both emotionally and psychologically, is vastly different. Try saying 'no' with the same routine. Now try a line of text. By just shifting the breath, your relationship to words becomes different. You own them more authentically, more completely, in the lower position.

Exercise 9: Expanding Breath and Support, Capacity and Flexibility

Next are a series of linked exercises designed to increase capacity and flexibility. Remember that these exercises are to give you confidence and more technical awareness. As you perform and use the techniques, you will forget them. The aim throughout is to have a breath support system that will respond to any performance demand – vocal, spatial or textual. Certain texts and spaces will require more of this work.

You can do these exercises standing centred, but also experiment with sitting, walking (in a dynamic way) or lying on the floor.

It is very important to remember to keep the shoulders free during this work. You should be able to move them without interfering with the breath. The jaw must also be free and the spine up. Also, always start each exercise feeling the readiness of the breath and support. Don't lock the breath but start an exercise when you feel the breath settle, not before or after.

- Using a gentle 's' (don't push the sound), breathe in and release the 's', feeling the contact with the support muscles for ten seconds. Repeat a few times.
- Feel the control of the release from the support system.
- Gradually build up this controlled release to 15, then 20 and finally 30 seconds.
- This may take time, several weeks even, but don't push yourself and get frustrated about reaching a specific goal until you've arrived naturally.

There used to be a view that a classical actor should be able to speak eight lines of iambic pentameter on one breath. I once had a speech teacher who insisted that we spoke a sonnet (fourteen lines of pentameters) on one entire breath. I don't think that is necessary at all. Some physiques are unable easily to travel that kind of distance on a single breath. But I do think that by expanding your release to 30 seconds you will gain a very solid working capacity. If you can keep yourself around that target you can always boost it up if the demands of the work or text require an even greater capacity. You need only do this for a few minutes a day.

Use 'z'. This will help your control. You might not get as long a release but try to control the sound on 'z' so that it doesn't wobble but sounds even. Concentrate on a strong, steady release controlled from the support muscles, not in the throat or jaw. It's interesting that by imagining the control coming from the rib-cage and abdominal muscles you will begin to monitor the sound from this region of support.

Now try a simple counting exercise that will give you a great sense of connecting to the support but also build up an awareness of only taking what you need – economy of breath.

- Stand centred.
- Breathe in and feel the support, take enough to count out loud '1'.
- Build up, count '1, 2', then '1, 2, 3'.
- Gradually build up over 10.

Never go off support!

As you feel more confident with the support and feel the power of the breath settling in the body, speed up the counting. As long as you stay free in the body you will be surprised how quickly the breath comes in. Invest in doing this exercise very quickly. Get the system flexible. To extend your capacity, build up over 20 or, if you really want to push yourself, 30, but never get ahead or behind yourself and go off support. Hold yourself always in the embrace of support.

What you are doing with numbers in these exercises is quite neutral. That is why I use counting, it has no agenda. Apply the same distance covered on one breath to text and you are probably speaking three or four lines of verse. It's strange, but when you think you have to travel a distance with a text, you freeze. First gain the confidence that you do have the capacity and equipment through the counting exercise, then move on to words.

As you work through these exercises and you can feel you are stretching yourself, you will feel work has been done on the breath system. It shouldn't feel strained, but exercised. The muscles of the rib-cage and abdominal area are being awakened. As you build up these muscles, counting from 1, you are also experiencing taking what breath you need. A small recovery of the breath is building up to a large full recovery. *Even when silently reading you can, in pausing, feel the muscular support in the stomach musculature*

Exercise 10: Full Recovery

Next is a full-recovery breath exercise. You are going to take in a full breath, use support and repeat the recovery several times. This is athletic breath work. The equivalent in text work would be speaking several lines on one breath, recover, several lines, recover, etc. This is also the kind of recovery you need to support a huge, continual release of emotion, or a singing position on the breath.

✗   You must be vigilant in this exercise and never go off support, but stretch yourself to the limits of the system. Jaw and throat should remain free, the spine up (never collapse this to squeeze more out). You will feel muscles work and after the exercise they will have been stretched.

Take in a full breath, but not with any sense of lock on the ribs or abdominal area. If you feel a lock, either sigh out and start again or try to release the ribs a fraction. Locks in the system can result because you are trying to go too far, but a lock just pulls you off the moment and freezes the system. There should be no lift in the shoulders or upper part of the chest. If this happens, stop and start again. If the abdomen freezes, stop and try the Kabuki exercise.

- Release on 'z' as far as you can but *before* loss of support.
- Recover again as far as you can, release on 'z'. Try three of these.
- If you are so fit that you don't feel the work, stretch on – 4, 5, 6, 7. As you get fitter, go further and further.
  My rule of thumb would be that seven recoveries, one after the other, serve even the most demanding texts very well.

During this exercise, if you feel the spine collapse, you might like to try the recoveries sitting on the edge of a chair or cross-legged on the floor. Sitting will enable you to feel greater support and allow you to control the collapse.

- Try all the exercises on the voiced sounds 'z' or 'v', or counting, changing the volume. As you change the level of volume, relate that change to the change of intensity in the support system.

Now play with modulating the breath support:

- Think of a number, let's say 3, breathe in and count over that number, then think of another number, say 7, and count over that number.
- Play with different numbers. Do this with easy counting only when you are ready and do the exercise at different speeds and volumes.
- You will suddenly notice you take what you need and that the breath is now organic to your need.

As you begin to feel connected to the support you can refine the system to get more out of it.

Wasting Support

One of the most common habits I encounter with performers is that of wasting support. Many actors, to get an immediate sense of power, will breathe in, pull the support muscles in, then vocalize. Effectively they have wasted a few inches of movement in their support.

Hone your support technique by becoming aware that you can use the muscles of support from the word go. The breath settles and you vocalize out on the first sensation of movement in the muscles – not grab and then sound. This technique might occasionally be needed to create an extreme sound, but this is not the norm.

Exercise 11: Taking the Breath You Need

As I've already said, the equation of taking what you need is: amount of breath equals length of thought and size of emotion and space. As we go further into voice and text work, I will be tackling the thought and emotion parts of the equation, but a simple exercise to experience the space factor is interesting.

- Stand centred.
- Put a hand about 9 inches in front of your face. Look at the hand and breathe to it. You will begin to take enough breath to touch and reach that hand. The hand could be a microphone, in which case the technique would be to breathe to the microphone but make imaginative contact with the audience.
- Now put your hand down and focus on a point across the room.
- Breathe to that point. The breath is changing. It's expanding. You are having to take more to reach the point.
- Now extend yourself further. Imagine the whole room. Breathe. Notice the change of breath.
- Finally, look out of a window and focus on a distant point. The greater the distance, the greater the breath needed to reach it.

This exercise constitutes a large proportion of what is called 'projection'. If you are free in the breath and you breathe a space appropriately you will not only take in the breath required to fill the space but you will make contact with the space and its perimeters. You will inhabit and own the space along with the words you speak.

Breathing the Space

This simple technique applies to many areas of life and control in speaking. The chairperson controlling the board room, the news-reader controlling the camera and our sitting-room, the actor controlling the theatre. As we breathe a space and extend the right amount of breath to a person, we touch them. You can sometimes sit in a theatre hearing an actor but not feeling part of that actor's process. You feel cut off. Most of the time when this happens the actor is not breathing the space.

A simple but basic exercise like the one above can bring you in contact with this problem. Whatever space you are performing in, stand on the stage when it's empty and breathe to the perimeters of the theatre or room. Not only to where the audience ends but the whole space from side to side, top to bottom.

In beautifully designed theatres this breath perspective is built into the design. If you were to stand in a Greek theatre like the one at Epidaurus, you could not help but take in breath and breathe the space. Most Victorian theatres, like London's Old Vic, also encourage this breath connection. Notice, too, that both these kinds of theatres wrap around and envelop the actor. Most modern theatres don't. If fact, most are so boxy and widely horizontal that they can often defeat the actor from taking in the space. The actor has to work consciously to make the connection between the space and the breath. The design doesn't do it for them. For instance, London's Barbican, Olivier and Lyttelton Theatres pull the actor's connection down to the back of the stalls. To include and breathe the circles and/or balconies you have to work to 'think up'. Your focus is constantly fighting a shifting battle.

However, larger theatres are often easier to breathe because the space acts as a breath liberator. A small studio space can cramp the breath. The audience is so close that the actor often forgets the whole space and is suddenly inaudible, speaking to just the first few rows. You must still think and breathe the whole space. In the National's Cottesloe Theatre, for instance, that means right up to the high gallery which is on a steep vertical plane. Only then will you reach your audience vocally and imaginatively.

When you finally feel at home in a space, your breathing within it will be organic. That is why you must take every opportunity to acquaint yourself seriously with every space in which you perform, even if it's just a small school theatre. Get into the space before the show; at lunch, for instance. By breathing a space you will actually begin to feel less fear of it. You will feel at home. You can play a scene with someone intimately on-stage but still breathe the space and be heard. You can play a speech facing upstage, if that is required, but still breathe the space.

The same applies to radio. This time the point of focus for the breath is the centre of the microphone. So many actors rely on the microphone that they forget to breathe and support, and are therefore inaudible. Equally, the young television and film actors close down so much that they don't breathe in a scene and can't be picked up by sound technicians. Here the microphone will pick you up if you are breathing to a fellow actor, or to camera if you are addressing the camera.

Testing Your Breath

All the exercises we have been doing thus far are only possible if you are free in your breath. But it might be fun to try a selection of them with your own favourite breath habit or tension just to feel the constriction. Note that even with tension you can adapt the constriction to get some breath support. This is an important process as you will naturally play characters who have particular ticks and tensions. By starting from freedom you will be able to produce the effect without inhibition or damage.

Also experiment with holding your breath in these exercises or speaking without breath. This will very quickly give you a sensation of the fear that grips many performers. Complete terror! The root of this fear is to do with not breathing easily or taking what the body most needs – a deep, low breath. Take this panic to its extreme and the body will knock you out – you will faint, so it can get on with living naturally, i.e. taking the breath. If you suffer from extreme nerves or sickness before working, invest a lot of time in very easy breath work, keeping the breath coming and going without holds. Aim to place the breath as deeply into the body as possible, don't hold or rush the rhythm of the breath. If you feel locked or panicked, sigh out and calmly wait for the body to ask for breath.

Changing Breath Rhythm

I will be concentrating on this very important aspect of breath work with text work later, in Stage Three, but I want to mention the subject here first. I'm convinced that all great writers, consciously or unconsciously, hear the breathing patterns of their characters when they write. Each human being has a different breath rhythm. If a person lives in an oral culture that cares about speaking and language, uses longer thoughts and expresses feelings with passion, then he or she will be using more breath organically. As life transforms us we change our breath rhythms. All these things and more are hidden in a text to be revealed by the actor to an audience's ears.

Two thoughts from my daily working experience arise about breath rhythms: 1) many actors train their breath systems to get the breath low, strong and flexible, but never shift out of their own unique rhythms; 2) younger actors who have never lived with stimulating verbal exchange feel that to change their breathing rhythms – normally conditioned by short thoughts and passionless dialogue – to that of someone who speaks huge and complex texts sounds unreal. My response to both these common habits is that if you don't change the rhythm of your breath to suit each individual text then you will never begin to characterize fully as an actor must and should. When you change the rhythm of your breath to match the text, you have not only begun to characterize by means of the structure of the text but have permitted yourself to be changed by the text, beginning to breathe it the way the writer intended.

Exercise 12: Changing Breath Rhythms

This simple exercise will neutralize the breath pattern so that you can build a new rhythm into your body. You need only do this if you feel stuck when working on a text.

- Lie on your back, knees up, soles of feet on the floor.
- Thighs should be unclamped and shoulders released. Make sure that you feel comfortable.
- Spend a few minutes being aware of your breath rhythm. Now clear the pattern.
- Begin the exercise by sighing out, not a voiced sigh but a gentle, silent one.
- Keep gently breathing out until you feel no more outward motion of the breath.
- Wait until you feel the body wants to breathe. It is useful to think of this moment as a suspension between exhalation and the organic need of inhalation.
- Let the breath in and when you feel full wait until the body starts to let the breath out. You are letting your body, not your head, seek oxygen.
- Think of the holds more like suspensions. You are suspended with the breath, not locking it.
- Continue this pattern. You might initially feel panic but try to work through the panic. If you can face it you will begin to relax in a deep way and clean your breath pattern of your natural holds.
- After this exercise you will feel a bit drowsy, but it would be interesting to try at this point to speak a speech you know well and see if the pattern of breath has shifted at all.
- By clearing the breath of your habitual patterns the text might inform you about where it wants you to breathe and how much breath you need to take.

Exercise 13: Building Breath Support, Fitness and Strength

Here are a few exercises to build up fitness and strength in the breath support system. All these exercises should be done with freedom through the rest of your body, particularly your shoulders, throat and upper chest. You should only do these exercises after warming up the voice (see pp. 336–9). I'll be using 'ha' a great deal as this is an open sound. If you can control 'ha' you can control any sound. A text with the physical control of words will be easy after this.

If you know you have a vocally demanding role coming up you should start these exercises two weeks before beginning rehearsal. This will give you time to build up fitness.

- Increase capacity. Use 's' and aim to get a 40-second release that is controlled.
- Use 'z' up to 30 seconds to increase control. The release should be strong and steady.
- Work up to seven or eight full recoveries using 'z' or 'ha'. The recoveries should be effortless, one after the other and with no collapse of the spine. Always recover before you lose support. Never cheat by thinking you have got more breath than you can really power.
- Release on 'z' and then 'ha', pushing against a wall or holding a chair above your head or lifting a reasonably heavy object. After these releases just stand and release. On 'z' or 'ha' you should immediately feel more connection and contact with the support.
- Walk, releasing on 'ha', trying to keep the sound steady. Try different notes and different levels of volume.
- Run and get yourself out of breath. Stop and release on 'ha', trying to keep the sound steady. Recover the breath until it settles down to its usual pattern. As you get fitter this settling process will happen faster.
- Release on 'ha', going from standing to sitting on the floor. Keep the sound as steady as you can.
- Now take this further by sitting into lying down on your back, then sitting into standing on one breath, releasing on 'ha'. This is not easy but very demanding and athletic.

At any time try one of these exercises using a line of text. After the 'ha' the text will be easy to breathe and control.

Now, for an even finer control of support, try these exercises. Again, these are only to be done after a warm-up. Remember to keep the voice placed forward so you are 'on' voice. Do not push anything from the throat.

- Over a count of 10, release on 'ha' but crescendo or build up the sound, all control of volume coming up from the support. Over a count of 10, diminuendo or decrease the sound. Try to build up these releases over 15 and 20. The diminuendo is harder and takes more control. In speech we rarely do this energy release. The crescendo rather than the diminuendo is more natural.

- Now take this support into a line of text. Intone the line, then speak it at moderate volume. Intone the line, then speak it bringing up the volume a notch. Repeat until you feel you are at full volume without pushing. You will feel your support having really to work. You might need to think of a yawn in the throat to keep free and it will also help if you elongate the vowels to aid the support. There might be a temptation to pull the sound back as many of us feel restricted when we make a loud noise – keep liberating yourself!
- Now reverse the exercise. Start on a moderate volume and gradually get quieter. You'll find that you really have to concentrate on keeping the voice full 'on' and placed forward. Don't diminish the volume by pulling the sound back, devoicing or using a whisper.

You will notice that to make yourself clear when speaking quietly not only takes very fine control of the support but requires a hundred per cent more mental and emotional concentration. It is almost the hardest thing to achieve technically – the Ph.D. of voice work! Only the most experienced actors can make this low vocal level work in space. Fine technique and superb concentration are required. For some reason young, inexperienced actors want to work on this level long before they achieve any strong, full-throated technique. It is so difficult.

Breath and Voice Planning

Just a tip. If you have a demanding acting job which requires lots of movement, support and voice, spend time working it out in advance. There is no shame in having to think out a moment on stage. It doesn't diminish your creativity. Otherwise you might end up always dreading a particular moment, or hurt your voice in performance, so plan it out. For instance, I had an actor who had to walk on at the start of the show and immediately suffer an attack. So the first sound he made on-stage was a huge scream. He was acting on a steep rake, which made the task even harder on the breath. The only way he could do this night after night was for us to plan the whole thing practically move by move. We had to consider where to breathe and support, where to be physical at any given moment and the exact position of his body when he fell. Through careful planning he didn't hurt his voice and eventually the sequence of moments became organic. Without doing this work he wouldn't have lasted through the show.

Dancing and singing, fighting, then speaking can all be worked out, keeping you and your voice safe. As you do this breath and voice planning you will notice that the body and breath learn very quickly and that vocal freedom is achieved remarkably smoothly. Don't endanger your voice merely through lack of preparation. Actors are constantly asked to perform hard and even unnatural tasks which combine speech with acrobatics.

Everyday Support

At this stage of my career I feel that the understanding and correct use of support is the most important aspect of good, strong, healthy voice work. Of course, I might change my mind in the next twenty years. Some years ago I used to say to actors that as long as they supported their voices in rehearsal and on-stage, that was all right. However, in retrospect, I think I was wrong. Not only is supporting your voice in everyday life the most natural and healthy option (and remember, it doesn't have to be this overblown position that announces you as an 'actor'), but I would say that if you don't use support in your daily speaking you will find yourself always 'putting on' a voice when you act. Support will never feel truly organic if it is used only when you work.

Try the supported voice in everyday contexts, perhaps not at first with people who know you well. They will notice the change in you. Our nearest and dearest are often

Noisy social gatherings

not at their kindest when we try to change ourselves. You will notice a lift in self-esteem when you support. Use support when you are in environments that are notorious for vocal exhaustion. The first night party with all that noise, smoke and alcohol is a cocktail for vocal damage. Many actors hurt their voices at parties. They support in the performance and forget at the party!

There will be much breath and support work later, connected to text work where support really comes into use. All this first stage is about is building up vocal awareness and learning about technical preparation you will begin to use regularly. Later you will be throwing caution to the wind and using all breath muscles vigorously. That will mean they will gradually become organic to the text and you will forget the work because it will be there for you naturally.

Rib Reserve

I would now like just to discuss a breath technique called rib reserve. Many older actors have been trained in this method of support and younger actors have heard it discussed enough to wonder what it is and if it has any benefits. So I think it is important to explain this method that has existed in Western singing and speaking for decades.

X   The purpose of rib reserve is to create a strong support system by means of a continual reserve of air. All fine and good, but the method has real problems.

Before I went to the Central School of Speech and Drama I was taught rib reserve. You breathed in and went 'on support', which meant you held or you locked your rib-cage up and worked from the abdominal area of muscles, with the ribs staying up. We used to go 'on support' at the beginning of the class and let our ribs down only at the end of the lesson. A bit of string was tied around our rib-cage. If the string loosened the teacher could see our ribs had slipped. One of my teachers used to put her ribs up in the morning and down before she went to bed, breathing and living off the abdominal, diaphragmatic breath!

This high rib position is obviously unnatural. The locking of the rib-cage for long periods of time creates shoulder tension, abdominal tension (the stomach becomes taut) and back tension. At worst it can damage the back. Many actors and singers become barrel shaped. Numerous singers practising rib reserve will clasp their hands as they sing to lock the cage in place. Actors on rib reserve will often act in a rigid way. Shoulders can tighten to hold the rib-cage up. Clearly little movement or acting is possible.

So, are there any advantages to this technique? Let's place it in perspective. The idea of rib reserve comes from a very natural process. If we push (remember the wall exercise) or lift a heavy object, there is a moment after the inward breath when the ribs are suspended up. As we push, lift, punch, etc., the open position of the ribs mean we have clear and uninhibited access to all those powerful abdominal muscles: all those muscles supporting the outward air for maximum energy and incredible vocal power.

It seems to me the problem with the rib reserve system is that the ribs don't come down naturally. For very extreme moments in speaking, and more so in singing, you do need clear access to those muscles, so I encourage a performer to use the technique only in rare circumstances – e.g. speaking over music, extended screaming. Release the abdominal muscles first, followed by the ribs coming down. The ribs overlap the abdominal release. The tension and problems appear when the abdominal release finishes and the ribs are still locked and then come down.

I think it is fair to say that this unnatural technique might be needed when the art form itself requires the unnatural. An aesthetic in art is not always natural. Rib reserve does produce enormous vocal power and, if taught properly to a performer, can keep the lower throat open, minimizing vocal tension. But your voice will never sound real because the underlying support is so huge that the voice cannot be quiet or subtle. Rib reserve turns the voice into a power tool.

Some performers skilled in rib reserve find the position useful and never suffer from inhibiting tension. So if you do have an enormous vocal task you might like to experiment with this tool. Remember, though, never to lock the ribs. The benefit should be felt immediately if the ribs are not locked.

Exercise 14: Rib Reserve

- Take a full breath, feel the position of readiness.
- Release on 's', but by separating the abdominal area from the rib-cage. The abdominal area releases first. The rib-cage follows but overlaps the abdominal releases.
- You can try releasing an 's' from the abdominal and change the sound to 'z' as the ribs join in.

I do teach this release but only when a student has established a strong, free breath system. For some it will double their capacity and give them a new sense of vocal power. Others hate it. The students who loathe it can easily get by without it. It is only for rare occasions and, as I've said above, the ribs should always be able to move freely and never be locked in place.

Finally, I have a theory about rib reserve. The locking of the rib-cage tightens all the abdominal muscles and consequently cuts the actor off from his or her emotional centre. The tight abdomen makes accessing feelings almost impossible. I think that this technique helped to create all those clear, intellectual British actors who sounded to American ears rigid and passionless. Great voices, but missing real souls.

III   THE FREE AND PLACED VOICE

Freeing the Voice

Imagine the column of air travelling up through the body from the breath support muscles. The foundation support you have been developing should be able to propel or project the voice into the mouth and out into the air. However, what can happen is that your support power suddenly meets blocks and constrictions in the throat and mouth. It is in these areas that we hold and distort our potential power and freedom. That stream of supported air finds itself fully or partially trapped as it tries to place itself in the face. We find ourselves back considering what tensions are inhibiting this free passage.

Let's list some of the most common tensions that create these blockages. The voice naturally wants to travel in an arc – up and out – so these blocks are actually trapping and suppressing the voice and words in the body.

A. The Push Down

This is a common vocal habit in actors. The voice is pushed down into the throat and chest, rather than placed forward in the mouth. Actors love this habit because they can feel the sensation of their voice buzzing around in the throat and chest, but fail to realize that if you can feel the sensation of your own voice, it's not releasing out of you. It's trapped and denied to the listener. You have to work much harder with your support to begin to communicate across space. The push down tires the voice. It's the sort of voice you may be able hear even at the back of the theatre but you won't be able to distinguish what is said. The push down restricts the range of the voice. I think many actors adopt this habit to lower the voice quickly and therefore to give themselves an air of authority. It is akin to the vocal bluff habit we talked about earlier: 'I don't know what I'm saying or feeling but I'll bluff it out.' It's all growl but no definition or bite.

B. *Throat Constrictions*

These constrictions all revolve around holding or blocking sound in the throat and not fully using the vocal folds. They fall under a number of headings:

- *Devoicing*   A vocal position close to whispering. This creates a soft, less focused sound, common in actors who have done considerable amounts of television or film. It is a short cut to reducing volume but it is vocally inefficient. You are running the voice on half-power because only a proportion of the vocal fold is being energized. This quality muffles the voice and, in most modern, acoustically dead theatres, a devoiced voice cannot travel or be distinctly heard. Again it will restrict the range of the voice and tire it after a long show.
- *Glottal Attack*   This is potentially very dangerous as the vocal folds are being clicked or bashed together harshly, particularly on vowels at the beginning of words such as 'apple'. It is as if the first point of the word is hammered. Many actors do this to find energy, but the energy is smashing the voice, restricting range and always sounds to the audience hard and aggressive. Used with large amounts of support in big theatres you could severely damage your voice if this habit continues for long periods of time.
- *Squeezing the Throat*   You can do this in a variety of ways and it can be caused by vertical or horizontal pressure in the throat. In effect, the channel in the throat is narrowed, so the voice will sound thin and choked. This tension can grip actors when they are nervous or not breathing fully. By tightening the throat you can, falsely, control the air flow. The sound allows no emotional shifts and remains weak and drained of colour. With this kind of tension you can see the throat and neck tighten with the effort of holding the voice. It wants to be released but you are trapping it. This is often accompanied by a tight tongue or jaw. Look in a mirror and speak, and you can actually see the physical strain in your face and neck. Your face will probably redden and the veins in your neck become more pronounced. You are essentially disconnected from the entire process of breathing.

● *The Push* Very common amongst actors who have no sense of support. Instead of using their natural power of breath support they push their voice to fill the space and to create an emotional fact. Most people who are frightened of a space, a text, an emotional truth, or who are trying to be strong without a connection to breath and support, will physically push. The audience will experience a bluffed energy. They will feel attacked and be unable to hear specifics in language. They will also feel cut off from the play and often get angry with the pusher and begin to dislike him or her. It's very tiring to be pushed at all the time: hit over the head with a vocal baseball bat. Thwack, thwack, thwack! *It's very tiring to push too!*

Pushing can damage the voice. The voice falls into a monotone. The switch-off time is very short; within minutes no one listens or cares. Again, actors will often mistakenly think this position is good because they feel they are working hard. However, the more you push not only are the audience being cut off but you cut yourself off too. My image of a pusher is a dog chasing its own tail. The harder you work, the less we all get. I find many actors adopting this position out of fear and panic, or because they have no technique. Through pushing, they are trying to sound energized and interesting.

● *The Pull Back* Imagine beginning to let the voice or word out, then pulling it back into the throat in denial. Words are never finished. Mumbling is often how this position is described. The end of a word is never launched into space. It has become such a common feature in film and TV acting that I find it is now affecting stage work. The pull back is often connected to the falling line. The thought drifts off and retreats back into the speaker, or into the floor in front of his feet. I suppose many of us don't trust words and find it hard to commit. Both positions deny the energy of language and we lose syllables and sentences. The rhythm can only be boring. After all, everything is falling into a chasm. The sound drones on and on. Eventually the speaker bores himself.

Many theatre people call this dropping inflection and word energy 'minor-key speaking'. It seems devoid of thought or emotion and far from the major key that passionate acting must strike. From the actor's point of view it is harder work. Every time you drop off or pull back a word or line you have to summon more energy to hoist yourself back onto the text. I will often say to a performer that it is the equivalent of trying to surf: you catch a wave and yet are getting on and off your board mid-wave every few seconds. Not very efficient! These habits are useless in a theatre. As soon as one word is unfinished, or a thought isn't driven through, the audience will not only miss great chunks of text but will be lulled into indifference. Remember, if I miss one word, I'm so busy working out what I might have missed that subsequent lines have gone past me, unheard. Even on microphone this habit leads to incoherence because by pulling back you have lost words. You are asking the listener to do all the work and imagine what you are speaking and experiencing. But should an audience have to work this hard?

C. Jaw Tensions

Any tension in the jaw will obviously result in the sound or word being caged in the mouth. Muscles of articulation are clamped in so that they cannot work clearly. Also, because the jaw is connected to the tongue and throat, the voice sounds muffled and range is reduced. In the simplest way, if you don't open your mouth, sound cannot travel into the listener's ears. Muscles of articulation have no room clearly to shape the voice into words.

D. Tongue Tensions

If you have a tense tongue, speech will be a constant effort and the voice will stay trapped in the throat. Sounds and words are swallowed and muffled. Try out these tensions. Clamp the tongue in the mouth and try to vocalize or speak with ease. You can't. Suddenly you are gagged. The slighter the tension, the more you will be able to monitor it. Remember that any of these tensions can explode into profound problems under the added pressure of stress, fear or unhappiness. You might only experience one of these tensions when you are unhappy in a role, or with a director or a fellow actor. By understanding the tension you will have the power to trouble-shoot it throughout your working life.

All these throat and mouth tensions could lead to some or all of these results:

- Extra mucus after using your voice fully. If the voice is held then the body produces extra mucus to lubricate and protect the system. It's important to note that if after using your voice in an extended way you notice mucus, you are probably tightening or misusing your voice in some way.
- The voice will tire with tensions and you will suffer a restriction of range. One of the first things an actor might notice is that his voice doesn't respond to feelings or imagination. Then what can easily compound the frustration of having an unresponsive voice is to cloud it further with more tension.

These kinds of tensions arise from one common misconception: that the voice operates from the neck up and not from the deep breath support system that comes from below. Until there is a marriage between support and the means of articulation, the voice is always going to be trapped, confused and underpowered. It will never really be free and placed.

Support should control not only the voice but the volume of the voice. It enables us to move through range, it connects us to our emotions, it allows us to think freely, to listen and be in the moment. However, vocal blocks are often applied by actors because they discover that they can short-cut the work and quickly control the volume of the voices in their throats. The throat becomes a faucet. It is only a short cut and if you place control in vocal tensions, you lose the whole rich experience of breath and the wonder of your voice.

Exercise 15: Releasing Vocal Blockages

As you do this sequence of exercises, please stay connected to the breath and support, and never do them in isolation. Some actors may have to address one particular tension for ever and throughout their careers, so don't be frightened of daily work and repetition of exercises. Other actors will address a tension once, resolve it and never have to look at it again. In each of these exercises, work from the outside of the face and body into the throat and voice. And keep breathing.

The Mouth and Face

- Move all the facial muscles.
- Gently massage them, particularly the muscles around the jaw hinges.
- Isolate muscles, move each in turn and then release: forehead, eyes and eyelids, cheek muscles and lips.
- Stretch out the tongue.
- Gently massage the throat and the back of the neck.
- Introduce tension into the face by bunching it up, then release it. When you release the muscles, allow them to fall where they want to go. Don't control the release. Muscles will find where they want to be, not where your habits set them. Bunch up the face again and release. Feel the muscles fall over the bony structure of the face. Repeat a few times. The face should feel more open and surprisingly invigorated.
- Push your lips forward, then stretch them back to bare your teeth. Repeat a few times before releasing. The face should feel more active and alive.
- Smile a big smile and with the smile still in place, open the jaw to about a two-finger drop. Do not let the face drop in the second stage of this exercise. Still imagine the smile as you open the jaw. The space might feel huge but this is a stretch not only to free the face, but because the jaw is connected to the back of the throat you should feel the throat open and that might include a yawn sensation. This is a good sign. It means the exercise is working. You are opening the throat. When the release feels involuntary and uncontrolled this is a positive sign that you are now naturally released.
- During this exercise, if you open the jaw with a smile and concentrate on the breath, you should feel vividly the column of air coming up from the abdominal muscles and passing through the body and throat without interference. This is a great reference point of freedom. Try the same breathing exercise with one of your habitual tensions: place a bit of tension in your shoulders, upper chest, spine, throat or jaw. You will immediately feel and understand the blockage you are working to free.
- After smiling and opening the jaw, stretch the tongue out over the chin. Breathe. The throat is even more open as the back of the tongue is flattened. Repeat a few times. When you return to

a neutral position muscles should feel worked and opened.

- Now release the jaw and circle it gently around as if chewing. Always keep the jaw moving in this easy circular motion. Do not swing it or pull it into place. Any violent thrusting or swinging of the jaw can dislocate it. The jaw hinges are delicate. I once saw a singer force her jaw in such a way that it locked and refused to close.

- Smile and open the jaw. This time place the tongue tip behind the bottom front teeth. With the tip behind the teeth anchoring the tongue, push the middle portion of the tongue forward and release. Repeat. Now with the same tongue-tip position, say phonetically 'k', 'g' and 'ng'. This will exercise the soft palate and free it. If the palate feels sluggish the voice might be held back in the throat or you might sound nasal. Try repeating deftly any words ending in 'ing'. Even just one sound that is held can, in connected speech, pull a whole sentence back into the throat.

Opening the Throat with a Yawn

- One of the best ways to open the throat is to yawn. Yawning widens the throat horizontally. Try a yawn.

- Now, with a lot of breath, try speaking or perhaps counting on a yawn (1, 2, 3, up to 10). You should immediately feel the throat open and stretch.

- Now be more subtle. Count or speak just *thinking* of a yawn but not actually doing it. The throat will feel and stay open.

The yawn, or thinking of a yawn, is a great way of saving the voice if you feel you are trapping or pushing it. It might not be ideal but if you are hurting or restricting your voice either in rehearsal or in performance, you can just think of a yawn and it will help free and save the voice. A good trick is to use the yawn if you have to shout or scream and are not yet feeling sufficiently connected to the moment or prepared for it technically. The yawn technique will at least save your voice. Speaking on the edge of a yawn was an old technique once taught to actors. Although it probably made the voice sound strange, pompous and much too open, it did keep the voice open and saved it from abuse. This thinking of rather than actually executing the yawn is no more than a modification of an old, tried and tested vocal technique.

Test for yourself what a closed throat feels like:

- Stand or sit centred. Breathe in and out. You can do this through the nose, then through the mouth. If you can hear your breathing there is a barrier in the breath. A noisy breath is an indication that there is tension in the vocal passage. It would certainly be audible on a microphone. A noisy breath will also dry the voice. Be absolutely silent without any hint of a rasp. Feel how calm the silent breath makes you feel. Now make a rasp and feel your throat go tense. Go back to a silent and free breath – in and out quietly.

- Do not rush this easy, quiet breath. Keep the lips together, teeth unclenched with the jaw lifted and open. This feeling of freedom you have now is a very important reference position. Remember it. This is the feeling you will be aiming for to keep the voice open and released. Begin to feel the potential power of the breath support welling up freely through the body. It might be at this point you want to close off the power by tightening the vocal apparatus but keep opening the throat, checking the freedom of the shoulders, the jaw, the tongue, the upper chest and the spine. Check that you are breathing out when you feel ready and that the breath has settled in you before you breathe out. This state of calm defines a silent, yet still powerful position of the ready and centred breath. Whenever you to need to re-capture this sense of ease return to this sequence again.

Warming up the Voice or Vocalizing

You already began to warm up the voice when you worked through the physical blockages above in Exercise 15. It's good always to start your vocal warm-up with these releases. If you take your time to address any blockages you will shorten the actual warm-up time needed.

Several reminders before you start vocalizing. Keep connected to the breath support. Never rush this process. Many actors try to get their voices forward far too quickly. Always avoid placing the voice forward before the folds feel warmed. The warming process can be internal, light and easy. There are no guidelines regarding time. Depending on many factors such as humidity, temperature, fitness, or fatigue, you might need a minute, while on other days you could need twenty minutes.

How do you know when the voice is warmed? It's hard to be accurate. I think the best I can say is that a warmed voice does not feel tacky, sticky or held. It motors easily and freely. As an illustration of how it can be held and sticky try gently humming first thing in the morning. It will feel like a cold engine spluttering to life.

Exercise 16: Warming Exercises

- Staying connected to the breath support, begin gently to hum. At this stage the sound can be internal. Many people find that by pitching the voice a bit higher than they normally speak it warms up faster.
- Keep humming gently and when you feel the voice motoring easily start to play with different notes. Hum a tune. Move down through your range. Think of this process as a massage of the vocal folds.
- If during this warming process you feel the voice is trapped, think of a yawn or a silent 'h' to free it. Keep checking the shoulder and the jaw to ensure these areas are free.

Exercise 17: Placing the Voice

Once the voice is warmed it needs to be placed. This means moving up the voice forward into the mouth where it is released. This is the point when the voice leaves you. It is a key moment in voice work because you constantly need to place your voice before you can begin to speak or work properly on a role.

- Stand centred. A visual aid to help you place the voice is to fix your eyes on a point on a wall or out of a window above eyeline. Think to the point in an arc.
- At first breathe to the point. Imaginatively touch the point with your breath.

- Now begin to hum gently, aiming to feel a strong vibration on the lips. This might take a few attempts, so do not push at this, the throat should stay free.
- After you have felt the lips buzz, change the position of your mouth and focus the sound even more forward to the point above eyeline by using an 'oo'. Really purse your lips forward. This will help launch the sound.
- Breathe to that point and vocalize 'oo'. Again, stay free, no vocal pushing.
- Release on 'oo' any note you want and do not be frightened of the sound you make. As long as it's free the sound can't be bad. You should feel the breath support through the body, an open throat and the sound leaving you through the lips. This is very energizing and should make you feel confident and powerful.
- Move from 'oo' into the full open release of 'ah'. This 'ah' is the most open sound you can make. This openness and uninhibited quality of sound can be fearfully revealing, so it is very prone to being controlled in the throat by tightening or pulling back, resulting in a dropping of the sound, letting it fall or dwindle away. 'Ah' is also a very emotional sound. So out of fear we are tempted not to release it fully.
- Elongate the sound, but stop when you feel the support about to go. Open up and raise your arms as you move from 'oo' into 'ah', this will help the release. I recommend you keep this up for a good three minutes.
- Other exercises you can now do to help you feel this full release from 'oo' into 'ah' as you vocalize are to hold a chair above your head, push a wall, throw a ball or imagine throwing one as you move with the vocalization.
- If you lose the sensation of the sound being forward, go back to the hum, the 'm' on the lips. Move quickly from 'm' into 'ah' and 'm' into 'oo' into 'ah'. This will re-establish the placing and release of the voice: m → ah m → oo → ah
- Now try different notes for the release, different levels of volume, while still keeping the sound forward, which will consolidate this sustained release.

At this point in our work you have put into place the basic foundation stones of voice work – marrying support with the free, opened and placed voice. This vocal position can be reached within a few minutes after warming up. The more acquainted you are with feeling this freedom and experiencing placement, the better your work will become. By working properly to regulate support, freedom and release, you will perhaps have righted many restricting vocal habits. This newly released and placed voice must now become a new habit in its own right. I cannot stress this enough. In fact, the whole first year of work has been about developing this awareness. But until you reach and understand this initial stage of voice work it's hard to continue to the next level.

Exercise 18: Sustaining the Voice

Now let's spend some time sustaining this placed, open and supported vocal position. As you do these next exercises, try to finish the sound or words outside you and not drag them back inside you. It's rather the same as holding a verse line and not letting it drop. As this is pure sound you will be making, it requires more concentration, but this means that when you work on an actual text, holding the verse line or the thought sequence will be easier.

- Use the visual aid of the point above eyeline to help focus the voice.
- Cover a count of 10 on a full, open voice: the first count of 3 on 'oo' and then from 4 to 10 on 'ah'. Then, stretch this over 15. Then if you have the support, go for 20. (If 'oo' doesn't work for you try 'm' over the count of 3 to place your voice, then into 'ah'.)
- Try sustaining this with a physical release: pushing a wall, throwing a ball. These exercises will give you a strong sense of muscle underneath the open release.

You are now making a very open sound. Check that you do not start the exercise with a glottal attack. That is, a click in the throat. All the time, think that the control of the sound is coming from the support system. If you find this control difficult, put your hands on your support system. Think of your voice as coming from the centre of your body.

Imagination is a very powerful tool in voice work, as it allows you to reach for the ideal state.

Do the exercises using different notes in your voice and keeping the voice placed. Experiment with different levels of volume.

- Try this simple release to feel continually the placing of the voice. Start a release on 'm' over a count of 3 on the same breath, open for a count of 3 on 'ah', return to 'm' for 3, open to 'ah' for 3. You have covered a count of 12. It's a form of chanting.
- Build your breath support up in this exercise alternatively between 'm' and 'ah' to cover a count of 21 or even 24. This exercise requires good control and returning to the 'm' is a continual way to check that the voice has been placed on the lips.
- Using this exercise further, now crescendo (increasing volume) over 21, then diminuendo (diminishing volume). The crescendo and diminuendo are great control exercises.
- Next try to crescendo and diminuendo with the fully open position on 'ah'; do not push or glottalize but try to keep the sound smooth and steady. Stretch over 15 if you can.

Stretch your breath recovery with this open 'ah' sound. Never go off support during these exercises. Keep shoulders and upper chest free and unlifted. Feel the readiness of the support. Keep that sense of connection.

Exercise 19: Full Breath Recovery

- Release on a series of full breaths on 'ah'; if you can build up to seven full recoveries, one after the other, you are very fit. Vary the note and volume for extra control. Never go off the support, but you will now have to trust you can work the full recovery muscles in the body. Breathe in, release as far as you can go with 'ah', then recover, seven times. Afterwards, when you return to a calm, quiet breath you should feel that the muscles of support have been stretched. It may take a student actor three to four months to achieve this athletic recovery of the breath. An experienced actor should be able to do this at will.

Exercise 20: Fast, Low Recovery

It is very important here to keep the shoulders and upper chest free during any recovery exercise.

- Start touching sound off with a gentle 'ha, ha, ha', taking a breath between each 'ha'.
- When you feel that you are free and connected, speed up the process. Then you can take 'ha' up faster and on a higher vocal pitch, then down.

Now put both these two recoveries together: the full recovery and the short, low recovery. These two recoveries span the experience of the intake of breath. The full is the mighty breath and the short is the top-up breath. Between these two positions are many intermediary breath recoveries, all organically connected to your living, moving, speaking needs. If you exercise the two extremes, you will safely cover the full spectrum of recoveries. Breath recovery marries with connected speech, depending on length of thought, intensity of feeling and the space. After all, we take the breath we need to say what we have to say. When you master the twin poles of recovery you can move into a greater variety of vocal challenges with less effort. You have touched the very seat of vocal power.

Exercise 21: The Recovery Sequence

- Make up your own sequence but start with this. Count on support over 3, taking only enough to cover 3. Recover; then 7; recover, 2; recover, 9; recover, 12; recover, 15; recover, 1; recover, 4; recover, 20. Do this easily and swiftly and you will find that you are taking what breath is needed for the count and moving between a full and shorter recovery of the breath effortlessly.

These exercises are athletic, but should never take you to a point of strain. After the exercises you should feel worked, but never exhausted.

Exercise 22: Supporting the Word

By this point you have reached the moment when you can join pure breath support and voice work with speaking words. We'll start by intoning into speaking:

- Intone, counting over 10, recover the breath and speak over 10 before you have time to think. Intoning is the most fantastic means of releasing the voice into speaking. Build up, intoning over 20, going immediately into speaking. If you feel that the spoken voice after intoning pulls back, try starting to intone over 10 and go into speaking around 5 on the same breath, keeping the energy clearly forward and making the transition into speaking on the same breath. Be vigilant and avoid any pulling off or denial of the sound. If falling off persists, try pushing a wall. Intone, come off the wall and speak.
- Try this intoning into speaking exercise while standing, sitting or walking. Do these exercises, particularly if you have a vocally demanding job coming up.

Once you have aligned the open, placed sound with your breath-support system and begin to have control over the process, you have covered all the basic ingredients of voice work. The important point to recognize is that there are other areas of voice and speech work still to come. But this basic work has to be done before you can access the full potential of your voice. Do this work even when you are not working; that is when you'll need it most. If you are speaking in a theatre every day, then through performance the work is being done. The voice stays healthy when used, but withers when it is inactive.

In a three-year training I would expect the student to understand this work within the first twelve weeks. Eventually it should be so known and habitual that it becomes 'forgotten' by the end of the first year.

As young actors work through all the primary craft exercises of voice work, I constantly try to get them to focus on three other key skills which are vital to the actor: listening, looking and learning.

Listening

An equal part of successful two-way communication is not just speaking, but also listening. Most people need to be trained in how to listen. The noise around us has deadened most ears. An actor cannot survive without listening skills. This awareness of listening starts on the first day of training. Young actors in their enthusiasm to work on themselves do not easily listen to each other, but they must learn. You cannot work on-stage without being able to react aurally to other actors and even to yourself: hearing and recapturing different notes, stresses, rhythms, pace, vowels, consonants. I would go so far as to say that the actor who does not listen and react to others well cannot use his or her voice imaginatively. The non-listening actor may sound beautiful, but will inevitably sink under the weight of her own arias, like a great but remote opera singer.

All aspects of advanced voice-training emphasize listening skills. Like other craft work, the ability to listen has to become ingrained over time in order to sing a note, to respond to the other actors' words, to speak an accent. For some actors listening will be harder to achieve than it will for others. After all, some students have done more work on it than others. If you are musical or speak other languages, or have been encouraged to discuss and debate, you will already have some listening skills. Perhaps more poignantly, there are always students who have never in their lives been listened to; so for them this journey can be rewarding but also painful work. As one student said to me, 'Why should I listen to others when no one ever listens to me?'

It is always productive to have sessions of silence in a voice class to heighten the ear's sensitivity to sound. This simply makes you aware that we do not live in an aural void but in a world rich with sound. Rhythm can be explored through simple clapping games. Any monitoring of sound in a voice class will be training the ear to recognize, for instance, vowel shifts or resonance and range. To master voice, you must master the definition of sounds.

As an initial listening test, I get each student in a group to speak a simple sentence five times, changing the meaning each time. Not only does the group hear the different thought and emotion in each rendering, but they analyse the stress, pace, inflection and pause differences, training their ears thereby to hear the physical effects of meaning and emotion within language.

Looking

Listening and ear training are easily identifiable, allied skills for developing a voice. But looking and seeing are also a part of voice training. We use sight in at least three ways:

1. By looking at the body, the stance and the breathing pattern, we can actually see how someone's voice is functioning. Many bad voices and habits can be noted in the face, jaw, neck, shoulders, legs. You can actually see the tonal quality of a voice by means of its physical placing in the body.

   Placing speech sounds can be done effectively in a mirror. But you have to know how to look. British accents, for instance, are more forward in the mouth than many American ones.

2. How we see ourselves is another key indicator of how we use our voices. If I view myself as a victim, I might constantly de-voice. If I see myself as superior to others I will sound superior. You can see confidence expressed in the voice. You can also see silliness and vanity. The voice really becomes a mirror of ourselves.

   Any student's tell-tale view of himself is always evidenced in the way he or she speaks. The one who falls off every line views himself as a failure. As he becomes more confident with the voice and stays on the lines, this is usually signalled by a radical change in physical esteem. Throughout your work you really do have to put yourself under constant self-scrutiny in order to grow and change.

3. The last part of looking is directed towards the character. How does he or she view the world, view him or herself? Looking at what the character says and does will expose a vision that might be at odds with your own. But unless you really look and hunt the text for evidence you may never really come to know your characters. So the character, too, becomes a kind of mirror in which we can read patterns which will develop into vocal ones.

Learning

Very early in their training, young actors must develop a taste not only for learning in the widest sense but for learning accurately. By this, I mean learning substantial chunks of texts at least once a week.

I must admit that I am reluctant to have to give advice on what should be obvious. After all, an actor relies on being able to learn parts and scripts. Learning accurately is part of the job's fundamental territory. However, the last few years have taught me that young actors either straight from drama school or university rarely have this essential skill. Learning texts and passages by heart and with understanding (not by mere rote) seems too old-fashioned to be part of the curriculum. From childhood, when learning poetry and passages of scripture were part of daily routine, I was made to become skilful at learning accurately.

Accuracy with words must be taken seriously by performers training or starting out in the profession. Too many young actors 'paraphrase' a text rather than speaking it with assurance and comprehension. In fact, this growing habit draws the ire of directors and fellow performers who never seem to get the same cue lines from performance to performance.

The actor should work to learn a part as soon as possible. But to know a part really well you will have to work on the text accurately. The more you paraphrase, the harder it will be really to know a text and the easier it becomes to forget lines. Learning lines for the theatre has to be deeper than learning them for film or television. You always have a longer journey to travel with your learning.

Notes on Learning

- Try to learn a new speech or poem as least once a week. Read all kinds of material out loud.
- Always learn accurately. I cannot think of any advantage in doing otherwise.
- Never spend time learning anything you don't understand. Know what you are saying. Know what you need from the words.
- Learn thought by thought rather than sentence by sentence.
- Learn by speaking out loud.
- Use the form of the writing to help you (i.e. the lines, rhythm and rhyme of verse).
- Pay attention to little words ('but' is very different from 'and'; 'do not' is very different from 'don't').
- Be careful of plurals. The 's' at the end of words is often dropped or added at will.
- As an arbitrary average, most actors say that they can learn a sonnet (fourteen lines of poetry) in forty-five minutes.
- The more you learn, the easier the process becomes. For the actor, learning must become second nature.

I have seen tempers flare in rehearsals and breakdowns in communications among actors and stage management whenever a performer has not learned a text properly. In panic, performers who are still unsteady with a text will lash out at an innocent stage manager or fellow actors. So learning is a habit you should develop early and take seriously.

Sight-Reading

One of the most important skills an actor can learn is, paradoxically, one that is rapidly disappearing in theatre, film and television work – sight-reading. A few years ago, I would have placed this in the second stage of work. But I now feel that so few students can sight-read that they need to be encouraged to start working on it in the first few weeks of training. Every day, pick out a book, open it and read it out loud. Explore all styles of writing. Get used to reading on first sight.

This is a skill you can develop on your own. It's mostly to do with practice and regular commitment to reading out loud. It used to be a skill taught in schools, but most of my students have never done it and come to it as a new experience.

Actors who are good at sight-reading will often work more regularly than greater talents who do not possess this skill. On the one hand it is a very commercial skill, leading to work in recording, advertising and dubbing. On the other hand a career can bloom just because you can sight-read. I have seen directors take parts away from actors because of a performer's inability to pick up a text and instantly read new sections on sight. I've also experienced first days of rehearsal when the director is giving out an uncast section of a play or adaptation. Good sight-readers always get the extra work and, on three occasions I can think of, those sections have brought the actor huge success in famous shows.

At auditions, a director may decide that although you are auditioning for one part, you are more suitable for another (sometimes a better one) and the deciding factor will be how proficiently you can read the part on sight. It is sometimes appalling to discover an actor being unable to make sense of a couple of sentences. The bad sight-readers missed their break. In one case a very ferocious director took a part away from an actor on the first read-through because his initial reading was so bad.

You must learn to read aloud every day from sight and read all styles of writing – plays, novels, newspapers, poems, essays, sermons, letters. Particularly useful are writers such as Swift, Donne and Milton, those writers who have long thought processes which need to be sustained vocally. They will help you train yourself to think ahead and read calmly and accurately.

Recently I was visiting an actor with a reputation for tremendous sight-reading skills. Beside his toilet are piled books from all periods and styles of writing. When I commented, he grinned and said that was where he practised his sight-reading as part of his daily routine.

Use a tape recorder to hear whether you are clear or whether you are reading too fast, too slowly, sustaining the thought or not, making sense and not falling off the line energy. Practise variety and lifting your eyes off the text, coming back to find your place on the page with ease. All these facets of sight-reading are directly linked to repetition. As your confidence grows and you are achieving the above, you might even start interpreting material.

One of the key notes when sight-reading is to stay calm, breathe and be curious and interested in any text you encounter. Essentially there is no magic exercise you can follow, except to work on building a habit for sight-reading into your daily routine. The more you practise and read, the more not only will your technical skills develop but you will begin to understand the structure of a piece very rapidly, along with its essential style.

Use punctuation to move the process of thought from moment to moment, but practise looking ahead to where the thought ends, so that you can motor yourself along to that point, pausing where necessary. The instinct many actors have is to rush on and try to fight the tide, or merely finish. If in doubt, slow down. The common misconception of many readers is that speed is less boring, but the reverse is true. Speeding might be a bluff but it rarely pays off. Actors who read narrative over the radio or audio tapes, for instance, are always asked by producers to read at a slower pace. The listener, you must remember, needs the time both to absorb the story and to catch up with you.

If you are handed a sight-reading just before an audition

you might not be able to read it out aloud, but you will be able at least to physicalize it by mouthing it silently. One actor, very fearful of sight-reading, told me he always takes the text to the toilet and in that way gets the chance to read some of it out before entering the audition room.

Stage Two
EXTENDING THE VOICE INTO RESONANCE, RANGE AND SPEECH

If a beginner actor works well and willingly, within a year the body, the breath, the free and placed voice are set in place. You now have a foundation from which to work positively. As the actor enters Stage Two of training, all the major physical and vocal habits should have been uncovered and are in the process of being addressed. I do not expect these to be totally solved or obliterated. But you should be conscious of any habit that is holding you back vocally.

You should also know by this point how to prepare and warm up the voice on your own without encouragement or instruction. This should be a daily habit. All of this work has probably been achieved during the first stage of work. I do think most voice trainers would agree that if a student misses this initial year of work, is either away too much or doesn't work sufficiently hard, he or she never catches up in the training. You find yourself faced with a constant struggle to achieve with ease not only more advanced areas of voice and speech work but the more challenging aspects of actor training in general. The craft work never becomes fully organic and a fixed habit. Quick repair jobs can be done later but never again will a student have the luxury of working his or her craft in safe seclusion and by measured degrees. Later, if the voice has not been comfortably placed, the actor will have to repair it in public: in the rehearsal room or on-stage in front of a paying audience!

I am not exaggerating when I say that I regularly have conversations with professional actors who lament never having learned proper voice technique and who wished they could return to square one. But beyond a certain point there is no going back.

But let's continue on the assumption that the work we covered in Stage One is set in place and you are doing much of it as a daily routine. You have taken the responsibility of doing the work to help yourself. We can now move on to other areas of technique, building on this solid foundation. Remember that the very basic work of Stage One will always be your security and the knowledge which permits you to forge ahead into more advanced areas of acting.

During the past decade I've noticed that young actors are less willing to accept responsibility for their work and find it harder to enter into a process. In order to move on in any aspect of craft work, fundamentals simply have to be in place. I cannot extend either the resonance or range of a voice during the second year of training if I must constantly correct, say, your lack of support. It is impossible to work the voice safely if it is not free and supported. In order to proceed to work on resonance, range and speech, all the basics of breath support and the free and placed voice must be in place.

Resonance

You've built up the breath support to an organic state, you've freed your voice and placed it out of you. Now you can learn to use other parts of the body to help in making sound. As you venture into the areas of resonance and range, please keep the body, breath and voice work in place.

In theory the whole body resonates the voice, but the most obvious and important resonators are in the chest, throat, face, nose and head. Each human resonator acts as an amplifier. The more resonators you use, the clearer your voice will be and the easier it is both to sound and project the voice. Also, the more natural amplification you use, the easier it is to work in space. Always remember that one of the actor's functions is to fill space with presence and with voice.

Experiencing Resonators

Here are a few simple ways of experiencing the resonators you have in the head, nose, face, throat and chest.

- Sustain a hum into the head. Some people find it hard to feel vibration in the head. Imagine the voice going up there even if you can't feel it.
- Now move and place the sound of your voice into the nose.
- Then the face, throat and chest.

Each position will create a different quality of sound and will require a different intensity of breath support. Generally, today, people do not use the head resonators as much as those in the throat and chest. This has to do with our level of speaking commitment. We live in a society which places value on not showing passion or joy in debate or ideas. More and more, the voice's tendency is to stay trapped in the throat and chest only. This is using the conversational voice only, rather than the declamatory voice of the actor.

The higher the energy of the thought and feeling, the more the voice rises into the head. The greater the need to speak, the more we invest in the head resonators. Most plays in the classic repertoire are rooted in passion and intellectual excitement just bursting to be said and sounded. So to release these plays you will need to open up the head resonators. Certain parts of your voice might feel strange – you will suddenly think that it's not your voice. But it *is* your voice, though perhaps not your habitual one. It has just entered a new key of excitement. Imagine that the humming in your head is just you blowing cobwebs out of your voice.

Four distinct advantages of working your voice in this way are:

- If you use all your resonators your voice is being worked economically and efficiently.
- All reinforcements of sound are being tapped to send the voice into space.
- Speaking only in the throat and chest is much harder work than letting your voice percolate up into the head.
- The head resonators carry sound in space. They produce harmonics that can pierce with ease any dead acoustic. By investing in the head resonances, your voice will become clearer and more acute.

Many modern theatres are acoustically dead. This is a problem I will bring up later when we talk about acting in different kinds of spaces. You cannot be heard in many spaces if you do not use the high-energy head resonators. Boom away as much as you want in the chest and throat, but you will still not be heard clearly.

Humming into Speaking

- Just as you hummed above, now try to speak in each area – head, nose, face, throat and chest. It will feel odd and you'll notice a vibration, but experiment, then clarify the exercise a bit more by getting each placing out of you – 'think out' when you speak.
- As you work the head resonators you should feel the voice become free of the throat. Many actors might want to allow their voice full resonance but find it gets trapped. There are exercises to help unlock it. Even after a few minutes of placing your voice in a different resonance area you will feel it become richer. Speak a chunk of text in each area, then speak it thinking the whole voice. You should immediately notice a difference. The voice ought to sound fuller.

Exercise 23: Head Resonance

This exercise helps to open up your head notes and place the voice very far forward. I like to recommend it because most actors underuse their head resonators and overuse the chest and throat. Consequently, as you do this exercise you might feel that you are speaking too high, or that you have lost the lower tones. This might be true initially but please do not be afraid of the exercise as it is probably over-compensating for years of holding the voice down in the ✗ lower resonators (chest and throat). Recognize that you are just exploring a new part of your instrument and learning a new tune. This image might help you: most of us struggle to place our voice as though we are coming up from some-where deep rather than from on high. So imagine coming over the top of your voice.

This exercise takes you over the top of your voice and out, not up and under the voice.

- Stand centred.
- Breathe and find some deep support before you start; you'll need it!
- Connected to the breath, hum right up into your head. Place your hand on the crown of your head and see if you can feel a vibration. If you can't, do not worry. The hand will still be useful to place the voice in the head. Place the voice here for a couple of breaths.
- On one breath (do not cheat here), place the voice into the head, then let it move down the face until you feel it buzzing on your lips. As soon as you feel this happening open your mouth and release sound on 'ha'.
- The feeling of the voice travelling down through the face is vivid, rather like a waterfall of sound. You must be diligent and open into 'ha' immediately when you feel it on your lips. Most people have an overwhelming temptation to pull back even a fraction into the mouth, if not the throat. This fraction can make the voice sound as if it's behind a plate of glass. It is a vivid recognition of the 'pull back'.

OPENING THE THROAT. by using head resonance!

If you do this exercise correctly, the voice will feel freer than usual and very released. Your support will feel anchored low and the throat open. You might have to do this several times before you fully grasp and appreciate its power. When you do feel this clear, powerful sensation, take the next step in the exercise.

- Repeat the whole process: voice into head; move down the face onto the lips; out on 'ha'.
- Then on the same breath take the 'ha' into intoning over a count of 3, or intoning a piece of text, and then straight into speaking. (Hum → 'ha' into intoning 1, 2, 3 → into speaking 1, 2, 3 → then into text.)

Again, you might have to make several attempts at this but when you achieve it the spoken voice will not only be placed very far forward, but you will hear very high head resonances in your voice. Your speaking voice will have a top layer of vitality and vibrancy which should feel completely new. You are now experiencing resonance.

- Keep breathing and speaking in this position for thirty seconds or so.
- Your voice is probably much higher than usual. Gradually, maintaining the placing and resonance, speak and allow your voice to drop to a more normal pitch. You will keep the clear head resonances and marry them with the chest one. Suddenly you have discovered a richer and freer voice with a usable technique.

Range

Range is the changing of notes in the voice and the movement of pitch up and down. Range can also reflect emotional and intellectual excitement in a speaking voice. If we sound dull it is either because nothing is going on inside us intellectually or emotionally, or because the voice is so held that it can't reflect the speaker's range of creativity. Hence the actor's common defensive complaint, 'I am much more interesting than I sound!' The human voice can only sound interesting if it is free, moves and is connected to emotional and intellectual truth. We are what and how we speak.

The other potential hindrance to the range of the voice is the speaker's fear of being 'over the top', or sounding too committed to the text, or perhaps the voice simply has been underused and the actor has neglected to stretch her or his vocal imagination. I am always amazed by how many actors fear sounding colourful on-stage. And range is vocal colour.

Consider these important and creative points about the use of your range:

- I am not the slightest bit interested in the actor who shows off his or her vocal range. You might be as interesting to listen to as it is to watch a tumbler spinning across the stage, but the audience cannot hear the text. The embellished nature of the delivery impedes their understanding.
- The great texts are about passion and a fiery intellect, so it is completely unreal to speak one of these texts with a limited or fixed range. Your voice is communicating coolness while the text is indicating passion. A rich text deserves a rich voice and it would be unnatural to sound otherwise.
- No audience can listen to a dull voice for longer than a few minutes before switching off. They might switch on again, but might also have missed the most important part of the play. Actors can sometimes come off-stage angry with an audience for not listening, but if you haven't worked to make your voice more interesting, how can you blame the audience?

There are five technical considerations about range I would like you to consider:

1. When your voice is free, strong, healthy and flexible, it will move through range dynamically along with the text. Your voice will, if the thought, feeling and need to communicate are in place, sound appropriate to the text.
2. Like all areas of voice and speech work, the range is dependent on breath support. As range moves in either direction away from the speaker's habitual notes, you will need more or a finer control of your support.
3. I like to think of a voice as a whole. Vocal tags such as tenor, soprano, etc., will often lead us to imagine that the voice can be consigned to compartments. It can't or, perhaps more accurately, it needn't be so limited. Most unstretched and

underused voices have breaks or blips; small holes in the range. When young, our voices break in order to develop naturally. These breaks need time before they fill in, as vocal folds grow and settle. Generally, a man's voice is fully settled at around twenty-five years and a woman's at around eighteen.

Most breaks I deal with are caused by energy that is not fully placing the voice forward. I will be describing exercises later to eradicate both these breaks. This is the creative problem of having a break, whatever form it takes. The actor is consciously or unconsciously frightened of using his or her voice near or around a break. You are afraid that the void in your voice will be revealed. This sometimes forces the break to become more deeply entrenched in the voice. Only by working through these breaks will you understand your full vocal potential and have a greater range of choices in your acting.

Sometimes actors say to me, 'I have two voices, my top voice and my bottom voice.' Or three, four, five voices. The record from one actor is six! When I examine the range, there are breaks that divide the voice, cutting it down. These breaks have to be addressed to give the actor full use of his voice.

4. A healthy spoken voice can easily stretch over three octaves if not four (e.g. twenty to thirty notes). Most of us, however, employ only three to four notes as we speak every day. We only use the whole range when excited or happy or threatened.

5. As the voice is worked and stretched, you will find there is a part of it that is freer, easier and more accessible. This area has been described as 'centre' or 'optimum pitch'. What is interesting – and this is tied to the resonance of the voice and our social shyness in committing to its use – is that when most of us find our centre it is higher than the voice we habitually use. Social conformity has made us suppress our voices. Centre is a place of ease and release.

I always like to offer a range of choice to any speaker, and it seems essential in order for actors to serve the great texts and engage an audience that they work on physically stretching their range. In doing so you will open up your vocal imagination. I always tell actors that it is possible to sound richer, yet still be real. It seems our physical voices have been stunted as well as our imaginative ones. Do not let the voice of restraint whisper in your ear to stop your vocal experimentation.

Exercise 24: Range Exercises

As you do these exercises, remember all the physical free-doms and your connection to the breath, but also try to keep your head still and centred. It's very tempting to move your head up and down in this exercise. In effect, this movement of the head inhibits the work and can pull the voice into you. We are going to be stretching a network of muscles which help you to achieve greater range. You can cheat this process by moving the head so that it does the work rather than the muscles that stretch the range.

These are pure exercises and are stretching two areas of muscles: the vocal fold and the throat muscles. Without becoming too technical, think of the vocal fold rather like an elastic band. It needs stretching in order to become activated. If you hold an elastic band and ping it as it becomes tighter the note is higher and, vice versa, it is lower when it goes slack. The second area to stretch is the muscles in the throat that hold and move the larynx. Stretching these two areas will begin to make your voice flexible and ready to use creatively, and will give you a pleasant surprise about how much range you have gained. You might not dare to use the full range immediately, but it is there for future use and somewhere in reserve you know you have it at your disposal.

Throughout these exercises, think up to a point above eyeline. This is to keep the voice moving out of you in an arc. This point of concentration will be one of the main aids of moving through breaks. Think out, but connect low to the breath. If you feel the support go during these exer-cises – and you will be needing more support and control and a fine sense of economy in the breath – push a wall or hold a chair and reconnect to your power. Lastly, you might feel throat muscles stretch. This is not a bad sign, but do not work beyond the stretch feeling into effort and constriction.

- Stand centred, jaw free, head balanced on top of the spine.
- Concentrate and breathe to the point above eyeline.
- Hum and come down through your voice on a slide, not note by note. Think up to the visual reference point. Try this several times.
- Now use 'oo', then 'ha'. There will be breaks at either end of your range (the human range is large but not infinite). If there are breaks or blips in the main body of your voice let's try to iron them out. It is very important that you are concentrating the voice forward and not pulling back off your voice.
- Pitch above the break and come down through it. Do this at least seven times. The breaks should minimize. If they do not, try the process very slowly. Concentrate on the breath control and the point above eyeline.

  You've been moving down through your voice when you move the voice in this way. You are moving away from tension to openness so the movement is slightly easier than going up through the voice which is releasing into tension.
- Now, on the 'ha', go up through the voice.
- Then down and up on 'ha' several times. If the voice breaks, it won't hurt if you are neither pushing nor tensing up and using support and the outward focus.
- For maximum control, slow this movement of sound.
- Try the same movement on different levels of volume.
- Speak, coming down, then up. You could try counting.
- Speak on the highest note you can, keeping the voice free and forward.
- Speak on the lowest note you can, neither tucking the head in nor pulling the sound back.
- If you have access to a piano, play with your range. Many people freeze up when they have to make a note, but it doesn't matter if you pitch wrongly. Anything goes. Always give yourself permission to sound a bum note. It is interesting that people who fear the inaccuracy of their ear will pause a fraction of a second after hearing the note before attempting to make it. If you do not hesitate but enter the exercise with a spirit of play you will probably pitch accurately – who knows?
- Start around middle C. Play the note, pitch on 'la', then speak around the note.
- Play with notes above and then below middle C. Pitch, then speak.

Stop whenever you feel you are straining. Many of the positions might feel odd, not because you are straining, but because you have rarely stretched your voice in this way. What you are hearing is none the less your natural voice; only a different and unused part of it finding its own range.

- Now sound 'la' over three notes coming down through the voice. Start two notes above middle C – E D C, la la la. Then F E D, etc. going up, note by note. Every now and then, stop and intone, then speak around the note.
- Go as high as you can, then return to middle C and in the same way move down through the voice, stopping off now and then to intone and speak.

Stretching in this way will probably surprise you as to how much range you have – two, three, even four octaves.

The Value of Centre or Optimum Pitch

Generally, if the voice has been used off-centre, one part of the range has been exercised and the other stunted; the voice will need stretching. At this stage of my work I do not dwell too much on what is called centre or optimum pitch, as it is complex and dependent on many physical, vocal and emotional factors. A male actor in a three-year training programme, depending on his age, won't find centre until he is around twenty-five years of age, and he might only begin to be aware of ease in his second year. Centre is dependent on physical centring, breath and support, control and complete vocal freedom as well as emotional liberation. Hardly anybody I have ever worked with in Western countries uses the natural centre when speaking. It commonly has to be rediscovered. Oriental actors discover their centre very early, since so much of their vocal training depends on it.

Exercise 25: The Full Range Stretch

During this exercise you might experience your voice moving close to or even onto the centre of your range. If you experimented with a piano in the last exercise on pitch, you probably have already felt a part of your voice which is easy and full with minimum and effortless support. This area of your voice is the centre or optimum pitch. Discovering this is important, because it gives you a sense of where your maximum vocal efficiency resides. In most voices this is slightly higher than the habitual speaking position. Awareness of centre or optimum pitch can also indicate to the voice teacher how much range is potentially available to the actor around this note. In theory, the centre of the voice is exactly that: you have an equal distribution of notes around the centre.

All this exercise is going to do is stretch your range. It might give you some sensation of where the centre of your voice lies, but do not dwell on only trying to make that discovery.

- Stand centred.
- Fix on a visual aid above your eyeline. Think out in an arc.
- Draw a breath in low and before starting the exercise feel really ready with the breath. Throat and jaw are very open and the channel between breath and voice is clear. Keep your head still and balanced throughout the exercise.
- Count over 20, breathing when you need breath. The odd numbers should be counted at the *top* of your voice and the even at the *bottom*. Do this exercise quickly. Do not ponder on it. The voice should be moving rapidly from the top to the bottom.
- When you reach 20 take a breath (this is vital because the strange excitement of doing the exercise will often mean you forget to breathe) and immediately release on 'ha' on whatever note comes out. On that note go from 'ha' into intoning, using numbers or a line of text.
- Then speak around that particular note.
- At this point you should feel ease and be quite near your centre or optimum pitch.

The principle of this exercise is that you stretch your voice out and then it returns to its centre automatically without you imposing the pitch and placing it where it habitually goes. You should let your voice find its own way like a pendulum coming to rest. You are stretching it like an elastic band and it returns to its proper form and shape – its true note.

Try the exercise several times, but not so often that you feel tired or strained in the throat. Only go to the notes which are possible without too great a stretch or contortion. It is vital that you avoid this. Most of all, enjoy the work.

Falsetto

Most men and some women have a falsetto. This position gives the voice a higher range created by a fluctuation of pitch on the vocal folds. Not all of the fold is vibrating and consequently there is always going to be a break or gear change to achieve falsetto or 'false note'. Counter-tenors work all their careers to eliminate this break. Falsetto is a singing position; you can speak there as well, but it never sounds natural, but artificial. As you exercise the voice it doesn't matter if you occasionally move into falsetto, but try always to work with the whole voice. This keeps the range work relevant to the spoken voice.

Range into Text Work

All resonance and range work will be re-introduced later, in Stage Three, when it is integrated with text work. The exercises in Stage Two so far have been work-outs, designed to prepare your voice and accustom you to new vocal sensations and sounds. However, feel free to experiment and play with text at any stage of this work. You'll be interested to hear how words sound with your new voice.

For instance, take a speech (I would suggest one that is full of rich language and imagery) and speak it with minimum range. Then speak it held only in the chest and throat resonances where it will sound deep. Then place the speech high on the voice, then low. Isolate different resonators as you speak the lines. Then warm up all your resonators and range, speaking the speech with awareness of your whole voice. I think you will notice a difference.

Speech

This work is designed to exercise all the speech muscles so they operate with efficiency and economy. An actor aims to speak so that the audience is completely unaware of articulation or technique, yet can hear each part of every word with total ease and understanding. The larger the theatre space, the more energy and definition a word needs, though on camera you need to possess a great economy of technique so that the movements of your lips and tongue do not distract from the words. To serve many types of texts you will need strong and flexible speech muscles. The same applies if you want to perform in large theatres.

The process we call speech is simply one of physically breaking up the voice into identifiable units called words. This process is done in the mouth with the lips, jaw, tongue, soft palate and facial muscles. It is very precise physical work and speech is one of the most balanced and complex muscular exercises the body performs. It is easy to push speech off balance, which is why it is one of the first physical controls to go when we've been drinking or suffer a stroke. These muscles, if they are going to perform well, need constant work; *they need it every day.* Most of us, when left isolated for any length of time, have had the experience of not speaking for a day or more. We then know how hard it is the next day to get our voice going and to make our speech clear. The actor simply must exercise the speech muscles constantly in order to safeguard clarity.

Speech is really what I would consider to be the last stage of voice work. All speech work needs the breath and voice behind it and is not done in isolation from the voice.

Too much speech work is done without an awareness of voice. If the voice is not placed clearly by the breath in the mouth, then why should the speech muscles bother to work? They need to feel energy in order to perform their extraordinary and wonderful task: the task of making the voice, our thoughts and feelings specific through the physical and sensual power of the word.

In my experience, when the voice enters the mouth most people find their speech muscles begin to work as they come to grips with the energy and physical clarification of words. I'm sure when you've been intoning and placing the voice in earlier exercises you have already felt the face move more. With this awareness and movement, your speech has already begun to sound clearer. Plus you are now having a greater awareness of how you sound and how you can sound even *better*.

All speech exercises must be done with strong breath and on a fully energized and placed voice. If you are prejudiced against clear speech and consider it as rather posh or too proper, I hope I can persuade you otherwise. Formality and clarity in speech is neither élitist nor a class prerogative. We always become clearer the more we need words and passionately care about what we say. When words are important and we choose them with care, we never short-change them but speak them fully. So urgency will often prompt clarity. Unfortunately we often need to feel that our voice, our words or our being is under threat before we can bring a clarity to our speech. We can be clear in any accent, dialect or language. Speaking clearly has nothing to do with background or culture. It always amuses me that some of the most lazy and incoherent mumbles come from the élite sections of society; from those who have nothing to ask for.

For an actor, clarity is absolutely essential, not only because most dramatic texts demand it, but because the audience has to hear every word you speak. Writers provide clarity clues through the make-up of the very words and sentences they set down on paper. An actor who refuses to speak a text with reference to these notations is not going to release faithfully the acting clues embedded in the physical nature of the word.

Consonants and Vowels

Learning to work with consonants and vowels teaches you about the physical properties of words and how your articulation of them brings verbal strength to your acting.

A common postulate you can make is: consonants = clarity of thought; vowels = emotion. Pause, pace and intention are all embedded in the word. Remember that language is only partly intellectual. Speaking words clearly opens many more doors to the world of the mind, heart and soul. Certain texts will need more speech work than others, as we will see later in Stage Three.

I think it is interesting that most actors agree that older texts – classical ones – need good clear speech, yet they will mumble through modern texts in an attempt to make their speech more 'real'. No, clarity is a demand whenever and whatever you speak.

I have been lucky enough to work in rehearsal rooms with many great playwrights. I have never yet had a playwright say to me: 'Can you make that actor sound less clear?' On the contrary, they often say: 'Can you heighten the speaking of those lines to make them clearer to the audience?' Writers do not write words unless they want them heard.

Exercise 26: Speech Work-out

At this stage I am not going to work on accents. I will be dealing with accent issues and received pronunciation (RP) later on (see p. 122). This is a speech work-out aimed at acquiring strength, flexibility and ease of all the speech muscles. It is a preparation to speak any text in any accent as clearly as possible.

- Breathe, support and place the voice.
- Stretch and awaken the speech muscles. Sitting, move every muscle in the face. Move and isolate the forehead, eyes/eyelids, cheeks and lips.
- Stretch the tongue in and out, then open the jaw through a smile to a two-finger drop. Do this several times.
- With the jaw open and a smile in place, put the tongue behind the bottom teeth, then exercise the soft palate – 'k', 'g'. Do this quickly.
- Next exercise the muscles around the mouth by taking a series of vowels and over-speaking them (e.g. d<u>ay</u>, N<u>o</u>, o<u>ut</u>) Think that these muscles are pulling the voice forward and launching the sounds.
- Bunch the face up and release, repeat a few times. Shake the face out. Blow through the lips. If you can, roll an 'r'. Massage the face.
- Very gently, with your hands, pull the jaw open and then with the back of your hand, close the jaw until the lips touch but the teeth remain unclenched. Repeat.

After this sequence the speech muscles should feel more active, worked and flexible.

Placing Consonants and Vowels

I will be placing some of these sounds in a position that is called RP (received pronunciation). But please just think of these exercises as muscular work that will bring greater clarity to your speech. One of the positive characteristics of RP is that all sounds are clearly placed as far forward as possible. You can always pull back later into other accents. These positions are athletic, energized and useful as a work-out.

You will find that it is useful to do many of these exercises looking in a mirror. This will help you monitor any tensions in the jaw and to see if you are closing it too much or pulling back. Also check for ease in the lips and neck. In connected speech the movement of muscles should be fast and flexible, and never strained or laboured. During these exercises I will be encouraging you to isolate and precisely place different sounds. This could feel odd and unnatural, but the muscles are being carefully trained so that when you speak a text they work and do not get in your way. So the feelings are new sensations that you have to live through. Sounds must be tuned and familiar enough for you to forget them – this is the purpose of all technique. I also think, if you can, you should aim to work all these sounds with a free and open jaw. This might be tiring, so do not work for hours on these exercises. Short, regular periods are best.

- Aim for a two-finger drop with the slight smile across your face. When the jaw begins to ache, shake out the face or blow through the lips. If it is very tiring, stop and do more another day. The tiredness will vanish as the muscles become more tuned.
- When you work the speech muscles with this open rather than tightened jaw, they are working in a bigger space within the mouth and have to learn to be very strong and accurate as the placing in the mouth is so extended. In connected speech you will find, if you have worked with this open jaw, that words fly from you more effortlessly. A word of warning, however. Many actors when working with a free jaw experience a few days of slurring their speech. Do not worry. This is a natural part of the process. If you have been speaking with a tight jaw the speech muscles have been working in a very cramped space. They haven't been used to working in a free way and are untrained and imprecise. They will soon learn. Go through this slurring phase because clearer and more dynamic speech will follow.

Voiced and Voiceless Sounds

Again, I'm going to ask you to be very alert and specific about all the sounds you speak. The habit we most often have today in our uncommitted way of speaking is to take voice away from sounds that should be voiced, particularly at the ends of words and thoughts. This is linked to the pull back on words and the falling line, habits that we worked on earlier.

All vowels should be voiced. Consonants are divided into voiced and voiceless. Many go in pairs. The same placing one will have may just lead to a vibration in the throat and the other will only be sounded by a release of air. You can check voicing by placing a hand on your throat. You will clearly feel the voice vibrating, such as a vibrating 'z' and a non-vibrating 's'. The first is voiced and the latter is voiceless. If you take voice away from, say, a 'd' and change it into 't' (deb<u>t</u> instead of dea<u>d</u>,) then clarity in a large space is almost impossible.

All consonants, using the muscles of articulation, fully or partially block or impede or manipulate the flow of the voice and breath in some way. The release of the air on consonants can be as follows: an explosion (e.g. 'b'); a constant release of air (e.g. 'v'); a block followed by a release (e.g. 'chew'); a nasal release (e.g. 'n'); a narrowing of the air passage (e.g. 'r').

A Full List of All Consonants

Please speak each of the sounds below so you can instantly identify the difference in quality between voiced and voiceless consonants.

	Voiced	Voiceless
Plosives	b	p
	d	t
	g	k
Fricatives	v	f
	th	th
	z	s
		sh
		h
Affricates	dj	ch
Nasals	m	
	n	
	ng	
Frictionless	r	All voiced
	l	
	j	
	w	

Some of these sounds you will already do well. They do not need attention. In fact, many actors worry that all their speech is in need of work. This is never true. Yet some sounds will always require attention. You might have to concentrate on the consonants you find difficult or know you stumble over.* Some consonants are more physical and less easy to make as sounds and everyone has trouble with them. I'll point those out below when I deal further with each sound. Some need particular attention on a microphone because if they are not voiced clearly the microphone

---

* Many actors who have an innate fear of certain sounds in particular contexts will instantly drop out of an acting moment and organically disconnect from a text. So if you work that sound and the the fear of making it out of your system your acting will flow and become more spontaneous.

exposes them cruelly as crackles or pops. I'll highlight those below, too.

Many actors find speech work easier and more relevant when applied to a text, so I'll be doing a lot of work on consonants and vowels later in Stage Three. But I do think you should at least go through these sounds once, just to check whether you are working them clearly and efficiently. All the placings of consonants I'm recommending represent the most efficient way to make a sound in connected, rapid speech. You might be able to approximate a sound with sloppy placing, but I'm concerned that you should be able to move quickly into the next sound. That's why I'm going to be somewhat pedantic in how I suggest you make the sound. Well-placed consonants are not only more efficient and clearer in theatrical space, but make the mouth look better on camera.

I will never do these exercises before a performance, however. I think they belong in a technical work-out, not a warm-up, as they can easily make you tense. The resulting tension-meeting-adrenalin will probably propel you on stage or in front of the camera with more stress than usual. I've often seen actors in the wings before an entrance furiously mouthing their consonants hoping that it will help them. Instead they are merely tongue-tying themselves. So quick fixes cannot replace genuine craft work developed over a proper period of time.

What might be useful while doing these exercises is to push occasionally and gently against a wall with one hand. This push can be subtle. It will just keep the breath connected and give you that all-important sense of finishing each sound and word completely. Even if you are sitting, you can push up against a desk or down on the chair. Also, you might like to use a tape recorder to hear clarity, or the lack of it. This clarity will be most apparent as you go into words.

Exercise 27: Placing Consonants

- Sit upright and comfortably in front of a mirror. Make sure you can breathe easily and that your feet are making contact with the floor and are rooted. Use the mirror to check not only the mouth positions of each sound but to ensure that you are keeping the jaw open and free.
- Smile in place, a two-finger drop. Keep checking for this drop. Watch that you neither contort nor purse your lips, nor yank the sound back with the sides of your mouth. Keep the neck as free as possible, with your head evenly balanced. Imagine the mirror is a camera and, for the sake of vanity, you do not want to be seen contorting your face.

   All speech work and voice technique for actors changed considerably with the advent of the camera. Before cinema, actors in large, badly lit theatres could perform physically weird and contorted forms of enunciation without the audience noticing. Even today, when we look at a series of pictures of nineteenth-century actors or even early silent-film performances, we notice how grotesque the facial and mouth gestures seem. Actors had simply learned to strain in order to fill huge spaces. Today's actors cannot show the strain and can learn techniques to avoid it.

   During this work, whenever you get taut or tired, 'shake out' the face and massage the neck. Do many releases and stay connected to the breath.

- Vocalize a series of 'b's. Check in the mirror that after each performance of 'b' the jaw reopens to the two-finger drop. The lips should be meeting each other strongly but lightly without puckering or pulling. Now do 'p' with the same placing, but lightly and without voice. Place your hand on your throat to check that there is no vibration. Badly or tightly placed 'p's or 'b's will be clearly exposed on a microphone as a distracting popping sound. So this is a sound you have to really work at in order to produce it well.

   Important. Whenever you work on a voiceless consonant like 'p' you must be careful not to put the ending 'er' after it (e.g. 'p<u>er</u>'). That will vocalize the sound and not give you a clear sense of how you are making the isolated consonant. Sound 'p', then 'per' and notice the difference with the voiced 'er'.

- Now move on to a series of voiced 'd's. Jaw open to the two-finger drop and not bouncing around. Let's make the tongue really work by not closing the work space down! The tongue tip should create a clear and strong closure of air by pressing against the alveolar ridge (that ridge just behind your top teeth). This release should be muscular, not slushy. Next try 't', voiceless but very prone to slush! The 't' sound should be a sudden and clear explosion of sound, not 'tsss'. The 't' is another sound exposed cruelly by a microphone.

- Voiced 'g' – voiceless 'k'. Two-finger drop again, tongue tip wedged behind the bottom teeth. A series of 'g's and then 'k's. If you have problems with these sounds, it is likely that the back of your tongue is weak and muffling clarity. Stretch the tongue out and down across the chin a few times, then try again. Many of us can't be bothered to work the back of the tongue and so we swallow these sounds.

- The sounds 'v' and 'f' are often overworked and pushed. The placing is unique to each speaker because it is related to the shape of your lips and teeth. Look in the mirror and, from the jaw release of the two-finger drop, gently close the jaw, aiming to make contact in the easiest way with the top teeth touching the bottom lip. Do this with the smallest amount of tension. Many people overdo this sound by drawing the lip in or scraping the teeth over the bottom lip. The sound is much easier than that to produce. Try a series of 'v's and 'f's with this light and easy placing.

- Another difficult sound for some people, and one often forgotten in some accents or overdone by others, is the voiced and voiceless 'th'. Look in a mirror and ensure the jaw is free. The tongue tip makes contact behind the two top teeth. The tongue needn't be pushed out from behind the teeth or drawn backwards through the teeth. The sound should be easy and clear, with the tongue contained in the mouth so it can adroitly move back to the next sound. Do a series of voiced and voiceless 'th's. Say, 'Three free things set three things free.'

- The voiceless 's' is often called the speech teacher's nightmare. It is one of the highest frequency sounds we make, so it stands out in any unbalanced voice. Most audiences and directors will criticize an actor's 's' long before they hear other sounds in a voice. Again, many speakers overdo this sound in an attempt to rectify it, but succeed only in making it worse by pushing on it. Many intruding 's' sounds right themselves when the speaker starts to speak on a full, not half, voice. The full voice will often balance the acoustic property of the 's'.

     If you have a gap between your top teeth or wear braces, you can make the 's' by placing the tongue tip on the gum behind the bottom teeth. Do this with ease and without pushing. If you do not have a gap in your front teeth, you should be able to make this sound by keeping the jaw free and placing the tongue tip on the ridge where you placed the 't'. But unlike the 't', your tongue isn't so rigid, it's a softer position with tongue sides making gentle contact with the back teeth.

Release without pushing on 's' until you feel the air is flowing across the tongue and the sound is just a gentle release between the tongue tip and the alveolar ridge. If the tongue moves forward onto the teeth, you will lisp; if the tongue or jaws are too tight, you might whistle the sound. When you release the 's', move on to the next sound. Do so with a rapid but light movement. This 's' sound doesn't need heavy work. A misplaced or too intrusive 's' will also be very noticeable on a microphone.

The sound 'z' is placed in the same way as 's' but is voiced. This voicing obliterates any problems of the 's's penetrating harmonic. Most problems with 'z' are associated with not giving the sound full voice ('words' rather than 'wordz').

- A light touch is needed with the voiceless 'sh' (as in 'shoe') and the voiced 'sh' (as in 'leisure'). The jaw must be free and the lips move forward, with the tongue placed without effort between the roof and bottom of the mouth. Usually there are no real problems with the voiceless 'sh' but many speakers often forget to give the 'z' sound in 'sh' its full voice (e.g. 'measure', 'pleasure'). The sounds are rich and sensual and when spoken will release passion and colour in a text. Go from a series of 'sh' to 'z' making sure the 'z' gets full voice.

- The voiceless 'h' requires a slight friction (only slight, no glottal attack) in the throat. Some accents forget or drop the 'h' ('ello' rather than 'hello') You only really hear the quality of the 'h' when you move into the vowel after it (e.g. 'how', 'heat', 'happy'). If you do drop your 'h' sounds, work them by elongating the release on 'h' before you enter the rest of the word. Be very aware that you must move into the next vowel with voice but not voicing through attack. Working on the edge of a yawn is useful if you feel you are attacking the sound. The microphone will pick up an overdone 'h' so you are aiming eventually to place the 'h' before the vowel, gently yet clearly, without over-breathing it or giving in to glottal attack.

- The voiceless 'ch' is a combination of a 't' moving on to a 'sh'. So place the tongue as for 't' but with the lips slightly forward. Feel the release of the 't' and move into 'sh'. Not normally a problem on the voiceless one but the voiced sound 'dz' is often devoiced. Firmly voice 'dz' – 'd' into 'z' and check the vibration by touching your throat (e.g. 'judge', 'fudge').

- With the voiced 'm', 'n' and 'ng', problems usually occur when the soft palate is a bit slow and lazy and you nasalize sounds that should not be nasal. No other sounds in RP apart from 'm', 'n' and 'ng' are nasal. If this is a problem, the chances are that your soft palate should be fitter.

  Here's a test. Place a hand underneath your nose. Move rapidly between 'm' and 'b'. On the 'm' you should feel a blast of air come down your nose, on 'b' there should be no air. Do the same with 'n' into 'd', 'g' into 'ng'. This exercise will give you a physical awareness of the sound and also train the soft palate to move swiftly up and down.

  For 'm', look in the mirror and put your lips gently together in front of an unclenched jaw. Do a series of 'm's. The lips must come firmly together to create enough pressure for you to feel a buzz on the lips but they do not need to be pulled in or puckered or stretched back.

  With 'n', the jaw should be at a two-finger drop and the tongue is on the alveolar ridge behind the top teeth. When you do a series of 'n's, the jaw should remain still and you should feel the vibration in your nose.

  With 'ng', the jaw should be at a two-finger drop with the tongue behind the bottom teeth. As you make a series of 'ng's, you should feel the flexing of the back of the tongue. Keep the jaw still.

- The making of the voiced 'r' proves difficult for many people because it needs a narrowing of the mouth created by the tongue, though you do not make physical contact there. Consequently it is a subtle rather than physical sound.

  Look in the mirror and, if you can, roll an 'r' and as you do so, keep the jaw free. Bring your lips forward. As you do this, you should hear the sound become richer. In this position try speaking an unrolled 'r'. If you find rolling an 'r' difficult, try the above sequence only with the tongue tapping the hard palate in order to make the sound. To strengthen a weak 'r', move quickly from a rolled to a tapped 'r' but remember to keep the lips forward. Now go from a 'd' into an 'r' (e.g. 'dream'). 'Th' into 'r' (e.g. 'three').

  The weak 'r' communicates certain messages. For men it can be considered laziness or a public schoolboy affectation. It is immediately identifiable (and for some television personalities a lucrative affectation), but for an actor changing characters it's often reductive.

- The two 'l' sounds are both voiced. The light 'l' as in 'light' and 'low' and the dark 'l' found mostly at the end of words like 'boil', 'kettle' or 'wall'. The light 'l' normally has no problems attached to it.

Look in the mirror with the two-finger drop. Tongue on the alveolar ridge but not tight as in 't'. Quickly do a series of 'l's. The tongue should be moving rapidly, releasing and returning to the alveolar ridge.

The dark 'l' is more problematic and is one of those consonants that many young actors fail to make. The dark 'l' is a strong sound that carries a whole syllabic weight. So if you do not make it clearly (as in 'toil all day'), it pulls the whole voice back, causing you to swallow words and choke on them.

Start in the same way as with the light 'l', but as you vocalize into the dark 'l' you'll have to pull the back of your tongue up. Try 'ball', 'wall', 'call'.

It is a hard sound but not difficult to make clear if you are patient and really finish the word feeling that full syllabic weight in your mouth. You have to dwell on the sound and give it space to sound itself.

- There are two consonants that are termed as semi-vowels inasmuch as they are almost a vowel. They are 'j', as in 'year' and 'yellow', and 'w', as in 'we' and 'war'. With the 'j' there are no real problems. Just for exercise, though, try to say 'year' several times without your jaw bouncing.

The 'w' only goes weak when the lips are not making sufficient contact forward. In the mirror, look and see that the beginning of the sound is made with the lips pushed slightly forward, touching and then releasing. You have to commit to this sound, otherwise it does get woolly.

These are all the consonants properly placed. As I have said already, you will not need seriously to address the sounds you find easy to make. But it's worthwhile, in front of a mirror, giving the consonants and your speech muscles the work-out below to trouble-shoot any problems which will require further attention.

Exercise 28: Consonant Work-out

- The jaw should be at the two-finger drop position. Always remember to use that smile which lifts the cheek muscles.
- Keeping the jaw still, move the tongue to touch the alveolar ridge behind the top teeth. Move it to the bottom teeth, touching the gum behind the teeth. Then into one cheek and

the other. Top, bottom, side to side. Start slowly and build up speed.

- Stick out the tongue straight and move the tongue tip up and down. It should ache, but not fiercely. Release the tongue and face. Repeat three times.

- Make up strings of consonants, including the ones you have difficulty with, for a quick way of toning up all the speech muscles. Here are some I use, designed to get the whole system working. Keep checking in the mirror for an unnecessary tension and for jaw freedom. Keep the voiceless sounds voiceless and the voiced ones voiced. Also breathe and support throughout.

  Start with 'p' and move into 'b', 'm', 'w', 't', 'd', light 'l', 'r', 'g'. Then build up as much speed as you can: P–B–M–W–T–D–L–R–G. This sequence moves through all your speech muscles. Try others such as the voiced 'th', 'v', dark 'l' and 'k': TH–V–L–K.

Some people prefer tongue-twisters such as 'many men' or 'red lorry, yellow lorry'. You can get wonderful tongue-twister books that work out each consonant. I will be doing more speech exercises later with texts in the third stage of work.

It's worth saying that certain texts (for instance, Restoration, Georgian, Wilde or Shaw) will require more speaking dexterity and energy. So before you go into rehearsal, work out these muscles even more diligently. For until you can speak a high-energy text clearly and swiftly you won't be able to act it appropriately. If your speech muscles let you down you will be seriously undermining any text which is meant to be properly heard. The pace, wit and intent of the play will come to a grinding halt.

Vowels

The vowel is the voice. Every unconstructed sound the voice makes is a vowel sound (e.g. 'oo' or 'ah'). Different vowel sounds are made by slight shifts in the mouth, tongue and facial muscles. As I've said before, vowels are the emotional part of any word and making the sounds can be a huge relief. I'm not going to go over all the vowels in RP but only a few to help exercise both the face and the energy of specific sounds.

Vowels can be pure with one movement of sound, such as 'hand' or 'car'. And within that category, short as in 'hat' or long as in 'car'. They can have two movements within them (diphthongs) such as 'buy' 'dear' 'bare', or three movements (tripthongs) such as in 'fire and 'slower'.

Exercise 29: Vowel Work-out

When working vowels and exercising the muscles, try to keep to the two-finger drop position. I know this may feel false, but it is going to open up the vowels accurately. Try to place the vowels as far forward in your mouth as you can. Some sounds are made further back in the mouth (like 'e' as in 'eat' or 'i' as in 'idiot') so this forward concentration will keep the voice from naturally falling back. Avoid glottal attack, the push or explosion in the throat. You will have to be especially diligent with the short vowels as they are easier to attack. Always stay on full breath support and on full voice.

When working all vowels, try going from intoning to speaking them. This will give you a tremendous sense of voice and forward placing into speaking. Also exaggerate the speaking of a vowel before you return to speaking it normally. This exaggeration will work out facial muscles, making the whole process easier as you return and speak a text.

Try this sequence with all the above in mind:[*]

[*]For North American and Australian actors: although the pronunciation of some words may differ between the standard English of Britain, North America and Australia, the principle behind these exercises will still work.

- '*Ah*' Intone, exaggerate, then speak: 'castle', 'father', 'barn'.
- '*Ee*' Same sequence. Be careful not to pull the sides of the mouth back. Keep the two-finger drop: 'bee', 'meal', 'speak'.
- '*Or*' Jaw free but the lips moving slightly forward: 'door', 'order', 'warm'.
- '*Oo*' Jaw free, lips closer than for 'or': 'moon', 'boot', 'loot'.
- '*i*' Short and avoid glottal attack in back of throat, jaw free: 'idiot', 'bit', 'wish'.
- '*A*' Again short, jaw free, no glottal attack: 'apple' ,'cat', 'band'.

Diphthongs

Really enjoy these and as you exaggerate the sounds, feel all the mouth and facial area launch these sounds forward:

> 'go', 'no', 'lonely', 'road'
> 'rise', 'life', 'smile'
> 'day', 'away', 'stay'
> 'owl', 'mouth', 'loud'
> 'air', 'care', 'share'

After this work-out you should feel great elasticity in your mouth.

Exercise 30: Definition of Words

The need for the actor to say physically every part of a word – beginning, middle and end – is a passion of mine. Working towards a greater definition of words is a key element of the craft work in this second stage of voice work. We are getting closer to really speaking now with the utmost clarity. Many of us think we do define words clearly, but we actually miss sections of them.

Some of these exercises may feel too elaborately overspoken, but bear with them so that you can exercise the speaking of the whole word.

- *Starting Words* Learn to put more energy at the start of a word in order to launch it into space: say 'three', 'big', 'pat', 'dig'.

- *Multisyllabic Words* Speak all parts of a word, including the middle. Many of us skid through these longer words but each part of the word, even the unstressed sections, should be defined: say 'multisyllabic', 'integrity', 'wisdom', 'abundance', 'delight', 'courage', 'flexibility'. Take these words to pieces and make sure you are saying each and every part of the word, then speed up that definition.
- *Ends of Words* Remember all the voiced consonants we worked on above? What tends to happen today is that we forget to voice at the end of a word (as in 'wor<u>d</u>'). We either devoice it (drop the end) or just run out of steam (stop). <u>The actor should remember that clarity in speaking is married to need. Clear speech is not a fussy standard but a necessary tool that every actor must have in order to communicate clearly to an audience but also to release the truth within a heightened text. Say these, for example:</u>

ward	NOT	wart
end	NOT	ent
dead	NOT	deat
love	NOT	lof
live	NOT	lif
breath	NOT	breaf or brea
death	NOT	deaf or dea
scrub	NOT	scrup
rub	NOT	rup
singing	NOT	singin
laughing	NOT	laughin
speaking	NOT	speakin'
hat	NOT	ha
hit	NOT	hi
paws		's' is a 'z' here ('s' becomes 'z' after a voiced sound)
doors		's' is a 'z'
shuns		's' is a 'z'
gives		's' is a 'z'

This all might seem pedantic but by working the muscles fully you really begin to speak clearly, quickly and economically. If you can't say a word, or you are frightened of a word looming up in the text, avoid the temptation of skidding through it. What I always tell actors to do is to take the word to pieces and confront each part of it. This will educate the speech muscles to tackle the word correctly. Like learning a dance step, you work it out slowly and then gather speed, but retaining knowledge of the explored parameters. And gradually, as with any dance sequence, you release the patterns and rhythms of speech sounds and consequently own the words. If you are in doubt about the stressing of a word, every good dictionary provides a pronunciation and stress guide.

As speech muscles learn to speak clearly, the audience won't notice the making of the word, they'll just hear it whole. This attention to the whole word is particularly essential in any large theatre or an acoustically dead space. Without clarity and definition it won't matter how big or loud your voice is.

Think of sound definition as a benefit. By staying on each sound of every word you not only unlock acting notes given to you by the writer, but you stay in control of your speaking and solidly in the acting moment. Actors often lose control because the breath isn't in their bodies and the word isn't in their mouths. Whatever emotion is surging through you, a clear word will keep you held and safe.

The Bone Prop

I want to discuss the function of the bone prop because it has been used for years as an aid to defining clear speech. The bone prop is normally made of plastic and comes in different sizes, depending on the size of your mouth. It literally props open the jaw, either by being wedged between the top and bottom front teeth or by being placed on the alveolar ridge at the top of the mouth. The purpose is to keep the jaw open as you work consonants and vowels.

I have been encouraging you to check continually for a two-finger drop while you are working out the speech muscles. This check is doing, in a less demanding way, what the bone prop does.

As a child I used to have to work with this prop because of a speech problem of my own and I had an unfortunate experience with it. I hated it! It made me want to choke. And since it was left in the mouth for long periods of time, my jaw locked because I was afraid I would swallow it. My prop had a hole in it with a string that went around my neck; the string was used to yank the prop out if swallowed. I only remember the bone prop as an instrument of torture. Consequently I never use it in teaching.

However, a bone prop does help and some actors swear by them. As long as you don't use it for more than a few minutes at a time and you don't lock the jaw around it, you might find it can clear up a persistently weak sound. Recently an actor I worked with begged me to try exercising him with such a prop. I conceded and within a matter of days a sound he had been struggling with for weeks emerged clearly.

If you want to try a DIY version of the prop, trim a wine cork to fit your mouth, not holding the jaw too far open; remember the two-finger drop. Have a go, but don't swallow it!

Accents

When an actor understands and can use his or her own voice, native language and accent with pride and freedom, the time has come to encourage the performer to try using other accents. Not only is this work essential to broaden an actor's commercial possibilities but it will extend vocal range, pace, stress and listening skills.

Always remember that to live emotionally on-stage with an accent not your own is hard. It takes time and familiarity. When the acting heat is turned on, unless the actor has worked diligently in an acquired accent he or she will usually slip back to the native one. What is also true is that if an accent is neither breathed nor felt organically, an actor will act 'by numbers' in a stifled, disconnected way. As audience members, I think we have all witnessed these results on-stage.

Received Pronunciation and Other Accents

A war still rages in theatre and in actor-training programmes about whether or not to teach received pronunciation (RP). RP is a standard form of English with, supposedly, a neutral accent. It should not be confused, as it frequently is, with posh, upper-class accents. Here is a brief history of the RP battle.

There was a period in British drama training (roughly up to the 1960s) when every student actor was told that he or she must speak RP and that his or her own accent was irrelevant, unintelligible or, at worst, ugly. Actors who learned RP in this way could often sound disconnected and false. Their own natural voices, full of regional variety and sounds, had been lopped off crudely.

Since the 1960s most voice and speech teachers have accepted that this rigid and somewhat élitist attitude to RP is morally wrong and artistically unsound. Systematically to attack and undermine our natural pattern of sound can be psychologically inhibiting, robbing each of us of something special and particular in our natures. But then the pendulum swung to the opposite extreme. Some schools stopped teaching RP altogether, so many working actors never learned it. Complaints from directors came in thick and fast. Young actors without a grounding in RP were uncastable in certain plays and roles. Audiences also complained. Actors relying solely on their regional accents could not always be understood easily. This last complaint, however, is somewhat dubious, as I will explore later.

What I think is now emerging is a balanced middle ground, in which native accents and RP mix and mingle. For actors to work fully, and have as many professional possibilities as possible, RP is required. It must become another element in your arsenal of craft, to be deployed when necessary. What the actor must realize throughout his or her working life, however, is that RP, like any other accent, changes every decade or so. Some period plays (a Coward play of the 1930s, for instance) will require a heightened RP of the period. However much the theatre changes and accommodates itself to new styles and voices, it is still fair to say that stage and casting directors continue to require a performer to speak in RP and, for some unknown reason, will accept you can speak other accents but only if you initially present yourself in RP. What many do not seem to understand is that you can speak RP from another accent.

At an audition, if you reckon the part is in RP you should be prepared to speak it. It is wrong to say that other accents are inferior to RP. In fact, actors today need a whole repertoire of accents to work consistently. It is also wrong to assume that many parts traditionally played in RP should always be done thus. The battle continues over these points. The actor who survives these skirmishes is the one who is prepared to speak in many tongues.

I am willing to bet anything that Shakespeare's actors weren't speaking RP, but something rougher and coarser. And yet there is still a fuss when a well-known actor plays Shakespeare in a regional dialect or accent like Irish, Scottish, Welsh, Lancashire or Yorkshire. The same would be true in America if the dialect or accent were Hispanic, Black American, southern or mid-western, rather than American RP. Turn to any other country and you will find a similar clash over the 'proper' way to speak. This matter of propriety is rightly being challenged but only just recently. So there is still a long way to go. Not long ago, I encountered a production of Shakespeare in which the actors spoke in native South African accents (Afrikaans and the accents of the Black townships). It brought out new values in Shakespeare's text, but it did alienate some in the audience and caused controversy.

A skill still required in all aspects of acting is flexibility. To serve a play well, an actor might have to speak any accent in order to create a world and a theatrical style. Because of the politics connected with RP, this theatrical consistency is strangely more attainable in other accents. Recently I noticed a lack of cohesion in the speaking styles of a production even though all the actors were presumably speaking RP. But because there were different periods of RP, I felt the production was caught in several different time warps. This only illustrates that RP, as an accent, can be subject to challenge.

Young actors who resent RP often have a tendency to mock it or to do it half-heartedly. You are, after all, mocking some people's natural sound when you do this. Whatever the accent, you should aim to be well spoken in it without ridiculing it. Be honest with the accent and commit to it with integrity.

What I usually tell my students about RP is to never lose your own accent, but to learn thoroughly as many useful accents as you can. RP is an incredibly useful craft weapon in the voice and speech arsenal. If you don't wish to speak it, then understand that you have committed to a choice which will drastically reduce your professional working chances. It is as simple a fact as that.

Never disrespect any accent. Whatever accent you are working in, you should be able to converse in it off the text as well as on. You should be able to pass in it while being auditioned. Too often actors lose jobs because they cannot do this.

Exercise 32: Tips for Learning RP

I find that these notes have helped actors struggling to own RP. I am listing the generalizations, so there will be exceptions; these might, as always, be a dramatic clue to the character you are playing. Remember, no one is perfect in any accent. And certainly no one speaks perfect RP.

I'm adopting the notion that RP originates from a group of people who collectively and for years had the confidence and a right to speak. They were the movers and the rulers of an empire. So, with that in mind:

- Take time to breathe, feel the breath low and connected to the support while you practise RP. It's amazing how this breath confidence can free the RP sounds.
- Don't rush as you speak. RP is an evenly paced accent. Again, this pace comes from a place of certainty, if not superiority.
- Physically sit and stand centred as though you dominate the space.
- There is no glottal attack in RP. The throat stays very open. It is not an aggressive sound. Don't ever mistake RP for some of the conservative upper-class accents that can be closed and harsh, attacking one's sensibilities (e.g. the Restoration fop, upper-class twit, a high-tuned socialite or member of royalty).
- The RP resonances are well balanced and modulated. The whole voice does have an aesthetic quality: generations of actors finding the most appealing way to seduce an audience.
- The jaw stays free and opens evenly. Most of the 'off' sounds people make when trying to speak RP are physically created by tightening and pulling back on the sides of the jaw or mouth. Again, this is not an RP habit but an affectation we associate with upper-class accents in general.
- Place the vowels very far forward in the face, even more than usual into the head resonance, and continually feel them moving forward. Never drop them or pull off them.
- RP has a natural returning energy to the sound and placing of words. What I mean by that is, every sound continually moves forward. Even unstressed syllables bounce and springboard the stressed ones forward. You can feel this vividly with diphthongs ('out', 'no', 'day'). The sounds return forward and are not swallowed.
- Sounds and words are finished off outside you. Ends of words are particularly in place. RP speakers rarely apologize for the way they sound.
- RP is not casual but has a formality. Definition is a key word. Multi-syllabic words are fully weighted, not skidded over.
- Try beating out iambic with RP. This can stress the rhythm and the pace of RP for you.

● Some students find it useful to listen to very heightened or period RP (tapes of actors in the 1930s, '40s, '50s, or older British films such as *Brief Encounter*). By going to an extreme, the voice will often fall into the right position and energy.

RP constantly changes and, like any accent, no one speaks a perfect version of it. All accents will distort as you become emotionally charged. Once you have tackled any accent, you have to get to a stage where you can forget it and just play the role, not the accent.

The Audience and Accents

Here is a complex and highly charged subject! If you chose to do a part in an accent other than RP and the part or play had traditionally been performed in RP, you might experience hostility from some members of the audience. Many theatre audiences come from the barbican of RP speakers and resent what they think of as their plays being done in anything but the correct accent. I have received too many letters of complaint not to know there is this prejudice among audiences. By all means experiment, but do it with the full knowledge that some members of the public may be antagonistic to what they hear.

Accents carry the weight of such political fear that even when an actor is perfectly audible in an accent I receive letters of complaint that the performer is unclear. On many occasions I have had to conclude that the actor is clear but the audience doesn't feel compelled to listen, or is sufficiently stubborn about disliking an accent that they choose to stop listening.

It is hard for anyone's ear quickly to adjust their listening from one accent to another. Remember this particularly when you are playing in scenes with a variety of accents. This note also applies to starting a play in a strange accent. It will take the audience a few minutes to adjust and to hear what you are saying. In other words, don't take these moments at a huge lick or for granted. Make it part of your artistry to give them a chance to listen; they want to. You might need to place and pace these scenes differently so that ears can adjust.

It is also true to say that some accents are not so useful when it comes to projecting the voice. You might have to compromise the accent slightly for the sake of clarity. Remember, like any good speech, when the actor is completely connected to the text we hear what is being said and should not be distracted by the accent.

Exercise 32: Learning an Accent

Here are some basic tips for learning an accent:

- Always connect the whole body, breath and voice to any work on accent. If you just shift sounds around in your mouth the accent will sound cosmetic and false. So breathe all the sounds.
- Many accents have a physical quality and an inbuilt posture to go with them. This can be great fun to play with and will help you capture the essence of an accent. For instance, Joan Washington, the great dialect coach, always talks about American accents being more on the front foot. Italians use plenty of physical gestures when they speak. Certain high-status English accents look down their noses at you. Some London accents are punchy, with fingers pointed and heads jutted forward.
- Find out as much as you can about how an accent was formed. This can lead you to discover many interesting theatrical facts about it. When does it date from? Is it urban or rural? Does the geography or the climate affect it? What is the status of the speaker? High-status speakers often have more confidence and flow more in their speech than lower-status speakers. Then you can be so powerful that you don't even have to bother to be clear or coherent.
- Hum the tune of the accent. Does it rise and then fall? Constantly fall? Fall and suddenly rise? Is stress consistent or are certain words hit unusually hard? How are the words or syntax of the sentences distributed? Are verbs or nouns in commanding positions?

● Observe and listen to a native speaker of a particular accent. Notice any tendency to place the voice in a particular area: face, nose or throat. Is there much movement in the speech muscles? How forward is the sound? How wide does the jaw open? Does the jaw pull back or relax when making the sound? Is the speaker's pace generally fast or slow? What are the words per minute? Are there pauses in the speech and are these pauses common? Does it proceed, generally, without halts? How physical is the speech? Are words clear or unclear? Finished or unfinished? There could be a mixture of sounds: some heavy, some not even present. Are there non-verbal sounds in the accent? Are there certain sounds that they don't make (e.g. Cockney finds 'th' hard so it goes to 'f')? Are there particular phrases that crop up continually? Does the speaker enjoy speaking?

Doing this kind of work, you will have captured the essence of an accent. You might have to clear up certain vowels and consonants for complete accuracy on-stage, but I think you'll be surprised how much sounds have shifted. To 'hear' an accent for yourself, try to read any writer who writes well in it: e.g. D. H. Lawrence (Nottingham), Dylan Thomas (Welsh), James Joyce (Dublin), or Tennessee Williams (American South). But keep in mind what I said about accents shifting over the years.

Remember, finally, that no one speaks an accent perfectly. Not even native speakers. All our accents will shift when we are passionately connected to a moment. If you try to sound perfect, you will ultimately become rigid within the accent.

Compromising an Accent for Theatre or Film

Some accents, if done authentically, would leave the vast majority of an audience unable to understand a word. How far you take an accent is a debate for you, the director and the accent coach. You might want to make an audience listen to an accent, in which case you might really slow down the first scenes to give the audience a chance to adapt. You might keep a great body of the authenticity intact but clarify, say, ends of words and not slide through syllables. I think you always have to bear in mind that you want the audience to understand you. I've seen experienced actors lead an audience very gently by the hand and start a play with a slight accent and when they sense they've got the audience behind them become more authentic as the play progresses.

Some accents are harder to play in space: ones that are very physically contained or swallowed; accents that have a pronounced falling line; or ones that have a tendency not to finish words. These accents will have to be cleared up if you intend to be heard in a large theatre. I always take the line that all speakers in whatever accent become clearer and more defined when they are speaking in a heightened and passionate way. Most theatre is based on these moments of passionate feeling so it makes for a more heightened reality if you clean up an accent and speak clearly through it.

Any character that enjoys speaking and has a need to communicate will do so clearly through any accent. A compromise is necessary if the accent has qualities in it that can damage the voice. When you are communicating in a large space you will need more support. This support, meeting and hitting certain constrictions naturally present in some accents, could produce vocal abuse; glottal attack, for instance. You could speculate that native speakers of these accents have adapted sufficiently not to suffer this abuse. Generally, if you are working with a free voice and good support you can simulate any quality freely. Again, you must have that reference point of freedom in order to go to a place of tension in any accent and not harm your voice.

Heightening the Voice

The next two sections of work involve using the voice in extreme situations like screaming or wailing. This work may be possible to do at the end of the second year of training. Having said that, I do get some students who are so advanced that they manage it safely after only a year of technical voice and speech work. Of course, the reverse is also true and it may take an actor a few years to be able to heighten the voice properly.

The important aspect of this heightened-voice work is that the young actor knows enough about his or her own voice – its balance and centre – to be able to monitor it enough and to stop an exercise if he feels tension in the throat or pending vocal abuse. Although I can keep a pretty reliable ear on the exercises for those students who might not stop when in danger, if there are too many technically insecure students in a group then I prefer to wait until they are all ready before I do this work. Also remember that the adrenalin that screaming, for instance, produces can lower the monitoring process. So high levels of student responsibility for their own voices is necessary.

Physical Transformation, Vocal Freedom and Clarity

Acting methods continue to change. One particular performance area that is growing rapidly is physical theatre. Mime, performance artists and dancers are now speaking texts. Traditionally trained actors are being asked to transform physically and radically and to use their voices in unexpected ways and in unusual circumstances. Not only are actors having to move and speak, but extreme physical characterizations are more and more in vogue. I've had to work with actors speaking lines hanging upside-down from ropes, falling in mud, absailing, clinging to walls, walking up walls and standing on their heads. Obviously my work with companies like Theatre de Complicite and directors like Robert Lepage comes to mind. But their style of work is affecting many other ensembles and actors. I think performers nowadays should be prepared to make radical shifts in how they use their voices because the kind of work they may encounter could be very exciting to do.

The Reference Point of Freedom

I'm finding that I use the phrase 'the reference point of freedom' more and more in my teaching today, especially when great physical demands are being made on an actor. I really don't think an actor can safely speak while doing any difficult or vigorous activity unless he or she understands where freedom resides in the body and voice. And you have to be fit to do this work. In theory you can speak through heightened physical contortions and transformations as long as you start from a place of freedom. Then you can move towards an extreme physical characterization but still be able to monitor any unhealthy vocal tension and stop before the physical distortion blocks the voice or the breath support.

Always remember that from whatever position you choose to perform, you should still feel a flow of energy and the centred state of readiness we talked about in Stage One. It is vital that you are always able to access power and stay vocally free. As your body contorts, you will have to work even harder to keep the support passing through it, especially the neck, to keep your voice free and speech clear. Any extreme position you might try in rehearsal could tighten more with performance nerves. So be aware of this constraint as you work.

Exercise 33: Freedom in Physical Transformation

This work will take time and a great deal of repetition until you feel freedom with just a subtle shift of the body. The way I have always worked with strong physical transformation is to start from the highly energized but neutral centre and *gradually* encourage the actor to go into the extreme physical position. But safety must always come first. So go through each stage of this exercise very carefully, never advancing so far that you cannot quickly pull back and relax. Work with a safety net when attempting vocal gymnastics.

- Start at centre, but with enormous readiness. The body should be aligned, head balanced on top of the spine, weight forward on balls of feet, feel your big toe, spine up and breath and support feeling strong and ready. In this position the body, breath and voice are in the most economic place to work with maximum freedom and energy. This is the ideal reference point of freedom. This position is what we know as centre.
  Now let's play around and discover how you can change physically while still keeping enough freedom to be able to communicate safely. Working in front of a full-length mirror is useful here.
- Push your head forward. There will be a moment, as the head goes forward, when the throat closes, the jaw tightens and the breath becomes held. Go to this point and feel the chaos in the body. Now pull the head back until you feel the throat open again. This adjustment might only be a fraction in terms of movement, but if you appreciate and feel freedom you can create a character with its head jutting forward without strangling yourself.
- You can do the same with the head pulled in by performing the above action in reverse.
- Speak some text and check that the voice is free. In transforming yourself to the desired physical extreme, note any blocks in the body and voice, pulling back by degrees until you feel the right proportion of vocal freedom. It is a simple adjustment and works like magic for any exaggerated physicalization.
- Now slump through the spine. Everything in the body will be squashed in some way. It will be harder to support and there is pressure on the throat. Go quite far in the slump so that the blocks become very vivid. Then release enough by coming up through the spine in order to free the breath and throat. If you look into a mirror at this point you will still be physically transformed, but not completely blocking your voice. Sit and try the same process again. Then speak text and feel whether it

is possible to communicate easily. Are there still constrictions? Make further adjustments if there are.

- Stand extremely rigid, rather like a soldier at attention. Go too far and again you will feel all the restrictions grasping your body. Release enough to feel freedom and speak.
- Now go through the same process crouched over as though you are communicating to someone on the floor. Go to the extreme and then release enough to have the freedom to speak. You can try any physical shape in this way. You can walk, sit, run, lie, stand on your head – try and experiment.

The technical freedoms you will always need in order to speak through a physical transformation are:

- The ability to get enough breath support. The support might have been diminished by the physical tension, but you must have some, and be able to connect it to the voice.
- The throat must be free, so thinking of a yawn or an 'h' will help with freeing it in extreme positions.
- Always think up and out with the voice. This note will be most relevant when you are severely crouched over or turned upside-down.
- The jaw and speech muscles should be workable, again they might not be as free as in centre but you should be able to get clear speech.

Actors who have hurt their voices doing extreme physical work have no real ability to monitor themselves or have tried to launch too quickly into the physical transformation rather than by stages. This suddenness can create stressful and inhibiting tension. Go slowly with continual checks along the way, and as you begin to feel the slightest blocking of tension your monitoring will be the more successful.

Moving and Dancing with Speaking and Singing

You will need to prepare and get fit and strong to sing and dance or even do a very active, physical show requiring huge amounts of speech. The key technical facility you will need to develop is the ability to recover the breath as quickly and as low in the body as possible, alongside very fluent and full recoveries.

During this breath work you must keep the shoulders and upper chest released and you will need added flexibility in the back of the rib-cage and the lower abdominal muscles.

Exercise 34: Speaking through Movement

- Prepare to work with full breath recoveries, one after the other. Take a full intake of breath with no tension in the shoulders. Get the breath right down to the lowest position you can in the abdomen. Release on 'z' or an open 'ha'. Take yourself as far as you can and recover the breath the moment before you lose support.
- To build up proper strength, don't be shy of using all the support muscles to get the last supportable breath out of your system. For real strength and flexibility you will need to build up to at least seven full recoveries, one after the other. Understanding and monitoring the moment you suddenly go off support is also of prime importance. In your movements, never constrict the neck or jaw when performing.
- Fast Recoveries: You will need to be able to get breath in quickly and low without tightening the shoulders. Use the counting exercise: 1 – breath; 1, 2 – breath;1, 2, 3 – breath. Go up to 10, or even 15, but do the exercise with tremendous speed. When you get up to the target number, go back down, but increase the pace of descent. Keep checking that the upper chest is still. Put a hand there to ensure it is not rising. After this exercise you will really feel work has been done on the support.
- Control: As you move and use your voice, support will have to control the voice otherwise the movement will make it wobble. The danger is that you will stop the wobble not in the technically safe way, through using support, but by tightening the throat, jaw and thereby locking the voice. None of the latter is good or healthy.

So throughout the next series of exercises, keep a strong awareness that all the control comes from the breath support system, and make sure that the voice and its surrounding areas stay open. The aim throughout these heightening exercises is to keep the voice steady and clear within a pattern of motion.

- Use 'ha'. Remember 'ha' is the most open sound, so if you can control this sound, any speech, scene or song will be easier, as you will be using sounds and words that have an inbuilt control. Experiment with different notes and levels of volume.
- Release on 'ha' and walk. Keeping the sound steady, walk faster and faster. Run. On one breath, sit on the floor and stand up. The sound should remain steady. Sit, lie down, sit up, stand up – all on one breath. Dance, releasing on 'ha'.

What will become apparent – and this is a prime acting and rehearsal note – is that the more you repeat a sequence of movements with sound, the easier it is to keep the voice steady. The body helps you find the control and support. The muscles of support, as long as you are fit and flexible, learn rapidly to adapt to a sequence of movements. For this reason it is important to rehearse movement and sound very thoroughly and together. Precision will also be important.

As you transfer these exercises into, say, a song-and-dance routine, you will probably have to start slower than the final performance pace and build up the speed gradually as the physical routine settles into your body and breath memory. But it will settle and be remembered after enough repetition.

Many actors find it useful to time – or mark – where and when they are going to take a breath. This seemingly false positioning of the breath recovery will become organic with repetition. Some physical tasks are so demanding on you that it is not cheating to plan where and how – whether it is a full or short breath – you will breathe. I recently had to help an actor plot a series of intricate and athletic movements up and down a scaffold while shouting. The breath had to be planned early in rehearsal. By the time we got to the technical rehearsal these planned breaths were organic to the action the actor was performing.

Speaking with Singing – Singing with Speaking

In principle, the spoken voice is the same voice, with slightly different energy, as the singing voice and vice versa. However, what is true in theory can be troublesome in practice.

Many singers are frightened of speaking. Many speakers are frightened of singing. The two voices rarely meet and overlap with ease. There is often a grinding of vocal gears as a singer moves into speaking or a speaker into singing. Energy ceases to flow naturally and the voice can make alarming jumps in terms of placing and pitch.

Singers will often push too hard and be too loud, or go to the other end of the spectrum and not support their spoken voice. Speakers can freeze as they move towards singing, losing all flexibility in their voices and not knowing how their singing voices will come out.

Dramatically, these fears and energy shifts can take an audience by surprise and their belief in the dramatic action diminishes as the uncertain and noticeable vocal shifts shatter theatrical reality. Suddenly a performer's vocal struggles become more interesting than the show.

I realize that singing is, on one level, a very technically complex activity. Yet it is more natural than speaking. It has a fluency and a free flow that should be fun and more liberating than speaking text. This free flow has been stifled by very rigid notions of note, placing the voice, timing and the type of voice you have. The potentially joyous side of singing has been corseted with judgemental fears.

I only mention this here by way of introducing some simple exercises to bridge the spoken voice into the singing one. You must try to do the exercises without too much worry about your ability to sound a note, whether your singing voice is good or fits a fashionable aesthetic. As long as you stay free and supported, all will be well.

These exercises need to be repeated many times. Repetition will finally shift you into a sense of security and a matching level of energy and pitch and placing between the two voices.

Exercise 35: Singing into Speaking

This process is technically easier than the other way round, so we will start here. You will need the lyrics of a song and a few lines of spoken text. Choose something from a musical, perhaps.

- Intone the spoken text several times as though it were a song. Intone the text and midway through the text, and on the same breath, move into speaking. As you repeat this exercise, be very careful that as you move into speaking you keep the same sense of energy as you have in the singing voice. The tendency will be to drop the energy as you start to speak. Try to minimize that energy drop because it falsifies the commitment of the acting and the bridge between voices.
- Secondly, check the transition between placing and pitch. The voice might change placing and pitch as you move into speaking. By repeating the exercise again and again you will gradually be able to make the transition smoothly without jumps or vocal blips.
- With all the above checks in place, now sing your song, immediately intone text, immediately speak the text. Sing – Intone – Speak.
- If transitional bumps are still there, make each transition – singing/intoning, intoning/singing – on one breath. The other technical trick you can use to eliminate transitional blips is vigorously to 'think out' to a point just above eyeline throughout the exercise. Whatever the note or placing of the voice, this will help knit the singing and speaking voices together.
- Now eliminate the intoning phase. Sing the song and go straight into the spoken text. Both singing and speaking should feel equally filled. When you experiment with matching this dual fullness you are achieving the task without bumps.

It is important to mention 'need' here. It will always help if you need the words of both the song and the text. Singing is a notch up from speaking in terms of emotional expression. You can experiment with this idea by shifting quickly between prose, poetic verse and song. You will notice how you move up in emotional notches each time. We've been working the other way round, singing into speaking, because technically you are going down a mountain instead of up it which is the more difficult way of travelling.

Exercise 36: Going up the Mountain – Speaking into Singing

- Take up your text. Speak it and before you have time to freeze on the thought (again, doing it on the same breath will help) move into intoning the text. The voice might shift in pitch or placing, but keep it free and focus up and out, not worrying about the sound that you produce.
- Now speak, intone, then improvise a tune with the text. Now cut out the intoning. Speak and go straight into an improvised song on the text. Now speak the text, sing the text and immediately go into singing your song. Now speak the text and sing your song. Both should feel equally full.
- Now let's sweep the voice in all directions. Speak, then intone into singing a song. Sing a song, intone a text, then speak it. Sing a song straight into speaking a text. Speak a text straight into singing a song. With repetition, all these transitions will start to feel seamless. As this happens dramatically on-stage, the audiences will know that a greater intensity is occurring, but without observing the technical shifts which will suspend their disbelief in the story you are telling.

How to Do those Big Vocal Moments

Let's now turn to work on some of those vocal tasks which actors dread most. They go by the technical term 'extended vocal positions'. Actually, that means shouting, screaming, crying, laughing.

In theory, if an actor's voice is well supported, free and released and she has the right motivation, a scream, for instance, will not hurt your voice. For many reasons this theory rarely works. Why? Well, most of us think or believe that these extended vocal positions can damage the voice. That knowledge is often enough to stop the freedom needed to ensure safety. Often in rehearsals I have noticed actors who have made a very free scream become so shocked by its quality that they closed down immediately afterwards. Nothing has happened to their voices; something has happened to them.

Extended vocal positions are extremely demanding vocal moments and will expose any small tension in the voice or hesitancy in connecting to the breath support. So they do need very strong technical awareness in order to be correctly performed.

Younger actors are often ashamed of approaching these moments technically. They feel the approach through technique is fraudulent and compromises truth. A scream must come of its own accord, they think, and cannot be prepared for. They fail to understand that they will have to repeat the sound night after night during the run of a play and it is simply too risky not to get it right through practice. When you are using great amounts of support through your voice, even the smallest vocal tension can be potentially damaging. When all that power hits a slightly tense throat, it will hurt.

In short, please don't be ashamed of working out these moments very carefully. Your voice is too precious to risk damage and your career is too important to curtail because of a careless moment when you were technically unprepared. To make matters worse, actors are often asked to do these vocal feats from the worst possible physical position, which hinders them even more.

It is not natural to repeat these moments again and again, but in rehearsal that demand can be made on you. Consequently the voice finds itself put through a ringer which damages it because of the unnatural repetition.

One important awareness I want you to grasp is that every extended vocal sound we make is physically created by the same process. Laughing and screaming operate the same set of muscles. The sound quality is changed by the emotional experience pumping through the body. After a good laugh or scream, we feel the same ache around the centre of the body, the abdomen, and the same stretch in the throat.

Exercise 37: Technical Preparation

- The support must be strong and prepared. Work to get the breath low into the body. It is very important not to have any tension in the shoulders or the upper chest. Even a small amount of tension will create a vocal block as you release a large sound. Get the ribs swinging freely and the back of the rib-cage open. You must keep the abdominal area released.
- One of the most important moments in releasing extended sound is to use the support underneath the voice. The co-ordination of the support connecting to the voice is essential. Problems will arise if you either start the sound a fraction of a second before the support moves in, or if you pump or pull the support in before the sound. This contortion will close the throat and create a constriction which is potentially dangerous. Trust in this work is essential. You will have to get to the point when you can know the support is there and will move in simultaneously with the voice.
- A completely free voice is one which has been thoroughly warmed up. No pushing or devoicing as these extreme positions will freeze a voice on the verge of being heightened.
- A well-placed voice is one that isn't going to pull back on itself. One of the most common habits that afflicts actors who hurt their voices while releasing in this way is that they release and then pull into themselves, rather than carry through completely. Sound must go out and not reverse inwards. You can see this physically happening. The body and voice clench around the sound and the voice is then instantly abused.

Before you do some basic exercises to launch yourself into this extended vocal world, you should know what has to be avoided. Stop the exercises if you feel any of these things:

- Any distress, pain or effort in the throat.
- Any disconnection with the support or any sense that the breath isn't ready and behind the sound.
- Any pulling back either in the body or the voice.
- You will need to drink water as the support passing through the throat will dry you out more than usual and a dry voice is more susceptible to damage.
- Never do any of these exercises for a long period of time. Muscles will get tired rapidly and you will need to rest them. Actors often hurt their voices when they are exhausted. To extend your voice night after night will require extra fitness.
- You can hurt your voice in performance, yet because you are so charged up and in the acting moment, you might not feel the pain for some minutes or not even notice it until you finish playing. A simple exercise that will help you monitor any potential damage is to release very quietly on a 'ha' after each major use of the voice. In doing this release you will feel any constriction or if the voice wobbles or hesitates more than usual at this level of volume. You should not push yourself further if the 'ha' signals danger.
- Any increase in mucus or phlegm on the voice is also a warning sign. The phlegm is a lubrication being produced naturally by the body in order to protect the throat. If excess phlegm does occur, be extra careful. Your body is speaking to you, so don't keep clearing the mucus and continuing. Swallow it down or clearing it will only cause more tension.

Exercise 38: Preparing to Release

- One of the most useful tricks you can employ is, just before you release on a large sound, to 'think of' a yawn or a 'ha'. This adjustment effectively opens the throat and can save the voice from harm. Use this trick whenever you feel the throat is closing or in danger of being abused.
- Be very aware of staying as physically centred as you can. You can imagine how easy it is to pull back even a few inches as you release the sound. These physical shifts can tighten the throat and the breath. The body, like the sounds, should be moving imaginatively forward.
- The jaw must remain released. Again, the nature of the sounds you will be making is aggressive and this encourages the jaw to clench. Another reason the jaw might tighten is because the sounds can be shocking and the jaw closes to apologize, so to

speak, for the enormity of the expression you are making. If the jaw does clench, it will constrict the throat and create problems. Stop the exercise if this happens and re-release the jaw.

● You will find that lifting the jaw through the smile will not only open the throat more but will place the voice onto the hard palate and consequently pick up the hard vocal quality that we associate with the high-energy vocal tone of emotionally charged moments.

● It is going to be essential to place the voice very forward, up and out, and not pull back on that position. You must be aware of a point of release above eyeline to simulate the arc of sound you will release.

● Even if you have all the support and vocal freedom in your technique, pulling back or off the sound can still hurt you.

● The most important part of this preparation is to get the breath in low and the support securely under the sound. So many actors try to enter a great emotional release without taking enough breath. This is wrong. It's as though the excitement of the moment stops that natural instinct. Take the breath, this can be dramatic, feel the support, and only then execute the sound.

When you are confident these things are in place, you let the whole process happen and go!

After doing all the basic breath stretches, remind yourself of the strong support position by pushing against a wall or holding a chair above your head. In this position, release air without using the voice in order to check the power of the support. The air passing through should be silent in the throat. This is a good check as to whether the throat is open. Closure in the throat can be heard; a slight rasping sound, for instance. Warm up the voice, particularly concentrating on the head resonators. You will be needing them more than usual.

Monitor these exercises and if you feel any throat disturbance or tickling, stop. Don't try to burst through any tension. You might feel a stretch in the throat. This is fine as long as there is no pain. Never do these work-outs for more than ten minutes at a time. Muscles will get tired and at that point you should not go on. The weakened support and throat muscles need rest and if you continue they won't be able to save your voice.

Exercise 39: Swearing

If the use of obscenity goes against your nature, perhaps you might want to avoid this section. Let's start with a good stream of profanity! Most of us swear, probably under our breath, though few of us do it as a full release of the word. We pull the words back and, consequently, diffuse anger yearning to be expressed. Voicing a good swear, therefore, will often uncover all your potential habits of blocking high emotion. Without meaning to sound too amoral or blasphemous (and the danger of using swear words in public comes from its roots in blasphemy), one use of swearing is the words themselves. Most swear words are very physical, lusty and onomatopoeic. So we should get some earthy satisfaction in saying them and releasing the words into space. In many contemporary plays you cannot avoid the use of this kind of language; sometimes it comes in torrents.

- Choose a stream of expletives that is manageable on one breath. Mouth the words really to appreciate their physical qualities at the front of the mouth.
- With full support and a very open throat directed to a point above eyeline, intone the words.
- Take the intoned position immediately into speaking. Not only feel the consonants but slightly elongate the vowels to get more mileage out of the increased support.
- Now have a full swear with all the volume you can muster. Be aware of any tensions or pulling-back sensations that might cause any of the sounds to fall off. Keep the sound moving forward and fully stressed. Be brave and non-judgemental.
- Now try to add to this very technical use of words an emotion – anger, frustration, jealousy, grief, or despair. Check that you still feel free. You will need to be liberated in every area of your being – physically, emotionally and intellectually. It might be fun at this stage to use some of Shakespeare's cursing.

CORIOLANUS. You common cry of curs, whose breath I hate
As reek o'th' rotten fens, whose love I prize
As the dead carcasses of unburied men
That do corrupt my air: I banish you.

Coriolanus, Act 3, Scene 3, 124–7

Exercise 40: Shouting

Volume is directly linked to the amount and quality of your support. As you need more energy for shouting, you will need that extra oomph from your support system. You might also have to invest in a violent motion of the breath to create the aggressive sound that some shouts have. With this increased support activity and its violence, you must be very vigilant about any vocal constriction in the throat and jaw, being mindful also of any tendency to pull sound back into yourself. At any point of feeling constriction in the throat, stop the exercise. The same applies to any sense of not being sufficiently connected to the support.

It is essential, as you stretch your voice into these extended exercises, that you are very conscious of this connection. Any pulling back physically will impede the voice and support. Try to stand upright and stay open across the chest. You will also need to have excellent physical contact with the floor. Think up and out in an arc. Thinking of a yawn or an 'h' before the initial sound will help to keep you free.

- Avoid glottal attack. The more violent the sound, the more tempting it is to glottalize. You can simulate that violence by lifting the upper cheek muscles into a suspicion of a smile. In fact, if we watch people expressing themselves in any extended way they lift that area of the face and jaw into a sneer. This lift pulls the sound up onto the hard palate which instantly hardens the sound.
- Use the violent consonants of the word. By hitting certain sounds with vigour ('t', 'd', 'v', 'p', 'b', 'ng') you will not only sound aggressive but even feel more violent. It helps the acting.

- The increased support will use more of the vowels to release the sound.

Exercise 41: Calling into Shouting

- Start with a few gentle calls – 'Hey you!' Imagine someone across a field. Staying physically centred and breathing with good support connection, wave to them. When you feel well connected and sense in the imaginary distance the same physical expansiveness, imagine throwing, overarm, a ball or a spear. As you release the imagined missile, release vocally on 'Hey you!'
- When this feels free and the throw is working with the voice and the words, stand still, but feel all the breath activity of being filled and alive. Then just call with the freedom. Use 'o'. Really extend and open up your arms to the skies. Call to the gods. Shake out and check with a light hum that the voice still feels free and unheld before the next stage. You will now be prepared to shout.

It's always important to remember at this stage of the work that many of us have certain inhibitions which make it difficult to release a strong emotional statement. If you are like that, perhaps you should try an extension like this in the open air or where you can't be heard.

- Phrases like, 'How dare you?', ' Where are you going?' or 'Let me go' are good to start with, as they are full of open, easily released vowels. Move on to more violent words: 'What studied torments tyrant hast for me.' Or 'Don't ever do that to me again!' Trust your technique. Pinpoint the person you are addressing across the space – the arc! Breathe in and feel the support. As soon as you feel ready, shout at the person. Throat open, words in the mouth and let them go. At the first sign of any perceived vocal tension, think of a yawn.
- If the sound is too pure, return to the smile to place the voice on the hard palate and find the violence in the words. If you do feel a blockage in the throat, go over the basic check-list of physical freedom: shoulders, neck, jaw and connection to the floor. Never press down on the larynx or swallow sounds. The support is underneath the sound and ready, and you are using enough of it.

The next image I'm going to give might offend but I think it is vivid and important. A huge vocal release is like vomiting. All this work is really about purging yourself of emotion without apologizing, pulling back or retreating from the feeling. When we vomit, we are releasing unwholesome bits of food or drink from our system. A purge is necessary in order to restore health. The same is true of emotional sound. We don't swallow the vomit, we let it go. Harsh and violent sound cannot be swallowed. After several attempts with aggressive shouting, try a whoop of joy. The joy will make the release easier. We can all remember the feeling of release and relief after genuine emotional purges we have experienced in life – the real stuff, not the acting bits. This is precisely the same emotional memory you must bring to your work.

Exercise 42: Screaming

You will need every technical exercise and security that we have explored up to now in order to scream. This is the most demanding vocal release not only technically but psychologically. It can alarm you even to go here. A scream is also potentially the most damaging vocal position. So you must only do it with confidence and never attempt it if you aren't completely inclined to go there. You should definitely only be doing this for a limited amount of time.

- Go and push a wall until you feel strong support connection. Come off the wall with that energy imprinted in your body.
- Tap out a small 'ha, ha, ha' from the support. At this point, check that your jaw, throat and body are open and released. Increase the support and volume of the 'ha, ha, ha'. If all is well, start to elongate the sound and pitch it higher and place it into the hard palate. Stop after a few releases, just to check all is well.
- The next stage is for you to breathe in and feel that support and let out a scream. Use the yawn to keep the throat open. After these exercises you will feel a stretch in the throat and the support system might ache. Shake out and have a gentle hum.

- Three vital points:
  1. All this technical work must be organically linked to texts and the feelings they contain. This will not only make the work easier and more sensible, but it will shift any purity of technical sound into a more meaningful acting context.
  2. As you work technically, the nature of the breath and voice work can disturb and stir you. It can also mean that as you allow huge waves of emotional energy to pass through you it might be hard to stop the outpourings. It's rather like trying to rein in a galloping horse.
  3. All human sounds can be made freely, but because of habits, fear and inhibitions we might only have experienced these sounds in life through trauma and immediate breath and voice restrictions. You have to battle this one out. One sobering thought is that if you do not learn to work with this freedom you can seriously injure your voice and your career. So take care!

Exercise 43: Crying, Wailing, Laughing

If you have achieved the technical releases of shouting and screaming, then you have the ability to enter these next areas of work safely. However, it is not that simple since all these releases are very reliant on your acting and the imaginative motivations behind the release. All I can do is suggest certain exercises and springboards which give you the physical potential to do these emotional releases. The imaginative circumstances must come from you. Again, be aware that these releases can stir you up and expose a raw place in your being.

Crying into Wailing

Some actors are able to cry at the drop of a hat. Some never stop! Again, this emotional release must be linked to the text, but here is a simple preparation exercise.

- Sit on the floor, if it's comfortable, sit cross-legged.
- Flop forward as far as you can and release the back of the neck. Sigh out, at first silently, then with sound.

- Start to rock up and down, keeping the sound going. Continue, and as you come up begin to hum and release into a 'ha'.
- As you finish the sound and rock down, breathe out any excess air.
- As you come up, breathe in, then, on the suspended height of the upward rock, release the sound. Continue.
- Hold in your arms, then stretch, then out with the sound. Within a few minutes you will be wailing.
- When you stop, lie down on your back and continue to breathe with the rocking rhythm and start to let out any sound you want. The chances are, you are close to a cry or wail.
- Stand and try a few moments of text: 'O, my tender babes' or 'Woe the while'.
- Never fight or try to control the breath. This is how we stop the tears, the motions of grief. Clamping down in the throat is another means of blocking. If this happens, yawn and the feeling will come out.

Laughing

Laughing is one of the only emotional releases our society freely allows us to perform in public. Consequently many moments of laughter are not reflecting joy but a host of other less wholesome feelings or attitudes. Widen your scope of laughter by playing with different types of laughs. As long as you stay free, each type of laughter and the feeling and thought behind it will create a different quality of laugh. Snort at a smug intellectual notion. Mock with a laugh. Be sarcastic with a laugh. Titter to cover a stupid mistake. Show embarrassment. A filthy laugh – think of a smutty joke. Flirt with a giggle. Seduce with a laugh. Insult with laughter. Suppress a giggle, release it, suppress it. Try an 'in' joke and a laugh that excludes others. If the voice and breath are free, every thought or emotion will produce a different laugh.

The technical side of these emotional extensions is only the physical manifestation which must be triggered by an inner experience. The above exercises are to help you build up confidence in your voice and an emotional range, and to help you do the release safely.

The acting note in all these areas might be to experiment to the full with your voice, then bring it down in order to be as subtle as possible, so you are filled with an emotion but not over-expressing it all the time. Dramatically, one full release in a performance is often more effective than a constant display. Audiences tend to turn off very quickly if the actor shouts, cries or screams his or her way through a performance.

The display of real passion in performance has to be finely judged and monitored. I personally love actors who have the courage really to explore their passions, but the work on feelings must be in tune with the word and the clear communication of the text. Often we watch an actor 'feel' but because the text is clouded with emotion we have no idea of the specific nature of the thought. The word specifies our experience, our emotions.

Strange Requests

As a voice coach, I am frequently confronted by actors with strange vocal challenges they are being asked to face. Again, I am looking technically at work which has to be based on truth and anchored to an organic connection to the text.

Dying   There are usually two main concerns connected with dying: the death speech and after dying, lying on stage dead, but without the audience seeing you breathing.

There are many ways to die on stage. Many deaths are accompanied by a speech and there lies the problem. I only have one major note to actors who are dying and having to speak. I'm sure that if you are speaking your last words you are going to (a) make every word count and (b) make them clear. Unfortunately many actors chose the option of acting the moment through such anxiety, tension and pain that they become incoherent. In extreme circumstances like sickness and dying, even though we feel weak we never want to repeat ourselves because speaking takes such a tremendous effort. We are more careful and more clear in our speech, taking the time and breath needed to say it. Each word is precisely placed. We might be fighting for breath and against pain and weakness, but the moment of speaking has to be economic and precise to combat all the other barriers. This is the last moment you have to speak and generally what the dying person on-stage has to say is of immense importance to the plot and the emotional journey of both the character and the play.

Technically you should think about why you are dying and how that affects the breath and the voice. Obviously the breath is going to stop, but how and where does the pressure on the body begin? If you've been stabbed, where has the knife or sword entered you? It's very hard to breathe close to a wound so if the point of entry is in the stomach then you would be breathing in a swollen chest breath. You will have to link the dying breath to the words.

The next problem is how to lie dead on-stage (perhaps for a long time) but still be able to breathe. There are staging and lighting tricks to help shroud you. It will always be easier if you are moved to be partially masked by the set or other actors, or if you are moved out of light. To be covered with a blanket or coat helps or, if you haven't had to speak before your death, to die on your stomach.

However, whatever the director can devise for you, you could be lying there for many long speeches. The aim is to get the breath as calm, as slow and as still as possible. This will all be dependent on how you fall and where you can get the breath. If you are crumpled up it will be harder. The bits of the body on the floor will be impeded, so you can only use the free parts.

The other obvious problem is that you might just have had a very exhausting athletic fight so you are out of breath and need to take more air, not less, to recover. The first thing you must try to do just before death is to use the breath dramatically and sigh or groan out. This will clean the breath and give you the opportunity to place the breath as low as possible into the body and into the breath apparatus least exposed to the audience. If they can't see your stomach, go for that area.

After the cleaning of the breath, try to slow it down. Wait for the breath and take it in as slowly as you can. Breathing through the nose will help to take and release the breath with minimum muscular activity. During this process you might panic. If this happens, thinking of a yawn will release some of the anxiety. Remember, if you do need to take a large breath because of panic, there is evidence that the rib-cage can shift after death. So tell the audience members who have noticed you breathe that you are being anatomically correct!

Illness Consumption is a very popular illness in nineteenth-century plays. Heroes and heroines are constantly wasting away in a slow death. Now, of course, we have characters in plays dying from Aids. Playwrights have always commented on the plagues sweeping across society. The Jacobeans were ingenious at poisoning. The Spaniards used torture. Ibsen was conscious of syphilis.

Whatever the illness or disease, actors now want to record the progress of their characters' illnesses accurately and with compassion as well as truth. I ask you to do a bit of research into the pathology itself and find out how the illness progresses. Its effect on the breath and the voice would be interesting to know. The effects of any medicine, the levels of pain and how constant that pain is. Remember you might find that the modern equivalent and its treatment are not applicable to the period you are playing. Our painkilling techniques are very different from those in Shakespeare's time. The Jacobean forms of madness were not dulled or drugged into passivity as ours now are.

Pain and illness debilitate us and this will eventually weaken the support, followed by a weakened voice. Even after a flu bout our voices suffer from this weakness. Consumption is all about the struggle for breath, as it is in an asthmatic part. The danger in these roles is that you forget to connect the struggling breath to the voice and the voice dries out. Any infection of the lungs will be accompanied by a noisy inward breath. As you do this you will dry out quickly, so keep drinking water. Check on the connection and make sure when off-stage you drink water and breathe more through the nose.

Remember there is often more vigour in illness. The good days are highs so don't play the whole part with a mournful low energy. The body is fighting to regain health or struggling to stay alive. And this focus is always most noticeable in the way someone makes efforts to breathe.

Illness will automatically affect our movement, the pace of all our actions and speaking moments. Rather like my note on speaking just before dying, I would suggest that if you have limited amounts of energy you acquire incredible focus and economy of movement and speech. The last thing you want to happen is to have to repeat a task or sentence.

Coughing (those consumptive roles)   If you are required to cough a lot, be aware that this can hurt your voice. Keep well hydrated and support the cough. Even with the slightest hint of tension, cough thinking of a yawn. If you want to achieve one of those phlegmy coughs, get a lot of saliva – biting your tongue quickly achieves that – and swallow it just before you cough. Use the effect economically.

Playing Drunks   There are certain distortions of behaviour, physical and personal, that transform us when we drink. These distortions are quite easy to overact. The first question you might ask yourself is: is the drunk a habitual one or is the experience new? Experienced alcoholics vocally cope in a very different way from the innocent drunk. Generally, drink makes us bolder and more vocally liberated. That's why drunks will often sing. The confidence makes us louder and we believe everything we say is of enormous interest. Barriers drop, so we speak and behave in a way that is more of everything in our character – more mean, more jovial, more promiscuous, more morose. The drink gives us the right to go to those places with a vengeance.

Physical motor skills are diminished. The first set to go will be the complex speech muscles. Slurred speech happens even before we start to wobble and topple over.

The 'me' aspect of our being takes control, so we become very bad listeners and unaware of how obnoxious, embarrassing or vulgar we are being. Drunks are not interested in others' sensibilities, but are self-obsessed. Responses deaden. We slow down. The eyes become less seeing, the ears less hearing, the touch less meaningful. Our spatial awareness and reality are not sound, we bump into things. We are isolated in our own world and if we do reach out we can't accurately gauge the world's responses.

The habitual drunk has learned to control and focus him- or herself through these effects. Many experienced drunks get clearer, walk with more focus, touch and listen with more deliberation before collapsing. Years of drinking will coarsen the voice, particularly if the drunk has regularly vomited. The less experienced drunk will go quickly from confidence to a descent into slurring and falling about and complete incoherence and collapse.

The Youthful Voice   One theatrical cliché says, 'You need a very experienced actor to play a young role.' And sometimes that cliché is true. Whatever the truth, older actors often have to play 'young' and a danger can lie in the actor changing his voice cosmetically without understanding the real organic nature of a youthful voice.

Voices break early. A girl's voice breaks around nine, a boy's more dramatically around eleven. Surrounding this potentially traumatic physical change in the voice are the often more painful psychological, emotional and sexual changes that follow children into adolescence. Chattering and inquisitive boys and girls can become shy, aloof, moody and 'a problem'. This can be the time when girls begin to slump and hide their bodies. Boys sit down on their voices, making them deeper and more gruff. Whispering, giggling, secrecy are all part of the initiation process. Healthy yet disturbing for parents are the challenges and the rows. All these things (and more) will affect not only the quality of voice, but the delivery: the body language, the focus, the not listening, the aggression. Dive into the text and see if there are any clues underlying the way a youthful character speaks.

Most recently I had to work with a thirty-six-year-old actress who aged from twelve to twenty-eight. This is what we did together. The girl the actress was playing was an uncomplicated, joyful, innocent child. All the best qualities of youth. She had curiosity and the text was good enough to help insofar as the girl's language and images were childlike. It's important to note that the actress was very strong technically and open vocally. As we worked on the text to uncover the curiosity, the joy, the wonderful innocent images, the performer's voice changed. She sounded like a girl. The voice organically rose and she vocally found that spontaneity of pace and thought that children have. Through the journey of the character, her life changed and she became weary and cynical. Life let her down and again this was reflected in the language the writer used. The weariness, the disillusionment went organically into the actress's voice and she gradually aged.

I remember only being given a short time to make an actor reduce his age from thirty to eight. The actor wasn't skilled technically but we worked it in one day when he discovered a way of walking, skipping and jumping as an eight-year-old. Suddenly the actor's voice shifted and he was eight.

Dennis Potter's *Blue Remembered Hills* is a play which requires the whole cast of adult actors to be seven. In this text the key is in the unrestrained cruelty of childhood, the fast-changing alliances and the cruel remarks made without apology. The whole company started to sound like children once they physically allowed themselves the freedom of that kind of childhood liberation.

One last note. All of us contain all ages within ourselves. The adult is never far away from being an adolescent. Some children look at you with all the wisdom of an eighty-year-old. The text will tell you and if you are vocally free and warmed up the energy of ages will transform your voice.

Ageing the Voice   Many actors have to age through the course of a show and, like drunkenness, this process can be easily caricatured and rather embarrassing when not done properly. Most drama school teachers have sat through auditions with young actors doing 'old man acting' – wobbly voice and shaking body. I remember sitting on a panel with a very sprightly seventy-year-old director who asked a young actor after his 'old man' audition, 'How old is the character you are playing?' 'Sixty,' came the reply. 'Well, I'm seventy. Do I walk and talk with a wobble?' The young actor never replied.

The point is that some voices do not age until very late, often well into the eighties. It all depends on physical, intellectual and spiritual fitness. All I can discuss are the possible effects age can have on the voice and you will just have to pick and choose alongside the evidence of the text or perhaps do nothing. These are thoughts that could be useful:

- If we don't keep fit, the body begins to weaken, particularly the spine. If this goes we lose breath and support power. If we slump we will also put pressure on the throat and the voice will lose colour. I've met students in their mid-twenties where this process had already begun.
- A hard life and years of relentless physical work will also embed themselves into the body. Many older people who've spent a life working with a particular tension will suffer a more rigidly

set body that will also rob power and colour from the voice. A ninety-year-old friend of mine spent most of her life in service and by the time she was sixty was bent over.

- Age slows us down, our walking and speaking pace is probably not so fast. This is neither necessarily negative nor a sign of senile dementia. Age will often give us confidence. Priorities change, so we might not be pushing so much or hurrying our lives along. We might look out at the world with more consideration and less judgement. The vocal manifestation of this might be taking more time, being less judgemental, less aggressive when we speak. On the other hand, age could make us more rigid. Perhaps, like drunkenness, it brings out our true character without so many barriers.

- Our hearing does diminish. We lose the higher vocal notes relatively early. As our hearing becomes less acute we will miss conversation or remarks and perhaps speak with less ability to monitor the volume of our own voices. Many people as they begin to lose their hearing do not notice it themselves for a time. They just think that everyone around them is speaking less clearly. People can learn to lip-read without even knowing it themselves. The world can seem to be in a conspiracy against them – hence the grumpiness.

- All the work you have or haven't done in your body and voice will become more and more apparent as you get older. Vocal habits will become more entrenched and locked into the body. This could mean the habitual placing of the note we speak on in the voice will wear out and it moves to a new place to compensate. Shakespeare talks about a man's voice piping – presumably after years of it being placed low. Women's voices equally can drop. But a well-trained voice can age beautifully and actually can become richer, like a fine vintage wine.

- Years of smoking or alcohol will take their toll, coarsening the voice; and with the breath fighting to get in, we can begin to wheeze.

- If the voice does wobble or swoop around the range it's because of lack of breath control.

- Physical frailty will often lead to being too careful and protective. This will reflect in the power and economy of the voice.

- Dentures, unless they are very well fitting, will affect the placing of all the speech muscles and the consonants. The removal of teeth will change the relationship you have with your facial muscles that place vowels.

The good news should be that as you live and if you have kept physically and vocally fit and open in yourself, your voice will only become richer. Life will inform it and transform your communication to a point of greater harmony.

Abused Voices   Often you have to recreate on stage a character suffering from vocal abuse; one of those rough, harsh voices. I've recently worked with a spate of actors playing tramps, requiring a very abused and aggressive voice to characterize. The immediate problem is how realistically to create a sound that is abused without damaging the actor's voice. The qualities we were after included the broken voice, strong glottal attack, a voice with a wheeze, or a clamped voice.

You can do the following safely as long as you follow a few guidelines and appreciate you should always compromise on the side of safety and be able to communicate clearly in space. I had to heal a damaged voice a short time ago. The actor had been playing a homeless character with a drink problem and before each show he had been screaming to break his voice for the part. He nearly had broken his voice for life.

Whatever you do when playing a character with an abused voice, always:

- Support, get the support into the body even if you are stooped over. Find out where you can breathe – the back, one side, the abdominal area – and make sure that connection is always there. Most of the time you will be needing more than usual.
- Keep the throat open, thinking of a yawn immediately helps.
- Even if the voice should sound low and trapped, keep imagining the voice up and out. This will stop it being locked and trapped. You will need more support to do this position safely.
- Use the violence of articulation to make the voice more aggressive. Overdo articulation to stress the violence and abuse.
- You will need more moisture in the mouth and that will help you get that phlegmy quality. All abused voices make phlegm rattle around.

- Croak the voice. Children play with this position – a creaky door sound. Speak through that sound and the voice will immediately sound broken.
- Try groaning but with all your technical awareness in place (support, open, out). Then go into speaking through the groan. Again you will probably be creating a broken sound.
- Never go beyond a point that hurts your throat. You might have to face the fact that to do these voices safely you will have to work more technically than normal in rehearsal. All voice work should eventually be organic to the text and the part, but the more extreme the position you are working on, the earlier the technical awareness has to be in place.

Spitting You need saliva to spit. A quick tip. Bite your tongue and the saliva will rapidly gather for a good spit. You can make a noise as you gather the saliva!

Speech Characteristics

A lisp: Fashionable for young women to have in the nineteenth century – the 's' goes to 'th'. You simply move your tongue forward from the 's' position on the alveolar ridge onto the top teeth: 'A thweet girl.'

The weak 'r': Fashionable in British speech of the 1920s and '30s with young men from the public-school system. The 'r' moves to a 'w': 'Wound the wagged wock.'

The one tap 'r': Fashionable among the smart set, including actors, up to the 1950s. The 'r' is almost rolled. Try to get to a point from rolling the 'r' when you hit the 'r' once: 'Verrrry rrrright.'

Stammering Stammering and its causes is a huge and contentious subject still being researched. A stammer can take many forms, appear sporadically and might only happen in certain sounds. All are dependent on the character's well-being, state of relaxation and confidence. Research this carefully and the text should give you the evidence of what type of stammer you should be doing.

Some stammers are slight hesitations, or repetition of a sound or word. Some stop the voice in full flow, particularly when the organs of articulation come together. They become clamped for a second or two – 'p', 'b', 'm', 'n', 'g', 'k' – a glottal in the throat, the words then burst through.

It is as interesting to note when the character doesn't stammer. Researching the stammer of Charles Dodgson (Lewis Carroll) for a play about the author of *Alice in Wonderland*, the actor playing the part was suddenly released and informed when we discovered that Dodgson mostly stammered in the company of adults but rarely in the presence of young girls. He felt comfortable with them.

Stammering physically starts with the breath, so always investigate the rhythm of breathing. There is normally a lock in the system before the stammer starts, then the throat, tongue and jaw will follow and the words are caught in the body.

With all these extreme vocal characterizations, please try to make them real. I've watched too many actors create a sound and leave it there; a cosmetic and possibly insulting re-creation of someone's battle with their voice. The work must always move into the organic and be compassionate. The text should be enhanced by your vocal choices, not masked. It is often enough to play with an idea, take it to the extreme, then let it settle. There is always a deep reason behind every vocal habit we have in life and it is the actor's job to search and discover why that habit is there and make it inform the character.

After having taken the actor through a deeper use of the voice, the time has now arrived for the performer to use his or hers in relation to a text. The third and last phase of technical training will follow the actor through a journey into the language which he or she has been training to speak.

Stage Three
VOICE AND SPEECH MEET
WORD AND TEXT

The Marriage of Voice and Language

All through the first year of training the voice only flirts with words. But by the second year the student actor is focusing primarily on text. From the third year and through the rest of your professional career, speaking texts, for all script-based acting, will be your primary concern. In order to be able to communicate words with authority and imagination, basic voice and speech work must be a given by this point. The techniques we have worked through in the first two stages of training must be firmly in place and secure in order for you to challenge yourself with speaking texts and being heard by the audience.

Actors return to every basic stage of their craft throughout their career, but the constant return to voice and speech work should be a kind of secure and familiar haven where you can prepare yourself to work on any play.

A highly skilled and brilliant older actor once asked me, 'Why do younger actors always feel that they have to show you their technical work? Patsy, I don't go to the theatre to see *how* people speak, I go to *hear* what they have to say.' He's right. If an actor has not crafted his or her working habits to mastering voice and speech skills which can then become hidden and transparent, then the audience will always be watching how it's done. I'm regularly asked, 'What's a good voice?' I often answer, 'One that I don't notice.' I would also add, one which makes me notice things about a spoken text.

Bridging Vocal Technical Work into Text

In this third stage of work I want to introduce a series of exercises which connect the voice work we've been doing to any kind of text. On one level all these exercises are technical; they will help you breathe, vocalize and speak a text. But on another level these exercises will help you act a text in a more informed way. They will aid you in discovering the hidden intentions in a script that can only be revealed when you speak and fully commit to the words. We shall be working from the outside in, seeing how the very structure of a text – its form – reveals its content.

When I mention speaking, and this particularly applies to this section of work, I mean speaking on full support, from an always open position that is fully forward in the mouth, and without mumbling. I cannot tell you how many actors I listen to in rehearsal who think they are speaking and rehearsing but are not. What they are doing is mumbling. Mumbling is a habit which does not release any power in a text. When you mumble you leave yourself no way of excavating the acting clues embedded in a text.

Many actors will describe a feeling of powerlessness when it comes to how best to apply voice work to the earliest stages of role work. They do not know how to work outside a rehearsal on their own and, in the worst instances, are totally dependent on a director for guidance.

All the exercises I recommend to actors to use with texts can be done outside rehearsal and will free most texts; especially the kinds of period texts that are meant to be spoken and heard because their use of language is so acute.

It's important to say at the outset that you should never approach voice and text work expecting an instant result. In the product-driven world of theatre, actors have become very result orientated. This is not compatible with the discovery and creativity which ought to be the process of acting. You have to learn to work and search, not expect instantly to find. Enter these exercises with that notion and you will discover clues. These exercises will also help you to learn a text. Many actors find them useful to do while in a long run. They can help clean up the text and break monotonous rhythms to spark and rekindle the energy in stale speaking and keep your performance in the moment.

Most of us, I would say, think too much before we speak. The process of thinking too self-consciously censors our connection to a spoken text. But words contain emotional and physical properties which actors can work with and expose in performance. And it is this emotional, physical and sensual content in a text that I am trying to release alongside its thought.

Appropriate technique exercises allow you to enter a text clearly and without barriers. After many years of work I have come honestly to believe that you are not out to 'act' a text but to speak and understand it as simply as possible so that you (and the audience) are transformed by it. Rather than control the words and dominate them intellectually (something which some actors do to great but often cold effect), I would like to see the actor painted by the words as though he or she were a canvas gradually taking shape from outside stimuli.

No actor or director works in the same way, so you will have to mix and match the exercises for your own needs and those of a director or production. Actors often have to take what stimulus a director gives them, then fill in what is not offered in the director's text work. One kind of director, for instance, might spend hours or weeks sitting and analysing a text, in which case you will need to do many exercises on full release of the words to make up for the lack of using the language in space. Another director might work in the opposite way by staging the play without working in any detailed way on the thought or specific qualities of a given script. You will have to do the Thought

Exercises later in Stage Four to compensate for the lack of close analysis.

All good actors will be organically linked to a text after doing their own work first and then in combination with that of a director. Once an actor knows how to speak a text, this work will naturally fall into place. The ultimate aim of voice-meets-text work is to discover a process that is so known that the work is forgotten. However, given the short number of rehearsals which most productions receive (four to six weeks), this knowing a text might not happen until long into a run.

Warm up before Starting Work

Before doing any serious work on speaking a text, you must warm up both the voice and the muscles you will be using to speak. I cannot stress this enough. The pattern of warming up before doing any work has, by this third stage, become repetitious. I have included an extensive warm-up on pages 336–9. Go there right now and work for about fifteen minutes before going further with the following exercises.

Once you come back to continue the work below, the golden rule is to do the exercises, then speak before you have time to think. If you ponder too heavily between the exercise and speaking the text, you can again build up habitual barriers, rather than break them down. Work that should be spontaneous and free suddenly becomes too self-conscious and negates the work.

Exercise 44: Opening to the Word

This exercise is one that I always use with actors who are new to or unfamiliar with a text. It is simple and effective. Actors love to do it and use it constantly. Some will do it with all their text work, others only when they are stuck on a problem speech or when they feel frustrated and blocked by a particularly knotty text.

- Intone a text on full support, the voice placed fully forward, the throat open, sound focused up and out.
- Go straight into speaking before you have time to think. Intone → speaking
- If, when you speak, you find your voice pulling back, try going from intoning into speaking on the same breath. So intone and in the same breath go into speaking.
- If the voice feels in any way constricted during the exercise, use the visual aid of fixing on a point above your eyeline to lift the voice up and out in an imaginary arc. This is a great cleaning and motoring exercise because you suddenly find your voice leaves you cleanly and confidently.
- You will feel all the muscles of articulation are active if your voice is very forward. Otherwise the effect will be sluggish.

By releasing words so freely and vividly into space (without hesitating to think about them), you will be informed instantly about their form and physical content. Acting clues within the words can be discovered. Say, for example, 'No longer mourn for me when I am dead.' In saying this line you should be able to experience the mournful quality of the words.

As your voice feels the muscularity of words and gains confidence through the impact with new words and phrases, you are ready to move away from pure play and towards a state of readiness with words.

Exercise 45: A State of Readiness with Words

- Speak a speech by pushing against a wall or better still, an acting partner; the partner should play the role of a heavy and unyielding obstacle which has to be shifted. This is a very useful way to release a blocked scene between two characters. Before you start speaking, check that your shoulders are free and that you are not tightening in the throat or jaw. Don't look down. Look directly into the wall or at your partner.
- Breathe, and you should feel vividly not only the support power but the readiness to speak.
- As you speak the text, feel the physical pressure of the push. This relates directly to the physical release of a word and a thought. Words and thoughts are physical. As you begin to

sense this more regularly, you'll find that their energy has to be released. This pressure will also help you sustain a line of verse without pulling off.

● After you have spoken the text pushing, you should release from the push, centre yourself and speak the text, remembering the energy you found while pushing. You will begin to feel that wonderful sense of the power in the breath and the power of the word.

This is a great exercise for anyone who falls off words and thoughts (a common problem), because you will quickly feel that fall, rather than a pressing urge to continue or to put across your point. Suddenly, the pressure of pushing will make you finish words strongly.

You can extend this exercise to help you fill pauses but still stay heightened and ready.

Exercise 46: Filling a Pause

● Speak, pushing against a wall or a partner. Come away and walk across the room but still feeling the power before you speak. You can experiment with waiting many minutes, sitting, walking yet still breathing and retaining that power and finally speaking. Stay filled and connected all the time.

This pause exercise is a good one to do with verse. You can, if you stay filled, pause during a verse line and then pick up the line where you left off without losing its power or rhythm.

I often use the analogy that speaking heightened text is like pushing a rock up a hill. You can push the rock in different directions, you can push it at different speeds, you can pause, but you cannot release pressure or allow the weight to go slack, otherwise the rock will topple backwards and squash you. The same applies to speaking heightened text. Only on the last syllable of the play is the rock finally pushed over the top of the hill. Then it can be released and rolled away, but not before. In individual scenes each actor has to take up his or her part of shouldering the responsibility of passing around the rock without dropping the energy.

Exercise 47: Physicalizing the Text

- Start speaking a text from centre and return to centre as a reference point after each phase of the exercise. Start and return to centre.
- Speak the text with physical bluff (e.g. with a lifted chest). Gauge the different points of energy. Does this reveal anything about the text or the character? Return to centre.
- Speak the text with physical denial (e.g. the body pulled in and slumped). What does that reveal? Remember that negative discoveries are as important as positive ones. Return to centre to speak. You might learn that centre is not useful in some places. Your character might bluff or deny, causing you to be off-centre.
- Walk and speak a text. Walk with clear energy and purpose, as though you have somewhere to go. Now do the opposite and walk without purpose. Which walk matches the text? If the clear energy walk helps, it is probably because the language is very focused and apt; no useless words. If the ambled walk matches what you are saying, the text might contain unclear or unfocused language that pads or diffuses the action and actually holds you in check. Generally speaking, a heightened text marks emotional and intellectual transitions very clearly, so the words and thoughts move you in a focused way.
- Speak the text moving in different rhythms. As you do this, see if one physical rhythm helps the text more than others.
- Speak the text moving at different speeds (e.g. from running to walking slowly). When you come back to simply speaking the text, feel where the text is fighting you or trying to release you.
- Sit and speak. Try all different positions, lying, crouching, etc.

You might discover in the above process how you wish to place yourself physically during these exercises in relation to a given text. The most important realization I hope you will have is a sense of movement and energy in the text which can be used even if you are standing still in a very prescribed way. The movement in the text might not be reflected actually in performance, but only felt inwardly. This movement will enhance the words and the structure of the text. For instance, a text might work best spoken from a standing position, but the scene calls for you to sit. So you know that there is a particular energy you must find in sitting. The same could apply if you are standing and speaking a low-energy text. To explore the opposite energy when speaking a text could be a great acting choice as long as you have experienced the text's fundamental energy.

Breathing the Text

On the most simplistic level, breath and voice work in the following way: I breathe in, I speak out. In a more complicated way, the breath is linked to the length and quality of thought and feeling. These experiences hopefully will unlock that simple, natural breath. Every human being has a different breath pattern which will change according to different circumstances. As you change, your breath changes. Our physical and emotional transformations are reflected in transformations of breath. A finely wrought text will have these changes and rhythm shifts built into it. Different styles of text have varying lengths of thought and consequently will demand different lengths of breath.

Today most of us tend to speak in shorter thoughts with a fractured rhythm using faster and shorter breaths. A lot of my work is about breaking and extending the short breath pattern of an actor in order to release the thought and emotion of the text.

Here are some exercises to solve this endemic problem. All these exercises will work on two levels:

1. The technical, by building up technical strength and flexibility.
2. The creative, by releasing any acting notes implied in the structure of the text.

Exercise 48: Full Recovery with Text

- You already have worked full voice recovery with a 'z' or a 'ha' (see p. 61). This time apply the recovery to a text. Remember never to go off support and always to recover before you feel constriction. Keep the shoulders and upper chest relaxed and stay physically alert. You can move during this exercise, but keep the movement dynamic and focused.
- Breathe in and begin to speak the text, but instead of snatching the breath in any of your habitual breath patterns, motor the text along until you need to breathe.
- Breathe in and continue speaking as far as the breath takes you.
- Repeat all the above until you find a length of breathing appropriate to the text. Do at least three of these recoveries. You should feel your breath has been stretched.
- Then go back to the beginning of the text and speak it again, concentrating not on breathing but on making sense. You should find that you are breathing more with the thought and feeling of the text.

For extreme breath fitness, you can build this exercise up to seven recoveries.

A great variation of this exercise is to do it with a verse text in iambic pentameter. Use at least twelve lines of verse. At first this may be frustrating because you will be feeling out of synch breathing against the thought. But that can only be a great lesson in learning how to breathe with the text. For the purpose of this and later text exercises, I am using the opening speech from Shakespeare's *Richard III* (Act 1, Scene 1, 1–13):

> Now is the winter of our discontent
> Made glorious summer by this son of York;
> And all the clouds that lour'd upon our house
> In the deep bosom of the ocean buried.
> Now are our brows bound with victorious wreaths,
> Our bruised arms hung up for monuments,
> Our stern alarums changed to merry meetings,
> Our dreadful marches to delightful measures.
> Grim-visag'd war hath smoothed his wrinkled front,
> And now, instead of mounting barbed steeds

To fright the souls of fearful adversaries,
He capers nimbly in a lady's chamber
To the lascivious pleasing of a lute.

- Start speaking the verse, taking a breath after each ten-syllable line: one line → one breath; one line → breath, etc. to the end.
- Now build it up to two lines: two lines → one breath, etc. Motor that pattern a bit. Then build up to three lines on one breath, four lines on one breath, building up as far as you can go naturally on one breath without losing support or tensing. Don't rush or speed up in order to achieve more lines. Keep a fully voiced position throughout.
- As soon as you have gone as far as you can, return to speak the text without thinking of breath. Again, you should be amazed at how free the breath is and that the places you breathe are more organically linked to the text. Perhaps they are the places where the playwright breathed when he wrote!

The traditional view of the breath and verse speaking was that an actor ought to be able to speak eight lines on one breath. I do not think this is practical for many actors without appearing artificial. Most people aiming at eight lines contort themselves, squeezing the text out and not sounding real. So, if you can do eight lines without squeezing or losing connection to the words, that is a fine feat, but if you cannot achieve this don't despair. Stretch as far as you can without constriction. Just learn to control the length and pace of your own breathing, rather than fit pre-scribed rules.

However, in the course of the above exercise you might be surprised at how many lines you achieve. And the number will increase as you exercise over time. When you enter into the spirit of the play, rather than 'I've got to get there on one breath', you begin to work without punishing tension. The creative discovery you should make is that by stretching the breath out you return to speaking the text without thinking of the breath; different breath patterns can be used to vary the experience of thoughts and emotions in a text.

Exercise 49: Building-up Support

Pick a line which is one complete thought to work through. It is interesting to do this exercise with a long and a short thought (e.g. use lines from the *Richard III* speech above or the first two lines of Hamlet's speech: 'To be or not to be, that is the question. / Whether 'tis nobler in the mind to suffer / The slings and arrows of outrageous fortune, / Or to take arms against a sea of troubles, / And, by opposing, end them.' This exercise can be particularly informative about a thought that troubles you or that you don't fully understand.

- Build up the thought breath by breath and word by word: breath → 'To'; breath → 'To be'; breath → 'To be or'; breath → 'To be or not' etc.
- Gradually build up the complete thought. <u>Never speak until you are ready.</u> When the thought has been worked through in this way, speak it straight through and see what you experience.
- Now move on to a longer thought and repeat the same pattern: breath → 'Whether'; breath → 'Whether 'tis'; breath → 'Whether 'tis nobler', etc.

You've already done this exercise in the general work-out with counting (see p. 80). The technical benefits here include (a) the extending of the breath and (b) exercising the shorter breath recoveries needed for short phrases within long thoughts. Speak when you really feel ready and can support each word, then release it.

This exercise can also produce wonderful creative benefits. By building up the words on a deep, supported breath, you have to confront each word intellectually and emotionally. You have to stay in the moment with each word. You cannot dodge a word or slide over it.

Many actors say to me that they do not like some parts of text they have to speak. They will speak the words or half the lines they like but not confront the whole text. They are only actually speaking half the line or parts of the speech.

The above exercise makes you confront every word and line in the text. In a heightened text, like one by Shakespeare, every word and phrase moves you forward. Words are used actively to explore events and states of mind. So in this exercise you will feel that journey. Each word is like a stepping stones across a river. You stay in the moment and move forward word by word.

Owning Words 1

By taking breath deeply into the body and speaking each word, you begin to own and know the words differently and more organically. This notion of owning words and knowing them intrigues me because I think it sums up the actor's principal responsibility to the text. We can know words on different levels: in the head, in the heart and then in the whole body.

I believe, particularly in heightened text, that an actor should know words as deeply and thoroughly as possible. This process might take the whole run of a play to root itself, but the good working actor is trying to experience language this deeply. It seems to me that if an actor is not prepared to work on knowing and owning words, acting is a boring and uncreative job. You are merely a robot or a mechanical toy. When you watch great actors work in rehearsal, their knowing a word is very evident. As the rehearsal period progresses you can see actors drop words deeper into their bodies and they then access them from a more resonant place to sound out a meaning.

One of the most curious manifestations of this is that after a couple of weeks' rehearsal, having known the text previously, an actor will suddenly forget lines. This, I think, comes from suddenly experiencing the word differently and allowing it to enter from a new place. The actor's relationship to a text has changed. It has transformed him in a bold new way. Something has shifted which the actor needs to work through. The performer who learns a text by rote and has little relationship to it will simply rattle the words off, performance after performance, in the same way. The performer who is constantly word perfect is a dead one who never shifts onto new ground. By doing slow progressive work on chunks of text which are problematic for you, you can short-cut the rehearsal period and own words physically, thus igniting the emotional centre of the word.

I have found the next exercise invaluable when actors are rehearsing in a very unphysical way. Many directors today will spend weeks sitting around discussing a text. This work is often wonderful. Most actors are by nature active and need to act in order to experience and learn a text. At that point, making a text physical with the breath can help actors learn and experience it without being too intellectual. After all, speaking and engaging an audience requires every action of our bodies, hearts and minds.

Exercise 50: Fast and Slow Recoveries of Breath

This exercise might prove useful to shift different speeds of recovery. Technically, this is to build up different speeds of breathing without tensing shoulders or the upper chest. Keep the breath going in as low as possible.

The creative insight you might gain is one of status. Most high-status people take whatever time they need to breathe. They do what they want. Most of us today rush our breath, but many of the characters you will play in the classical repertoire are extremely powerful. They don't need to push when they speak. Under threat in high-cost or passionate situations, we all, in order to survive, gather breath low and at a fast rate, and perhaps young, 'cool' actors should explore that experience.

- Choose a high-status text and a high-cost one (e.g. the *Richard III* opening speech).

- Play with speaking the text; maybe it's interesting to start perversely and do it the wrong way so you can feel what it is like not to get it right.
- Then rush the speech before you slow down the breath and take as long as you need to gather your power. Reverse it and slow down the speech, then speed it up. Keep the breath low and the voice supported. You are playing with speed and the physical position of breath in the body.
- By changing the rhythm and speed of the breath you should experience certain phrases differently. It will work, because all human beings under threat shift breath around in a variety of ways. But in doing this consciously I think some new light will be thrown on sections of the text and you will feel different points of power.

Many directors working with a young actor who cannot sustain a long thought will try and circumvent the problem by asking him or her to speak quickly. I understand the thinking behind this request: thoughts, spoken quickly, can help communicate a lengthy idea. But this piece of direction has drawbacks. Asked to quicken their pace, actors frequently are panicked into gasping and losing their breath connection to the words. Sense is soon garbled. During the fast recovery exercise I hope you can experience fast breath without your chest lifting and your losing the support. Remember this and if ever asked to speak quickly do so with this vital breath correction.

Exercise 51: The Readiness to Speak

Again, this is a technical exercise, but also an acting one of being 'in the moment'. You did this earlier with counting (see p. 80) but now try it with text. It will work on any text, but it is very interesting to use with direct, concrete statements where any withdrawal of intention is most apparent. Again, use the speech from *Richard III* or any of your own choosing.

- Build up the line, word by word, then speak it with that clear knowledge which comes from only speaking when ready.

- Then play with the notion of withdrawal and hesitation. Breathe in, feel ready, hold the breath for even a fraction of a second, then speak. You will not only feel vocal tension, but that you are behind the text. The words are becoming redundant because you've experienced the line, then held back the energy, rendering the speaking unimportant.

- Next play with getting ahead of the text. Breathe in, start to feel that readiness, but speak before the breath has settled. Again, you will experience vocal tension but also suffer panic because, in acting terms, you are ahead of the moment. You are not on or with the text but, metaphorically, running after a rapidly accelerating bus leaving without you.

- Now feel what it's like to be weighed down by the text. Breathe in, feel that power, let out air or deflate the power and speak. Now you are under the text. It's almost sitting on your head, suffocating you, and you have lost your vocal energy and focus.

- In order to get back 'on' the text, go back to simply breathing in, feeling, getting ready and speaking. What a relief!

- Here's a further tip about this exercise. If you have learned a text well but suddenly dry or forget your lines on-stage, chances are that you have lost that spontaneous connection with the breath. When you next dry, be courageous and just concentrate on getting back the breath and feeling the connection it gives you. I bet you'll then remember the line. Drying and panicking only makes the problem worse. Under stress, we often react in an unuseful way and stop breathing and supporting, consequently depriving the brain of oxygen. No wonder we lose our way and can't think.

- With this connection and readiness, you can also right a scene that's gone off the rails. There is a myth among less experienced stage actors that if something is going wrong in a scene you are stuck with it until you leave the stage. Not true! Many times it is simply a case of you not being in the moment, connected to your breath. So stop and take that breath. Feel that readiness. The audience won't notice and you will have salvaged the scene.

Equally true, and I'll be exploring this notion with an exercise later, when you walk onto the stage, particularly those large, intimidating houses, never stop breathing. Get the breath low and only start speaking when you are completely ready. I've watched so many inexperienced actors walk onto, say, the National Theatre's Olivier stage or Canada's Stratford Festival Theatre thrust stage and freeze, stopping their power and their right to speak in the space. They then have no option but to push vocally and emotionally, or brace and pull away from their audience and fellow actors.

Exercise 51: The Push to Readiness

Here's an exercise to explore physically this state of readiness.

- Take a couple of lines of text; use lines from *Richard III* if you want. Push silently against a wall. As you do this, feel ready with the breath, then speak the text. Now push yourself away from the wall, walk a few steps, breathe, feel ready and speak the text.

This sounds so simple. However, be tough with yourself. Chances are that as you come away from the wall and walk you might pull off your power rather than carry it with you.

As you settle to speak, you might brace or physically shift back, maybe onto your heels or an actual shuffle backwards. Check these things, because if you are doing this you are denying yourself power just before you speak. Be careful, too, that as you push yourself away from the wall you don't pull away from your power by tightening and losing flow.

This last exercise is analogous to walking on stage from the wings. Actors should always want to get onto the stage to tell a story, but so many of them are fearful, hesitate and pull back, and this manifests itself in loss of breath and support.

Try the above pushing exercise off-stage in the wings before you walk on. Experiment on an empty stage. If working in a group, you can all stand in a circle, and one by one walk into the space. Keep breathing. Feel the support and the readiness before you speak. The group should always be supportive and allow each actor to take the time he or she needs. Once you have felt this ideal readiness to speak, you can always speed up the process. My experience is that actors go for pace before connection and never, as a result, achieve either.

Vocal Range and the Text

The technical purpose of these next exercises is to stretch your vocal range and experiment with the whole of your voice. The creative side of this exercise lies in releasing the emotional and intellectual vitality of a text and perhaps stretching the actor's imaginative experience of truth; a truth that can be vocally rich.

I am not in the least interested in an actor standing on-stage showing off his or her vocal range without a connection to truth. All vocal range should be organically linked to the text. Once the voice is free and supported it will go where you want to take it, and as we become emotionally and intellectually charged, the voice wants to move with these passions. You are not going to serve a hugely vibrant text with only minimum range; the result would obviously be unreal. Just listen to anyone speak with passion. The voice moves in tandem with the passion. I do not sit and think of the fact that the speaker has just used three octaves, but I am engaged because the voice, thought and text have all struck the same notes together. The voice sounds appropriate to the material.

I encounter so many young actors who are terrified of using their range because they are frightened of sounding 'hammy'. They have never used half of their voices.

I am passionate about two key issues with regard to range. If you are speaking a text in which characters care desperately about language and its tempos and rhythms, and you are using words ineffectively with a limited range, then you are denying your character's right to exist. Your limited reality bears no resemblance to the character's richer reality. The other vital point is that an audience can only listen for a few minutes to a dull voice. What they expect, in fact, from the actor is range. They switch off, they might switch on again, but imagine what they have missed in the meantime. Actors can come off-stage angry that an audience is not listening to them, without ever asking themselves the question, 'Is my voice putting them to sleep?' This may sound harsh, because few young actors ever get the chance to stretch or experiment with their range. Yet range reduction is inappropriate to any passionate communicator, especially an actor.

Exercise 52: Increasing the Range of a Text

Use the technical exercises in Stage Two (see pp. 96–104) to stretch your vocal range and this next exercise with a text to take your voice imaginatively into new realms.

- Choose a heightened text. Any of Shakespeare's verse (the speech from *Richard III* will do) or a speech from a Jacobean play. These kinds of texts will support any emotional release of range. Something Restoration or from Shaw or Wilde will reveal the intellectual range of a text. Stay vocally free. You will need a lot of breath and to keep the breath recoveries as low as possible.

- You will be speaking your text in three different ways. Make sure that each rendering follows the other. No pondering between the exercises.

- The first point of the exercise will drive you mad. It is meant to. Speak the text with minimum range. As neutral, dull and uncommitted as you possibly can. Deliberately corset and limit the text, reducing and keeping it down. You will feel the text wanting to expand, escape and free itself. Good. You will also experience a deadening of the emotions and the thoughts.

- Now go to the other extreme. Speak the text in the most exaggerated way you can, using your full range. But keep on support and don't push vocally. Extend the vowels, enjoy sliding through words and relish them extravagantly. Physically use all of your body, your movements matching the extremes of the voice. You might be tempted to get very loud. Try to vary the volume and not stay too much on one level. Again, volume should vary with range. Perhaps an image of an Edwardian or Victorian actor will help. Have fun!

- Lastly, after you've explored both extreme positions, go back and speak the text without any concentration on range. It's bound to sound richer and freer, and you will discover a new intensity in the language. The principle you've just been through is one of stretching the whole vocal instrument out, then returning to feel how free and rich your voice really is. If you can do this exercise in a group or in pairs, you should monitor each other. It will be interesting if the feedback tells you that after you returned from the extreme place, your voice does not sound false or hammy but just more interesting.

This feeding back is precisely what I do in class. After everyone has worked together I ask each actor to say one line first in the extreme way, then immediately go back onto the line naturally and speak it with sense. Invariably the voice sounds freer, richer and the sense more directly communicated. This feedback is necessary to encourage young actors to experiment with range, yet know when they sound unreal. The process gives an actor the permission to be vocally imaginative and interesting by comparing his or her range to other ends of the spectrum.

Exercise 53: Adding Resonance to the Text

These exercises open up those physical areas of resonance which allow you to use your voice with less effort. Character possibilities might also be discovered as you play with resonance. Dialect and accent might fall into place as you shift the voice around between areas of resonance. A large part of any dialect or accent work is connected to resonance and placing. The major creative discovery might lie in opening out the head resonators, particularly working on highly energized texts like Restoration, Wilde or Coward. The characters in these plays manipulate language, exploring it with intellectual suppleness and curiosity. If our voices are free and we feel no inhibitions when we speak, the voice would naturally percolate up into the head as language is explored at a highly intellectual pace. The higher the energy of the thought, the more the head resonance. Also, as you open up the head resonators notice how clear and effortless the voice is. The exercises are very simple.

- Keeping supported and open, speak a chunk of text in each area of resonance:

    Head – This will feel strange and to some people very alien.

    Nose – Notice the change of tone.

    Face – Feel the buzzing.

    Throat – Easy now, don't tighten!

    Chest – Watch that you don't push the voice down or clamp it. Return to speak the text with the thought that all the resonators are working. The voice will feel freer and richer, working with less effort as all amplifiers are switched on. On the character side of things, it always amazes me how quickly the whole vocal quality of the voice changes by shifting it around in this way. Parts of your voice might not feel like you. It is your voice, though not your habitual one. Your habitual positions will feel very safe, but as you invest in the other parts of your resonant voice you will feel very different. If you are lucky you might stumble over a possible characterization. Suddenly a new vocal resonance might fit the text and be more appropriate than your own tone.

After you have balanced your voice among all your resonators you might like to try this next exercise. This is for when you might work on a text from Restoration drama, Wilde or Shaw, as you are going to concentrate on opening the head resonators.

- Working with support, hum into the head.
- After feeling the resonance there, come down through the face resonator until you feel the sound on your lips. Open into a 'ha' and don't pull back, not even a fraction. Now speak the text in the same place. The life and clarity in your voice and the language of the text should be immediately apparent. You will feel the result clearly if you pull off or deny a word. The words placed in the head trip along and out of you effortlessly.

- Now speak into the chest. Suddenly the whole energy of the text will be muffled and the words will have to struggle to be free and effortless.

In reality those high-energy speakers who produce words effortlessly are working from the head. Whatever struggle they might be going through, it is not in the making of words. That part is easy.

Speech Work with the Text

These next exercises are essential. You should experiment with these on all texts. The technical and creative spin-offs are abundant. The important note to stress about speech work is that it must be connected to breath and voice. So often, actors work on their speech in isolation from their body, breath and voice. Speech is the tip of an iceberg. It is connected to the whole of us.

If you work on speech in isolation from this whole connection, you will sound false and the language you speak will neither be owned by you nor engage an audience. You will sound cosmetic. These exercises can be done with any accent. One of the notes I constantly give actors is that as our needs heighten and we have to speak from a seat of passion we all, whatever the accent, become clearer. On one level these exercises are about clarity, but the clarity must be linked to dramatic need.

The technical spin-offs of these exercises will be immediately obvious. You will be educating muscles to work clearly, economically and adroitly. Speech is one of the most physical aspects of communication. Your speech muscles have to perform one of the most complex muscular dances in the body. Any dancer will tell you that in order to perform steps easily you need endless practice. Many actors, when they fear a word or phrase, slide over it without confronting it or commanding their speech muscles to perform it. This next exercise will correct that tendency.

The creative spin-offs are also immense. The physical quality of spoken language holds many clues as to the meaning of the words. The physical nature of consonants and vowels unlocks all sorts of emotional conflicts which the language is articulating. It is a common adage that until you speak a great text out loud you cannot really understand it. I believe that and also that you cannot appreciate the physical and sensual nature of words until you speak them.

Whether playwrights are conscious of this or not, I do think they have an innate understanding of how human beings use language. This innate knowledge allows them to write what is most physically difficult for the rest of us to imagine, think, feel or say.

Texts are loaded with all kinds of signals which help us speak. Long before punctuation was needed for the printing process, speakers would have physically stopped, paused and added pace to their stories. For example, a 't' following a 'd' ('Save breed to brave') will instantly stop the speaker, heightening the effect of the word 'breed'.

Exercise 54: Mouthing the Text

- Choose a text to work on. Return to the speech from *Richard III* if you need one.
- Keep breathing and feeling the lower support.
- 'Think' the whole text but mouth it with no voice. Really exaggerate each word – every ending, beginning and middle or every word, e.g. John Donne,

> Batter my heart, three person'd God; for you
> As yet but knock, breathe, shine and seek to mend;
> That I may rise, and stand, o'erthrow me, and bend
> Your force, to break, blow, burn and make me new.
> I, like an usurp'd town, to another due,
> Labour to admit you, but Oh, to no end,
> Reason your viceroy in me, me should defend,
> But is captiv'd, and proves weak or untrue,
> Yet dearly I love you, and would be lov'd fain,

> But am betroth'd unto your enemy,
> Divorce me, untie, or break that knot again,
> Take me to you, imprison me, for I
> Except you enthral me, never shall be free,
> Nor ever chaste, except you ravish me.
>
> Donne, 'Holy Sonnet', *Poems*, 1633

- When you have silently mouthed the whole text, go back and immediately speak it on the full voice.

The first sensation you might feel is that it is much easier now to make every word. Muscles have been taught to move and work in the silent exercise. By taking voice away, you are left with only muscles to do the work and you will be amazed at how quickly these muscles respond to the challenge. Suddenly the whole word is spoken. You might have experienced, while mouthing the text, how many points of the text you forget physically to say and complete.

- Imaginatively, you will have noticed that there are hidden clues in the physical difficulty of saying groups of words. Review any line and thought that was difficult and you will observe that form equals content. The difficulty of saying the words matches, in some way, the content. Many actors ask me, 'Can I change this line? It's hard to say.' I always reply that you are missing an acting clue if you do that. Even the most flexible mouth in the world would have trouble speaking some lines. The trouble usually lies in the clue you want to change. I've worked with enough living playwrights to know that they make the hard things in life physically hard to say. So don't shy away from the challenge they give you.
- Mouthing also will reveal conflict and sense. By the consonants, you will intellectually understand the text. We all do that when reading a hard section of a book – we automatically find ourselves mouthing it.

Exercise 55: Vowel Work on the Text

The next exercise is one to use with working on vowels. The vowels are the main body of the voice. If you don't give sufficient weight to the vowels, you cut down your voice. The more volume needed, the more vowel weight required. This is equally true with the range of the voice. If consonants are the intellectual part of the voice, then vowels are the emotional stress.

- Look at these two sections of speeches from Shakespeare's *Othello* and work first with one and then the other:

  > OTHELLO: It is the cause, it is the cause, my soul.
  >   Let me not name it to you, you chaste stars!
  >   It is the cause. Yet I'll not shed her blood,
  >   Nor scar that whiter skin of hers than snow,
  >   And smooth as monumental alabaster.
  >   Yet she must die, else she'll betray more men.
  >   Put out the light, and then put out the light:
  >   If I quench thee, thou flaming minister,
  >   I can again thy former light restore,
  >   Should I repent me; but once put out thy light,
  >   Thou cunning'st pattern of excelling nature,
  >   I know not where is that Promethean heat
  >   That can thy light relume. When I have pluck'd the rose
  >   I cannot give it vital growth again.
  >
  >   Act 5, Scene 2, 1–14

  > IAGO: Thus do I ever make my fool my purse;
  >   For I mine own gain'd knowledge should profane
  >   If I would time expend with such a snipe
  >   But for my sport and profit. I hate the Moor,
  >   And it is thought abroad that 'twixt my sheets
  >   He has done my office: I know not if 't be true,
  >   Yet I, for mere suspicion in that kind,
  >   Will do as if for surety. He holds me well:
  >   The better shall my purpose work on him.
  >   Cassio's a proper man; let me see now:
  >   To get his place and to plume up my will
  >   In double knavery: how, how? Let's see.
  >
  >   Act 1, Scene 3, 375–86

- On full support and voice, just speak the vowels in the text.
- Some people find it very effective doing this lying on their backs so that they can really root the voice and breathe down into the body. Try this. Standing or sitting will also work.
- Go back and speak the whole text immediately.

I've chosen these two speeches because if you experiment with them you can feel how different they are. Othello is much more open and free with his feelings. Iago closes everything down emotionally. The moment Iago opens out, he quickly shuts down his language. As you speak Iago's vowels you might experience the technical sense of pulling away from sounds. You might not follow the vowel through but stunt it. Be as bold as you can with the vowel. Place and release the vowel as far forward in the mouth as possible.

Keep the throat open, otherwise a push or glottal attack, physical manifestations of closing down, might seize control. You might become very emotional; the sounds making you feel the speech without thinking it. This is good!

The emotional content of any speech emerges with the length of vowels. Shorter vowels are used to close down a feeling, longer ones open it out. The same applies to the thought. The longer thoughts generally surge forward with the abundant vowels. Naturally the consonants are also controlling the vowels, so when you return to speaking the whole text you should be feeling the marriage of consonant and vowel. On the return to speaking all the text you should discover your voice is fuller and richer.

These speech exercises should be done on all texts.

- Separate the consonants
- Separate the vowels.
- Gently push, with a partner or against a wall, as you speak. This will help you finish off words.
- Speak every part of the word, particularly observe the whole of multi-syllabic words.
- Physically confront the words or phrase you find hard.

Exercise 56: Variety and Volume

The following sequence of exercises encourages variety in the use of your voice. Obviously the space, the emotion and the dramatic situation should dictate the levels of volume you use. What I tend to find is that when an actor learns how to fill a particular space he or she can easily become stuck on a particular level of volume and find it hard to reduce. In theory, once the voice is working technically it is easier to speak with moderate volume rather than quietly. Once your instrument has found its natural centre or optimum pitch you may find it harder to be subtle, which is what is required when volume is reduced in space. To speak quietly and be heard requires incredible support, control and intensity of speech; almost a hundred per cent more technique plus intellectual and emotional concentration.

Many young actors want to sound quiet because it feels more 'real', but do so without the technique needed. They just go vocally soggy, mumble and forget to breathe.

The technical needs for volume control are:

- Always to stay on support with a very open throat which will help the release of sound.
- Always to stay on voice (the inexperienced actor goes off voice and towards a whisper which won't carry).
- To finish off every word and not allow any syllable to drop back into the throat.

Now take some emotionally charged text (e.g. Othello's 'It is the cause' from above) and work it as follows to decrease volume:

- Intone, motoring the text with full support and voice around a moderate volume.
- Drop into speaking. This might be an occasion when you go from intoning into speaking on the same breath.
- Bring down the volume a notch.
- Intone into speaking on this new level.
- Bring down the volume another notch, etc.
- When you've reduced to the quietest level on which you can still support and keep clear, then try speaking at that level.

Now try the reverse to increase volume:

- Start at a moderate volume.
- Intone into speaking.
- Bring the volume up a notch.
- As you increase volume you will require a lot more support. You might find it useful to relocate your support by pushing a wall, holding a chair, lifting a heavy object. but it will now be essential to be very careful about certain tensions.

If I am using my voice only at moderate-to-lower levels of volume then I can – I shouldn't but I can – still manage tensions without hurting my voice. But as soon as I kick in with greater quantities of power the whole voice is more vulnerable and under threat. So as you increase volume there must be no throat tension. If this creeps in, yawn. Think of an 'h'. If it persists, stop. No shoulder tension; all the work should be done from the support without physical lifting in the body. As volume increases you will need greater vowel weight to have something more for the support to work through.

You will need to follow words through and not be ashamed of releasing them. Any pulling back on words will now be felt in the throat. This liberation is vital. That is why drunks sound so loud and intrusive. They have lost the inhibition most of us have about sounding loud. They don't pull back technically or apologize but aggressively surge forth. Build up the volume as loudly as you can go, just to test your limits.

In both the quiet and loud phases of speaking, you may find that some bits of the text might seem better served and others are lost. I don't think you will discover earth-shattering secrets in the text as you play with volume but you will unlock variety and emotional intensity in your voice.

Crescendo and Diminuendo

Still in a spirit of play, crescendo and then diminuendo through a text. In rhetorical speeches (e.g. Mark Antony's 'Friends, Romans, Countrymen' from *Julius Caesar*) these up-and-down slides might prove interesting and match the text, but really it is just playing with volume that I am encouraging here. That, plus your giving yourself permission to work imaginatively with the volume of your voice.

Important notes about volume:

- Human beings don't naturally shout or speak at high levels of volume for long periods of time. The voice will tire if you thrash it out relentlessly.
- Audiences will quickly tire if you bash them with constant noise.
- Audiences will certainly lose concentration if they have to strain to hear you speak for long sections.
- Volume is linked to emotion. So, while I am encouraging you to experiment with volume, it should never be divorced from emotional truth. If the voice is strong, free and flexible it will move and travel through volume with a text. At all times volume should be serving the text. Many young actors substitute shouting or vocal pushing instead of real emotional truth. If in doubt, never push.
- A very technical note. I've always found that it is easier for an actor to fill a space initially by upping the level of volume. On first previews of shows I encourage that rather than risk the volume being under-powered for the space. It seems much harder for actors to rise than it is for them to come down to the required level. Actually, I've learned that note from all the experienced actors I've been privileged enough to work with. Find the essential volume you need to fill a space before you experiment with lowering it.

Exercise 56: Word Stress

In everyday life away from the stage, we only mis-stress words when we don't know what we are saying. Stress and meaning are completely united. Generally speaking, an actor always will stress properly when the performer fully understands what and why he or she is speaking, along with the subtext of a speech. Having said this, I have encountered situations when an actor knows the text and its meaning well, but is so overly tense or in such a state of fear that he or she constantly mis-stresses. Freedom in the body, breath and voice is linked to freedom in the mind and understanding.

If you are mis-stressing, check that you actually understand the text. Look up every word. Do you understand the situation? Is there humour or irony involved? If this work has been done and you have a coherent knowledge of what you are saying, here are a few exercises to help stress.

- Clean the text by intoning it very gently before speaking.
- Give a neutral reading of the text; that is, say the words without giving any one word special colouring (i.e. use a very neutral phrase like 'the cat sat on the mat').
- When you have a clean, neutral reading, this exercise is wonderful. You will need a partner. As you speak the text the partner should ask you questions concerning meaning. You can only reply using the text.

     Question: 'The cat sat *where*?'
     Answer: 'The cat sat on the *mat*'
     Question: '*Who* sat on the mat?'
     Answer: 'The *cat* sat on the mat.'

This interrogating for stress can be done with any text and through the exercise all manner of stresses and potential meanings are released. I prefer an actor to use this exercise to find the stress needed rather than telling her precisely where to stress. By asking the right questions you can release a text in many different ways and maybe even make valuable discoveries. Directors and fellow actors can help a struggling colleague to feel organically the stress pattern of a line or speech.

As a general observation, many actors confound the audience by over-stressing. We can't hear meaning because the clarity of a thought is swamped by too much stress. The very important words in a thought will have full weight. In verse, the good writer will do this with the iambic stress and when the iambic is odd or the stress irregular, the situation is difficult. A full stress on a word will include a fuller speaking of the word. An unstressed word will be neutralized.

'My friend is coming to supper.' Play with this line. If the meaning you want to convey is '*My* friend is coming to supper' as opposed to '*Your* friend' then 'my' will be fully weighted. The other words in the sentence move towards being more neutral. If 'supper' is weighted, the meaning shifts to supper, not lunch or tea, that my friend is coming to. We do this stressing naturally but if there is a problem with stress you might check that the words you really need have the weight, while the others are moving more towards neutrality. I understand this is one of the problems with getting computers to speak: the stress of the artificial voice sounds the same and therefore the listener gets confused.

Note that as a word is stressed we move into and out of that word with inflections – again a natural movement in the voice connected to meaning.

- With a partner, take a sentence and say it first as clearly and neutrally as possible.
- Then change its meaning through stress and inflection. Speak it again with a different meaning, stress and inflection. See if the partner can distinguish the different meanings.

You can get as subtle as possible with this part of the exercise. This is a great exercise for ear training, but it is also very educational for actors, because it will become apparent that you can never say a line exactly the same each time. The same meaning can be conveyed, yet if you listen carefully the voice, through stress and inflection, constantly changes. That is one of the reasons live theatre is so exciting and so constantly varied. The rendering of any speech in any play, even if the actors are supremely drilled, will always be different at each performance. The human voice as a reflection of the whole being will chart minute changes and we all change from moment to moment in life.

Respecting Writers' Intentions

In this section I will list some basic exercises to encourage the actor to serve the writer's intentions. There are many features in a piece of writing that you simply must learn to identify, respect and work with in your acting.★

I never mind an actor breaking rules; after all, great actors are often dangerous and sometimes anarchic figures who give a text a wholly original reading. However, what I do object to are actors who break rules without knowing what the rules were in the first place. Know first what you are doing and only then set off in your own direction.

The Length of Thought

I think many members of an audience sit and listen without understanding a speech or even a whole play because the actor or actors have not understood the thought, length of thought, or one thought's connection to another.

Two faults chiefly hamper understanding of text:

- Many of us no longer express ourselves in the kind of long, considered passages we sometimes find in plays. Yet most texts written before the 1950s contain extended and often complex thought processes. Many plays after the 1960s indulge in the problem of communications and use incoherence as a kind of dramatic device.
- Many of us have not been educated to connect ideas and thoughts together. This is a recent departure and a real problem for an actor when he or she approaches a text. All theatre-goers – and I am not just talking about the educated members of an audience – until recently knew that one thought had to lead to the next; that thoughts in structured communication do not hover in space like disconnected fragments, but are pieced together to form a coherent whole. Even the plays of Samuel Beckett are coherent when analysed and worked in performance.

★ Please see *The Need for Words* for an even more expanded version of this section of work.

With these two thoughts in mind, let me point out a few things which may help you:

- First, rely on a full stop or period, question or exclamation mark to indicate the end of a thought. (Let's not, at the moment, enter a debate about editors repunctuating text. We've got to start somewhere, so let's just rely on the guidelines you have in the printed text in front of you.) Commas, colons, semi-colons do not indicate the end of a thought but turns, pauses or different pulses in the thought before it is finished.

- A thought is physical and I express it as one completed movement like a dance step. Even if you are standing still, something inside is moving, is actively taking you a step further. To complete the movement, you might have many flutters, diversions or tempos. Once completed, it stops.

- Think of each thought as a journey from A to B to C, maybe across the room. I want to leave the room and I move to do that. I then have to stop off to pick up my bag, then return as I nearly reach the door, for my coat. The journey might metaphorically be in a car from A to B. In order to get to B, I have to turn corners, stop at lights, change gears. All these turns, stops, gear changes will be reflected in the other punctuation such as commas and colons.

- Let's explode some misconceptions about speaking long thoughts. You don't have to do a whole thought on one breath. We can delay thought and still breathe. The breath will invariably come on those turns, those stops, those diversions. Sometimes, it is useful to play with speaking a thought on one breath. This can make clear the thought's journey and enable us to recognize the wholeness of an idea, but some long thoughts would be impossible to speak on a single breath.

- You don't need to rush a long thought. You can stop and pause but carry on working with an idea. We do it all the time. Half-way through a thought, we pause, probably accompanied by holding the breath, then continue. On my journey along a road I can stop and admire the view, then walk on to my destination.

- Again, if you are not understanding the length of a thought it can be a useful exercise for you to speak it at speed. The speed will motor you through the thought and will often give you clarity. But speaking quickly is not needed all the time and is only a superficial solution. It is harder to hold a long thought slowly but it is possible. What is essential is that I feel and hear the actor completing the journey and that he or she is filled by the language. He doesn't stop thinking and working a thought until the thought ends.

- The intellectual vigour required to communicate thoughts implied in texts is tough, demanding and physical work. I dig a hole in the garden, working and digging until I get the whole root of the weed out. I pile the bricks one on top of the other until a wall is built. The same work – excavating and building – is required for holding a thought.

Exercise 57: Length of Thought

This works very well with a partner who will monitor you.

- Choose a long thought. (Pick a piece of text from Shakespeare, John Webster, John Milton, Shaw or Restoration dramatists.) Begin speaking the text, concentrating on its thought patterns.
- Your partner should monitor you and send you back when he or she hears and feels you stop thinking. This stopping, collapsing or not filling in a thought will be very apparent.
- You can also do this work on a tape recorder, if working alone, and play it back to hear the result.
- Start by sitting and begin to speak, not allowing the journey to finish until you reach the end of the complete thought; that is, when you arrive at the full stop, question mark or exclamation point.
- It is useful to physicalize the journey by moving your arm and continuing the movement until the thought finishes.
- What can help here is to push against your partner as you speak, your hand against hers. That will give you a sense of the physical energy or pressure of the thought. On your own, you can push against a table just by exerting a gentle pressure which will allow you to motor the thought. Once you have explored and held the thought, you can experiment. You can pause, wait, walk around but still feel that the pressing thought is unfinished and that you are actively working on ways to complete it; moving forward and searching even in silence. The car might have stopped but the engine is still ticking over.
- Examine how many changes of direction occur in this one long thought. Perhaps the thought is one uninterrupted arc or maybe it takes many swerves and corners. Recognizing one continuous energy of thought, or many changes in directions

within a thought, provides important acting clues. The more chaotic and tempestuous the thought, the more turns it will have. If the thought flows effortlessly, the character is probably more liberated in her thinking at that moment in time.

- Now look at the thought in the context of a whole speech. Maybe the whole speech is one thought, but find a speech with several thoughts. You might be amazed to discover that many large speeches just consist of three or four separate thoughts. Shakespeare's long soliloquies and his sonnets often work this way.

- Speak the speech, aware of the journey laid out in each thought. Begin to notice that each succeeding thought is connected to the previous one. Each thought completes part of the whole and moves you towards a conclusion. The movement is not only active but, like building bricks or boxes that open or close into and onto other boxes, it creates an edifice which is the play.

You can find this process governing most good plays. The individual scenes contain a building, as does the entire play. Some of the great writers, like Shakespeare, do something even more thrilling. As the thoughts move towards the resolve or conclusion, the focus zeroes in on a more concentrated issue and pulls you right onto the target. Suddenly, in a manner of speaking, the wide-angle landscape that began the play has isolated in close-up a bird sitting on a branch.

As soon as you understand the movement and direction of thought, not only will learning a text become easier, but you will be learning the text thought by thought and appreciating the connections.

Many actors are terrified of classical plays because they find them hard to understand. But if you stay calm and gradually move from the first thought to the second, to the third (speech by speech, act by act), noting the connections, you will easily crack the speech-by-speech movement of the text. I watch actors sweat over a fraction of a thought or one in the middle of a speech. If they would only go back to the beginning of the speech and start to build it up thought by thought, its meaning would become apparent.

The other creative exploration you can make when examining a text thought by thought is the varying lengths of each thought. Longer thoughts reflect a character whose intellectual juices are flowing along with emotional ones. If the thoughts are suddenly short, it is a clue that the intellectual and emotional gears are grinding to a halt or suffocating the character. Ask yourself if the character is flowing with long thoughts or is constipated with the shorter ones. Maybe he or she speaks a mixture of sudden movements forward, followed by stops and shudders.

Exercise 58: Walking the Journey of a Speech

I love this exercise. Watching actors do it will often reveal all their worst acting habits. The point of it is actually to walk the journey of a speech. Perhaps use the entire opening speech from *Richard III* here, or any long soliloquy full of complexity, vibrancy and colour.

- As you speak, trace out not only the length of the thoughts but all the diversions or pulse changes within each thought. You must stay open to the text and let it take you along in whatever way it wants. As you walk, you will feel the pace and rhythm of the thoughts or sense changes in direction. Some sections of the speech will hurtle you forward quickly, you might even have to run. Some will move you more slowly. In some thoughts you might experience twenty or more turns. Others will be so long and continuous that the room might not be large enough to contain you. If you were to look down on this exercise from above, you would see the physical journey of the speech mapped out by the actor.
- When you have physically walked and spoken the speech, stand still and speak it. You will still feel the movement in you and be filled with the motion of the text which has suddenly come to life. Your breathing will now probably match the thoughts. You may find that you are not even worried about your breath and that the range of your voice is most likely responding to the changes in the text.

- You should do this exercise several times, becoming clearer and perhaps tougher on yourself. The first time you did it you were probably aware that you were missing turns, or that there were many more than you thought. Try to find them all. Now you might have noticed that most heightened text has two key components:

  1. The language moves you forward. It is active. You don't dally and inspect your words but use them to shift events, not to prevaricate or ponder.

  2. Transitions or changes in the text, thought or emotional turns are achieved succinctly, mostly with one word: 'but', 'if', 'when', 'then,' etc. In less heightened, more casual language we make turns with several words. 'You know what I mean . . . ', 'Perhaps I might . . . ', 'I wonder if . . . '. This language difference should be transformed to your movement. You should be clearly turning on every word that turns. Many regular word turns result in a physically gentle curve. Heightened text has us turning clearly, cleanly and quickly. Lock this motion into your body and it will surface in the voice when you speak

- Walk throughout the exercise in a centred, dynamic, ready way. Don't amble or stroll. Avoid looking down; look out.

- I'm sure this exercise will reveal layers of meaning to you as you repeat it. The number of turns is somehow directly linked to the character's state of anxiety or need. Chaos in the walking is reflected in the head or heart.

- If an actor moves off on a turn and then speaks after walking a few steps, he tends to be ahead of the text or the thought – out of the movement, speaking before there is a need. If the reverse happens, speaking before moving, he is behind the moment and the thought. You have waited, felt the need, waited, then spoken. If you stop and speak long before you move, then you are one of those nesting actors: the sort who builds a nest with the words and examines each moment rather than actively moving on.

- Some actors, when they do this exercise, embellish their walk; they act 'walking'. This often results in your speaking with an embellished voice. Try to walk the speech as naturally as possible for a more straightforward result. Walk straight into the text with honesty and let it change you. You can always add refinements later, but investigate what the text is telling you now on an immediate level, not what you want to do with it. Discover how it wants to transform you.

Verse

It is easy to forget the thought when examining the physical forms of verse, so remember to do the thought exercise alongside any verse exercises. There are also physical factors to look at when exploring dramatic verse, like rhythm, line energy, and rhyme.

Rhythm In most English dramatic verse this will be the iambic pentameter. Iambic is the two-part rhythmic, 'de *dum*'. The second, heavy stress falls hard upon and after the unstressed syllable. It is like a heartbeat and therefore felt powerfully by all humanity. Pentameter means five, so there are five iambics to each line. In iambic pentameter there are ten syllables to a line.

I think it is essential for every actor speaking iambic pentameter verse to feel and beat it out. Not only will it thrill you and the audience – it's a momentous rhythm – but an understanding of it is essential to inform you of the writer's acting and thought clues. The heavy stress will usually fall on the important words. The rhythm will sometimes be irregular and won't scan into simple unstressed/stressed patterns. This indicates that the writer is changing the heartbeat of his character, or signalling a sudden shift in thinking. It is an acting note which you can use. Something unusual is happening to the language. What can it mean?

You should sound this rhythm until it becomes natural for you to speak it unselfconsciously. It is part of the craft of a classical actor to have the iambic verse beat instilled into his or her system. Once you feel the rhythm taking root inside you, you can start breaking rules. For instance, you can pause in the middle of a line and still hold the iambic beat, then pick up the rhythm and continue to a complete pause. The rhythm will continue beating and moving on silently just as your heart does. Suddenly words have a new power. You cannot not finish a word. The 'de *dum*' rhythm does it for you by moving up into a stress. The iambic has that surge in it. It urges you towards completion.

Be very careful as you beat the lines to allow the iambic its return upwards. I think it's because we write the iambic stress with a down stroke that people often speak it by pulling down off the word. Let the word return and that returning energy will move you on. If, for whatever reason, an iambic line ends with an unstressed beat, that can indicate a loss of power on the character's part.

Beat out a whole iambic pentameter speech and indicate where all the stresses lie:

> Two households, both alike in dignity
> In fair Verona, where we lay our scene,
> From ancient grudge break to new mutiny,
> Where civil blood makes civil hands unclean.
> From forth the fatal loins of these two foes
> A pair of star-crossed lovers take their life,
> Whose misadventured piteous overthrows
> Doth with their death bury their parents' strife.
> The fearful passage of their death-marked love
> And the continuance of their parents' rage –
> Which but their children's end, naught could remove –
> Is now the two-hours' traffic of our stage
> The which if you with patient ears attend,
> What here shall miss, our toil shall strive to mend.
>
> *Romeo and Juliet*, Prologue

Stay on support and full voice. You can walk, as long as it's dynamic and not a stroll. Many people find it useful to physicalize the iambic. Let the arms or the whole body move with it. Remember not to pull down in your movements: they should be up and out. One motion you will find in the above speech is that of conflict; two like households locked in a struggle. The pendulum, the conflict, swings from side to side. The dead lovers are actually buried in the speech. So that is a different kind of motion. Look for other patterns of movement like this.

As soon as you have finished the whole speech you can stand still and speak the speech just for the meaning, but you will feel the verse and rhythm are there. The iambic should not be dominating but hold you like a firm foundation. Don't be frightened to beat out every verse speech you have to speak. This is useful preparation. Eventually, after you have spoken acres of verse, you will feel it organically and not have to work so hard. As you beat out verse speeches and scenes, you will trip over two other important physical acting clues locked inside the verse.

- Caesura is a stop or pause in the middle of a line. This is a heavy stop in the verse line. The harmonious line is broken, the journey of the line is suddenly altered. It is like tripping over a rock.

> Gone already.
> Inch-thick, knee-deep, o'er head and ears a forked one!
> Go play, boy, play. Thy mother plays, and I
> Play too; but so disgraced a part, whose issue
> Will hiss me to my grave. Contempt and clamour
> Will be my knell. Go play, boy, play. There have been,
> Or I am much deceived, cuckolds ere now,
> And many a man there is, even at this present,
> Now, while I speak this, holds his wife by th'arm,
> That little thinks she has been sluiced in's absence,
> And his pond fished by his next neighbour, by
> Sir Smile, his neighbour . . .
>> *The Winter's Tale*, Act 1, Scene 2, 186–197

- As you examine the content of the speech you will see, like the physical difficulty of saying certain words expressed earlier, that this jolt in form is sympathetic to the content. The character is having difficulty or, as in this portion of a speech by Leontes, suffering insane jealousy. The unfinished line is where the remaining syllables of the line are left open and incomplete. The line is giving the character breathing space to suffer and react. It is rather like a rest in a tense piece of music; tension continues despite the rest. Again, the events, the content of the speech dramatically require some form of activity. A gathering time for a character in conflict.
- In playing a scene together you sometimes find the lines shared and distributed between two voices. Each one picks up and completes the other's line. This could reflect frantic division or peaceful harmony between two characters. Whatever we

observe here, the action is being taken forward by both parties
in a scene. Again, you might like to break these rules, but
please do so after experimenting with what is written. Look at
the next speech to examine what is at stake:

> CRESSIDA: Have the gods envy?
> PANDARUS: Ay, ay, ay, ay; 'tis too plain a case.
> CRESSIDA: And is it true that I must go from Troy?
> TROILUS: A hateful truth.
> CRESSIDA: What, and from Troilus too?
> TROILUS: From Troy and Troilus.
> CRESSIDA: Is it possible?
> > *Troilus and Cressida*, Act 4, Scene 5, 27–31

Line Energy – The Journey of the Line

As you do this work it is most important that you feel and
know the length of the thought. I want you to respect the
line energy, its start, middle and end, but I also want the
sense of the words to travel through each line. I've heard so
many actors speak perfectly energized lines, but because
they don't hold the whole thought, I can't understand what
the line is all about.

Take at least eight lines of iambic pentameter verse – the
first eight lines of a sonnet would do very nicely. You must,
throughout this exercise, breathe and think the whole text.

> O, how thy worth with manners may I sing,
> When thou art all the better part of me?
> What can mine own praise to mine own self bring?
> And what is't but mine own when I praise thee?
> Even for this let us divided live,
> And our dear love lose name of single one,
> That by this separation I may give
> That due to thee which thou deserv'st alone.
> O absence! what a torment wouldst thou prove
> Were it not thy sour leisure gave sweet leave
> To entertain the time with thoughts of love,
> Which time and thought so sweetly doth deceive,
> >   And that thou teachest how to make one twain
> >   By praising him here who doth hence remain.
> > *Sonnet 39*

- Speak the text three times. The first time, only speak out aloud the first word of each line although you are breathing and thinking the whole line and thought.
- The second time, read just the last word of the line out aloud.
- The third time, read the whole text aloud.

What becomes apparent is that the energy of the line is embodied in the quality of words that start and finish a line. The beginning words (O, When, What, And, Even, And, That, That, etc.) kick you into the line and you have to go on. The end words (sing, me, bring, thee, live, one, give, alone, etc.) in some way complete a thought. The energy of the thought might go into the next line or lines but in some way the journey of the line has ended. As you do this exercise it will become apparent that it is ridiculous to deny any word in a line. They are all moving you on. The punctuation is there to help you rest, and the scheme of alternating rhymes is there to help mark the journey. You might like to return to the breath support exercise, building up a line word by word. This will make the line's energy clearer still. Also notice the alternation between vowels (like 'o') and consonants. Great verse writers like Shakespeare guide the speaker through the text. We could all write iambic pentameter quite easily, but to do this, to start and finish a line with words that reflect beginning and ending within a line, takes tremendous craft.

Antitheses (Opposites)

To understand opposites and opposition within a line – love/hate, day/night, hot/cold – relies on understanding content and quality of language, and the various rhetorical devices which give language variety when spoken. But I'm putting antithesis on a more physical footing. This oppositional swing does create a physical tension in the line. There was an ideal in verse writing which encouraged the balanced line. Rather like those scales of justice, the line had to swing from one point of view to another.

> In the old age black was not counted fair,
> Or if it were, it bore not beauty's name;
> But now is black beauty's successive heir,
> And beauty slandered with a bastard shame.
>
> from *Sonnet 127*

If you speak these lines (take them slowly because this is a bit of a tongue-twister) and really mean each word as you speak it, completely in the moment of the struggle, try to experience the actual physical swing of the line as the struggle between 'black' and 'beauty' becomes engaged. The emotional pay-off will be evident. As you swing with the words so does your heart and your head. The antithesis of the line will place you on a see-saw, moving up and down emotionally and intellectually.

Whenever you work on a text, check to see if the antithesis of opposing words, thoughts or feelings is being engaged. I only mention it here because so many young actors will speak a text which is loaded with antithesis but only pick up one side of the argument. In doing that, they will often miss the balancing act of irony and the physical swing between poles that opens up the emotional and intellectual world of the character. The actor must remember that drama is about debate and constant struggle. There is rarely a rest between opposing forces.

Owning Words 2

When a great actor serves a text fully and gives a memorable performance, chances are that two strands of text work have been woven together. The effect can be like two mighty rivers meeting. Up to now I've concentrated on only one stream of work which is largely technical and which can be taught and learned.

We've been working on the physical power of a text as though it were a living organism. The thought, the structure, the rhythm and the line are meant to come alive through an actor summoning each of these components into physical life. You are working to respect the writer's forms, playing the text, matching your vocal patterns to some linguistic pattern in the text. Perhaps a simpler analogy might be that the skeletal structure is now in place but not fully fleshed out in detail.

Actors can feel quite threatened by the technical work we've been doing. They feel their creativity is being subsumed by the form of the language. I'm always at pains, however, to explain that form should reveal clues to enhance the actor's creativity. Performers will, none the less, somehow feel threatened when they work on form. Interestingly enough, dancers and musicians don't ever feel threatened by the stops or the notes of a piece of music. In fact, and this applies to acting as well, formal properties should release and liberate the artist.

However, I have some sympathy for this point of view because when actors have only paid attention to the form of a role, the thoughts, ideas and structure of the text may be clearly communicated but the performance can be devoid of any personal attachment or passion. I might, as an audience, understand the whole but feel little engagement with the specifics. Clearly we have a problem on our hands which no amount of technical skill can overcome.

So all this formal work has to meet up with another stream of work which enables the actor to bring into play his own unique and deeply felt experience of the word and of the world. The words must become personalized. As words pass through all of us, our experience naturally filters and transforms them singularly. Our relationship with words is our very own and constantly changes, hence the newness and exploration of words that a great actor can make every night. No one can ever experience words in quite the same way as someone else. When an actor enters this area of work, his or her imaginative contribution to theatre has begun. I like to call this second tributary of work 'owning words'.

Before we start on the process of owning words through exercises, I want to touch on four vital points:

1. If an actor merely does his or her emotional work on a text without the technical work we've been doing above, I will sit in a theatre understanding all the specifics and sense the actor's connection to language, but I probably won't follow a story or really know what is going on. It can sound extremely indulgent, usually because the performer's emotional attachment supersedes the needs of the text.

2. In a working process, you might lose half of the work in order to explore the other. For instance, form and thought might fly out of the window as an actor starts to own the text. That is allowable. In a working atmosphere you can always reconnect to other types of work. In my experience, directors who spend time on the text, exploring the specific nature of each word and the actor's connection to it, can easily add the form work into rehearsal. The other way round is more problematic. If actors have never been given time to explore the words and their feelings but have the form in place, it is difficult to connect the actor. If a director is leading you that way, you need to do a lot of the ownership work for yourself to balance it (see p. 208). Once words are sufficiently embedded in an actor he can speak them at any pace and easily obey the writer's form or any note given by a director yet stay completely connected and specific.

3. Please don't ever become too indulgent with owning words. Taken to extreme, I've seen actors become so selfish and 'me'-orientated with notions like 'I think this word means this' that they rule out all other meanings which might be equally valid. You have to respect the *real* meaning of a word before you have your own experience of it.

4. After owning the words for yourself, you must then go on to transform and own the words from the character's life and point of view. As characters change, so does their language. It's the same as in your life. As we transform so does the language we use. Through words the actor discovers new realities and new sensations. It's no good saying, 'I wouldn't say this; it's not real.' We all use words differently, depending on how we view

ourselves and the world we inhabit. What the character says
may be exactly what he or she means.

Some parts you are cast in will seem effortless because the
language is close to you (perversely, that closeness will,
with some actors, close them down). Some parts will need
time to grow before an actor can experience and own the
words. Lear uses language from a long-lived life. But any
wisdom he may have gained is tempered with folly. Points
of view are expressed that a younger actor might not yet be
able to savour. Juliet's language is youthful. Her imagination and language are innocent, yet she gains knowledge
and wisdom amazingly quickly and matures with speed. So
the performer must be naïve on the one hand and razor
sharp on the other in order to match the character's
changing pattern.

As characters heighten, another layer of language is
revealed. Careful language is scrapped and we view a
higher reality through words. An actor's job is constantly to
own and discover words afresh. In a great, densely written
text this might only be possible for short bursts, which is
why actors like to return to parts to try and own them in a
new way at different points in their careers. An actor should
always look at the type of language his character uses and
how it might change.

Asking Questions

Here are some questions to ask yourself all through a text,
moment to moment. We all have many forms within us and
it's the particular form in set situations that will give you
character clues.

- *Is the language formal or informal?* Verse is generally more
  formal while prose is informal. But these rules can shift. Are all
  the characters in the scene speaking with the same level of
  formality or is one disrupting the common language being used

(e.g. Hamlet in the court scenes)? The clues might be a formal use of verse or language being used to intimidate people who cannot speak formally. Or the reverse: informality being used to place someone at ease.

- *Is the language direct or indirect?* If it is direct the character might be very open. If it's indirect she might have something to hide.
- *Does the character use imagery?* If so, when and why? Probably as emotions heighten, the only means of expression is an image or metaphor. Shifting in and out of imagery will give you clues to what's at stake in a scene. How particular is the imagery? This may be due to the character's way of life or interests (e.g. Cleopatra's watery, sensual imagery contrasts heavily with the hard, rock-like imagery of the Romans).
- *Is the language concrete, full of very specific details?* If so, maybe the character is practical.
- *Is the language verbose or overblown?* Maybe the character is a pedant or a good politician not expressing a point of view but embroidering it to manipulate others (like Polonius in *Hamlet*).
- *Does he use analogy or academic references?* Sometimes this may be for comic effect. But you always have to look closely at the language to see how it helps clarify and characterize (see Ben Jonson's *The Alchemist*).
- *Does the character use more short than long words?* What does this indicate?
- *Does the character enjoy discussion and debate?* He probably likes being contentious, difficult or probing.
- *Where does she feel safe in language, where in jeopardy?* Perhaps the character wants to hide and avoid confrontation.

All these are simple and obvious questions but they will help any actor sort out the specific use of language which confronts him or her.

Exercise 60: Owning Words

This exercise may appear laborious, but never be frightened of taking as much time as you need in order to possess a text. One ten-line speech, for instance, might take an hour to go through but is well worth the time and effort. You will definitely come out of the moment and break up all forms – thought and structure – but this fragmentation can be put back together later. The important point to remember when working through this exercise is: if you really experience a word you will never lose the sensation of it later. Many actors prefer to do this work alone, lying on the floor, but you can also do this exercise sitting or standing. The important technical aspect is to keep the breath as low as possible and speak with support, on voice.

- Choose a text you are having difficulty with or one that is totally unfamiliar.
- First speak the speech, waiting to experience, in some complete way, every word and phrase. Do not utter a word until you sense a knowledge of it.
- Use all your senses in exploring the words: you might see, smell, hear, taste or touch the word. Imagery is perhaps easier to recognize and activate, but don't cheat on any word.
- If the word is a noun, imagine it fully and make it concrete.
- If the word is a verb, imagine the action it portrays as something incredibly active.
- If you are having trouble with a particular word or phrase, be tough. Do you really *understand* the word or is it one of those words you just 'sort of' understand? If so, look it up and be sure. Find synonyms for it so you feel truly comfortable with it. This is a point which really takes time to reconcile since few of us will be familiar with every word of a complex speech, especially one from a different time from our own. With Shakespeare, we may have to look up lots of words!
- Perhaps you are faced with a word you do not want to confront, such as 'kill' or 'death'. It may be a word that stirs up a deep emotion. Be honest with yourself and let yourself react. Own the word.
- Is the word the name of a person? When Orlando names Rosalind in *As You Like It*, he does so with resonant feeling:

> O Rosalind, these trees shall be my books
> And in their barks my thoughts I'll character

When Macbeth utters Duncan's name after he has murdered him, it is in horror:

> To know my deed 'twere best not know myself.
> *Knock within.*
> Wake Duncan with thy knocking. I would thou couldst.

- Do the words and their actions denote a mythical persona or scene? Who, and why is this person important as a reference to your character? In *Cymbeline*, the lascivious Iachimo quietly approaches the sleeping Imogen, likening himself to Tarquin who approached the bed of Lucrece only to rape her:

  > The crickets sing, and man's o'er-laboured sense
  > Repairs itself by rest. Our Tarquin thus
  > Did softly press the rushes ere he wakened
  > The chastity he wounded.

  It is in this area of the word work that actors must use their imagination and begin to think the thoughts and words of the character. So many actors use all their imagination to deny the word, not make it real and meaningful. But without the wholeness and potency of the word, most theatre would expire.

- When you have finished the whole speech, return and speak it straight through, staying on the word actively and in the moment. Do not worry if all the work doesn't instantly show results. It will become richer and, as you dig in, that richness will intensify. Your connection to the word will change all the time, which is fine and good. As long as there is a connection you will be communicating specifically.

An actor has to gather the power of the word, then release it into space, moving both herself and the audience forward with the richness of owning every second she exists and speaks.

Every Word You Speak

What is always in place when I watch great actors perform is their capacity to own every word they speak. They have taken someone else's language and have made it their own. Moment to moment, the words, as spoken by the actor, appear to be uniquely discovered and freshly minted, as if spoken for the very first time. The greatest actors are curious about language to a fault.

There are different levels of knowing a word. And in order to own a text fully and let it take root in us we have to move down through layers of dialogue so that we may know the words on a very deep level. That deep knowledge is an actor's most fundamental and yet hardest task. We all go through life rediscovering words and knowing them differently as life transforms us and changes the relationship we have with language. We might use the word 'love' for years and know it in some way, but then fall deeply in love. Suddenly the knowledge of that word has deepened and we will speak it differently, possess it more completely.

An urban student working on the fairy goddess Titania in *A Midsummer Night's Dream* came back from a trip to the country with a new and more vivid knowledge of the line: 'Met we on hill, dale, forest or mead.' She had discovered what a 'dale' and a 'mead' are, never having seen or experienced them before. Suddenly as she spoke the line those places were imprinted in her voice. The same happened to a boy speaking 'Sonnet 12': 'When I behold a violet past prime . . . ' He had never before seen a violet, much less one past its prime, so he went out, discovered one and began to know the line. While speaking 'Sonnet 27' ('Looking on darkness which the blind do see . . . '), a New York actor, brought up in a city where nights are never completely dark, came back from holiday in Montana and suddenly knew how blindingly dark night could be.

Examples like these could roll on, but the important point is that every word has to be known and experienced before it is fully owned. In order to begin the process the actor has to be honest about the words he doesn't own. He has to be prepared to excavate the text.

In some ways the more concrete words are easy to clean and own. A dale is a dale. A violet is a violet. Research might have to be done on archaic words which are difficult. They have to be looked up, but with a short journey of the imagination you can grapple with them ('fie', 'lo', 'surcease'). A word might be understood intellectually, but as it's not in common use you might have to move towards imagination. Classical and biblical allusions are not so commonly invoked, so to need them and use them with knowledge will take more work.

All these things are possible, and when you have connected to these words they will remain part of your experience and never abandon you. The words that are harder to grasp and are sometimes too painful or revealing to own are the huge and often simple words. Words that express feeling, or touch on personal experience, and make the actor look at herself in a raw, uncompromising light. Denying words will of course deny you ownership: an actor playing Lear who will not own the word 'Nothing'; a young, seemingly gentle boy not wishing to own the word 'savage'; the strong masculine actor not owning 'I fear you'; the feminist actress struggling to own Kate's last speech in *The Taming of the Shrew*.

For the moment, let's just connect owning words to the voice and, more importantly, to the breath. When an actor owns a word there is no clutter in the voice or speech process. The word is spoken cleanly and efficiently. It is there. The audience hears the word clearly in the most profound yet simple way. The word is free, but informed by the actor's unique experience of it. It is a place of enormous simplicity, but underneath that simplicity is a whole world of experience.

Many writers and directors will ask an actor who is confused about words in a speech to 'just say the words', which I take to mean just know and own the word enough so that you can trust and experiment without bluffing or denying. It makes sense. Either bellowed or muttered, the words invariably get lost and have no real weight.

A lot of this work is 'chicken and egg'. The voice and breath have to be free in order to own the word. Yet you have to own a word before the voice and speech are *completely* free. Much of the technical work I do with actors is to short-cut the process of owning a word. If the rehearsal period is long enough, good actors will get there of their own accord. The technical work, though, can short-cut the process. By simulating a free breath and open vocal position, you can connect technically to a word, the 'outside in' factor comes to the fore and will often inform the actor of how the word should be owned. Ownership of words has a lot to do with the connection and placing of breath.

As I watch actors rehearse a rich text, the same curious pattern often happens. They 'know' the text; that is, they have learned the text. The text is in their heads and they start to have a passing acquaintance with the words. As the rehearsal progresses you can almost see the text moving down into their bodies and taking possession of their breath. They begin to know the text on a deeper level. Then the most curious thing happens – they start to forget the text. When I first observed this happening I was alarmed and couldn't understand how someone who had known a text so well could lose it. But then, after many years of observing this process repeat itself in rehearsal after rehearsal, I think I finally began to understand what was happening. In their heads, these actors came to know the text intellectually. The forgetting occurred when they moved from that level of knowledge to a deeper one in their emotional and spiritual centre. When the words begin to grow roots in the heart and soul, in a sense they have to be relearned. Deep ownership starts to happen.

You forget words as they span the chasm from intellectual enlightenment to sensual, emotional and spiritual knowledge. When the actor begins to remember the text again, it is invariably fuller, richer and deeper. Great actors will speak of using a run to try to own more and more of the text. And during a run the emotional roots may drive down even deeper. Ownership for the actor never stops.

Let's return to the physical manifestation of owning words. Somewhere along the line when we own a word we take it deeply into the body – that drawing in is commonly through the breath. The lower and deeper the breath, the more we connect and feel a word. Here's an exercise to test this notion:

Exercise 61: Owning Words Deeply

- Take the word 'no'.
- Breathe high into the chest or lift the shoulders and say 'no'. We might hear the word, but how does it sound or feel? Weak or uncommitted.
- Now take the breath low into the body and say 'no'. You should feel differently about the word and perhaps feel more connection and have more knowledge of it. This is a very simple way of working 'outside in'.
- You can plunge the word deeper for even more resonant meaning.

I will encourage an actor to breathe sections of a text in this way if he doesn't feel or sound as if he is owning the words. The physical manifestations of the breath making a connection with the word will often trigger a real owning, both emotionally and sensually. Try other phrases in the same way: 'nothing'; 'savage'; 'I fear you'; 'I love you'.

Please be aware that this work on very emotive words can be disturbing. Words are powerful explosive devices that can easily stir you as you re-engage with painful memories. Never force yourself into a place you don't wish to go. It will happen when you are ready for it to happen. Your voice will find the need.

Exercise 62: Taking Time to Own Words

You can do this next exercise with any speech. I will be going through a Shakespeare speech to give you some guidelines, but the most important thing is that you experience the words on your own.

Some thoughts about the exercise before you begin:

1. You must take as much time as you need to experience a speech fully. One speech could take you an hour. So give yourself all the time in the world. If you find there is a word that you just cannot experience, move on after a few minutes. You can return to it later.

2. You must breathe as low as possible throughout the exercise and when you do speak, use a fully connected support system.

3. Keep the voice free.

4. Keep clear articulation so that you can hold on to each word physically. This is going to be important as the exercise can become very emotional. If you hold on to every word and speak it with full weight, you won't break down or come to a grinding halt emotionally.

5. Don't be alarmed if you lose all the work you've done on form or structure. You will get that back later. You are picking out the detail of words so you will lose the outline of the speech.

6. Many great Shakespearean directors talk about speaking a heightened text in this way: you should think, feel and speak *simultaneously* every word as you mouth it. I absolutely agree with this notion but in this exercise you might find the experience of the word comes a fraction of a second before you speak it.

Now let's get on to tackling the speech:

- Take your speech and sit or lie in a safe place where you won't be disturbed. Some people report that darkness is useful. It's up to you, but silence is important.

- Breathe low and continue to breathe in this way even when you are not speaking. You might have to wait some time for a word to settle in you, but do keep the breath going through these moments.

- Only speak any word or phrase after or as you have some experience of it. The experience can be visual or physical or emotional. You must in some way reawaken the word in you. You must sense it, even smell it. You will come across words that you thought you knew, maybe intellectually but which you are not really specific about. That's good, you can research them after the exercise.

- After you have finished the speech, stand up and speak the speech at full pace and intent. I think you will be amazed at how rich the text is and how many experiences of the language are still there. You will know and therefore own the text a great deal more. Equally useful will be your awareness of the parts of the speech you don't yet own. Maybe half a line here and there, maybe a whole chunk. Now you know where the work lies.

Here is a speech by Titania from *A Midsummer's Night Dream*. Try it, then I will give you my subjective reactions and experiences of the speech. You might not want to look at my subjective comments, which is fine, but I want to give some guidelines, although the only real guideline for an exercise like this is your own personal experience of the words.

> These are the forgeries of jealousy
> And never, since the middle summer's spring
> Met we on hill, in dale, forest or mead,
> By paved fountain or by rushy brook,
> Or in the beached margin of the sea,
> To dance our ringlets to the whistling wind,
> But with thy brawls thou hast disturb'ed our sport.
> Therefore the winds, piping to us in vain,
> As in revenge, have sucked up from the sea
> Contagious fogs; which falling in the land
> Have every pelting river made so proud,
> That they have overborne their continents:
> The ox hath therefore stretch'd his yoke in vain
> The ploughman lost his sweat, and the green corn
> Hath rotted ere his youth attain'd a beard:
> The fold stands empty in the drowned field,
> The crows are fatted with the murrain flock,
> The nine men's morris is fill'd up with mud
> And the quaint mazes in the wanton green
> For lack of tread, are undistinguishable.
> The human mortals want their winter here:
> No night is now with hymn or carol blest,
> Therefore the moon, the governess of floods,
> Pale in her anger, washes all the air
> That rheumatic diseases do abound,
> And thorough this distemperature we see
> The seasons alter: hoary-headed frosts
> Fall in the fresh lap of the crimson rose
> And on old Hiem's thin and icy crown
> An odorous chaplet of sweet summer buds
> Is, as in mockery, set. The spring, the summer,

The chiding autumn, angry winter, change
Their wonted liveries and the mazed world,
By their increase, now knows not which is which,
And this same progeny of evils comes
From our debate, from our dissension:
We are their parents and original.

After writing out this exercise, several thoughts suddenly struck me. Although I know the speech well, I discovered words that I had taken for granted, some of the small words like 'met'. It was suddenly shocking for Titania to meet with Oberon. It sounds to me as if they met in combat, not romance. I had to return to my childhood visits to the countryside to recapture certain words like the ploughman and the lamb's fold. I saw those things many years ago. Time evaporated and I had to encounter my childhood again.

I was also as struck by the wind's and moon's feelings as I was by Titania's compassion for the little lives of mortals. What seems, and is, a very poetic speech suddenly became concrete and real, so much so that when I was confronted by 'this same progeny of evils', I was truly encountering a destructive force which was destroying the world I had just described. Instantly I felt protective. My world being destroyed by Oberon's and Titania's debate and dissension.

That was my personal reading. Now here is a line-by-line charting of my experience of the speech:

- 'These are the forgeries of jealousy': I did find myself returning on the word 'forgeries' to a visit to a forge. All smoke, heat, sweat, fire and noise. A very violent and chaotic memory and that coupled with 'jealousy'. Any memory of jealousy is uncomfortable because it is such an ugly emotion.
- 'And never, since the middle summer's spring': I not only discovered the word 'never', which is so final, but also realized that I didn't fully know what 'middle summer's spring' was in actual time. I assumed it was the beginning of Midsummer, but it suddenly could be the 'spring of day'. I was left wondering whether time was different to the immortal Titania from how it was for me.

> Met we on hill, in dale, forest or mead,
> By paved fountain or by rushy brook,
> Or in the beached margin of the sea,

It took me a long time to travel across and visit the geography of
each place and find my own hill, dale or forest. The difference
between the paved fountain and the rushy brook was vivid.
'Met' was also a shock – in each place they met.

> To dance our ringlets to the whistling wind,
> But with thy brawls thou hast disturbed our sport.

'Our' brought in all the other fairies and I heard the whistling of
the wind. The ringlets waiting to be danced are so gentle
compared with the violence of 'brawls' and 'disturbed'.

> Therefore the winds, piping to us in vain,

The plural of winds suddenly peopled the planet with wind and
that same wind is calling to us in vain.

> As in revenge, have sucked up from the sea
> Contagious fogs; which falling in the land
> Have every pelting river made so proud,
> That they have overborne their continents:

As often happens at this stage of the exercise, normally about a
third of the way through a speech, the images and sensations of
the words come thick and fast. It's as though an imaginative
muscle has been activated so that suddenly the confrontation of
each word and its effect are heightened. The 'revenge' of the
winds sucking the rain from the sea. The sucking suddenly the
reverse of those cheeks blowing on ancient maps of the world.
The fogs carrying illness and every small river now so proud. I
remember vividly drawing childhood charts in geography class
of the evaporation of the sea into rain on the land. The image
of rivers having a continent – a given territory and boundaries –
suddenly reflected throughout the play. Almost every character
mingles across their continent.

> The ox hath therefore stretch'd his yoke in vain
> The ploughman lost his sweat, and the green corn
> Hath rotted ere his youth attain'd a beard:
> The fold stands empty in the drowned field,
> The crows are fatted with the murrain flock,
> The nine men's morris is fill'd up with mud
> And the quaint mazes in the wanton green
> For lack of tread, are undistinguishable.

My basically urban existence had to be pulled right into the countryside, probably specifically the English countryside, to search for memories of all those activities. It was to the Indian countryside I had to go to see the ox and I realized that although I knew the 'nine men's morris' was a game, I didn't visually know what kind of game. I needed to look up that one after the exercise (it is a form of open-air draughts, played on squares cut into the turf).

The human mortals want their winter here:

The 'human mortals', that's us. This is a view of the world through the eyes of an immortal. Winter suggests something bleak.

No night is now with hymn or carol blest,
Therefore the moon, the governess of floods,
Pale in her anger, washes all the air
That rheumatic diseases do abound,
And thorough this distemperature we see
The seasons alter: hoary-headed frosts
Fall in the fresh lap of the crimson rose
And on old Hiem's thin and icy crown
An odorous chaplet of sweet summer buds
Is, as in mockery, set. The spring, the summer,
The chiding autumn, angry winter, change
Their wonted liveries and the mazed world,
By their increase, now knows not which is which.

This section is such a vivid description of the world and nature turned upside-down. Oberon's and Titania's power struggle is shifting the order of the planet. I once heard a great director working on this scene. The actress couldn't understand this section of the text at all. The explosion at Chernobyl had just happened and he likened the text to that event. It is the same mighty power that changes nature but is out of cosmic control. It seems likely that the year when Shakespeare wrote *A Midsummer Night's Dream* was a year of unnatural rain and flooding. To any rural community, such uncommon catastrophes are an epic show of unharnessable power.

And this same progeny of evils comes
From our debate, from our dissension:
We are their parents and original.

After experiencing the chaos and the destruction on the planet, it is a fantastically revealing character note that Titania takes full responsibility for her actions, along with Oberon's. I experienced such compassion from her to the mortals – mortals struggle on unknowing and unable to chart their lives like an ant train crossing the terrace!

Return to the text now and speak it with the needed energy and flow. Eventually in performance the aim will be to experience and discover the words and images as you speak them. On returning to the text, try and let that happen. I think you will be amazed at how much of the exercise stays with you and how rich the language becomes, even if you have to speak the text at a fast pace.

You might have to do this owning-the-words exercise many times, each time finding new depths and experiences within the language. You might only need to do the exercise on parts of a text that you feel is alien to you. You might even discover that the work has to be done on only half of a line. The bit you don't like or want. This is, after all, about finding the text in *you*, before you speak it out to the audience.

After planting the language in yourself, you might find it useful to go back to an exercise that releases the length of thought, the verse line or the iambic. This will help you experience the two rivers meeting the technical and the personal.

The actor has to experience and own words before sharing and giving them to an audience so that they may also own them. Here is another wonderful acting paradox. You have to own something enough to let it go and not control its effect on the audience. We've all experienced the self-indulgent actor who is so into owning each word that he won't share it. 'This text is mine and I'm not giving it to you. I'm having such a good time up here.' This is an actor who has only done half the work. If he paid more attention to the form and structure of the text it would help, but it also smacks of not really trusting your own experience of the language.

One great actor I know, who always shares with the audience and is so generous with words and their universal impact, once said to me (we had been discussing this idea of trusting the words enough to share them), 'What I always think is that there is somebody out there in the audience who understands the experience of my character better than I do.' It's a wonderful note for any over-indulgent actor. Someone in the audience knows more about those words than you. Give them the words so they can have their experience. The owning-words exercises are the stage of plugging in to the language before you release it.

Your Words Meet the Character's Words

The other exploration you must now do is to make the imaginative connection that your character makes; not your imaginative connection but the *character's*. You have to transform from your experience to his or hers by gathering everything you know about the character and using it to serve his or her needs. In this exercise it is useful to list what makes the character different from you. Concentrating on the character's use of language will be a vital key because you will instantly see some crucial differences.

Working on a speech with an actor recently, several words came up that had been wrongly owned by the actor. Richard III talks in his first speech about 'war' and 'peace'. The actor liked 'peace' but hated 'war'. He was owning the words well, but *not*, however, from Richard's point of view. The actor and the character were at odds over the meaning of key words and phrases. Richard loves war and hates peace. The speech continued to have no real truth or impact until the actor changed his own relationship to those words and decided to adopt Richard's attitude. At that point the actor was able to transform himself into the character.

Another actor playing Iago was so ashamed of saying 'I hate the Moor', piling on his politically correct fear of racism and apologizing in his acting attitude for saying such words. Again he had to move radically away from his own attitude and adopt Iago's if the speech (and character) was to work.

'Honour' is a word that comes up in the speeches of many Shakespearean and Jacobean characters (and also Spanish and French plays of the seventeenth century), requiring from the actor a whole investigation of the importance of 'honour' as a code, a concept and a cultural norm. Contemporary actors who have no conceivable experience of the notion 'honour' have much digging to do in order to release the full weight of the word. Some years ago I was teaching an actor who I strongly suspected had family links with the Mafia. He had a very potent idea of what honour meant.

'Cuckold' is another word that comes up in classical plays. An actor recently using the word in a rehearsal knew the actual meaning of the word, but had to do considerable work to unlock the real horror of a married man's fear of infidelity and ridicule at the hands of a specific society. The fear also had to take into consideration a bastard child not his own; in fact, a whole kingdom was being given to a bastard and one who was not his. The actor eventually admitted to feeling no jealousy whatsoever. Furthermore, and because he was gay, he had no concept of either marriage or fathering children.

The actor can never take words in speeches for granted. They may denote something very urgent and frightening. A young woman playing the character Phoebe in *As You Like It* says to Silvius, 'I will not be your executioner' and suddenly realizes that Phoebe may actually have witnessed a real execution. A young man playing Bassanio in *The Merchant of Venice* mentions 'the rack' and knows that the character himself may have been a victim of torture. A non-believer playing the holy and virtuous Isabella must believe fully in her character's connection to 'God' and all that is moral in Isabella's universe.

Now let's return to the Titania speech above. Redo the exercise, trying to understand the character's relationship to the words rather than your own. In fact, here is an instance when it would be good to try some cross-gender role-playing. As I said before, some words will be the same but others could be radically changed. Titania describes her world. A rural though purely imaginary world known intimately to her. Her experience of the elements and the moon is personal and she knows and respects their power. The landscape of that world has to be owned *by* the actor, but *for* the character.

This movement towards a character's ownership of language can be the most exciting adventure in acting. You may have to change your whole vision of the world sometimes, along with preciously held beliefs, your status or your social and political views in order to accommodate the character's system of values. This never means that you have to condone the character's actions or words, but you do have to understand them in order to work with them. But all this is part of acting's great challenge.

Questioning the Character

Here is a check-list of all the questions you should be asking when you investigate a character and his or her language. It's a long list because there are simply so many lines of inquiry you can be making.

Are there things about the sentences or words which are linked to the status of the character? Is he better or worse spoken than you? Does she speak higher or lower than you? Care about language more or less than you? How might this affect the voice? What do these things mean in voice and speech terms anyway? Is the speech urban or rural? Urban speakers generally speak faster than rural ones and snatch words more, with a tight jaw. Where does the character come from? Does this mean a particular regional accent?

Does the character speak verse? A combination of verse and prose? Only prose? What idiom is he most fluent and comfortable in? What words does he alone use? What do special words expose about him (e.g. Shylock's use of the words 'bond' or 'ducats')?

How is the speech rhythm different from yours? Hum the rhythm. Does it rise or fall? Is there continuous flow or disrupted flow? How musical, how varied? Rhythm might mean varying range. Does the character use more extravagant language than you? This is directly linked to range (i.e. Restoration and Wilde). It would be unreal to use fantastic language and not use range. Extravagance in speaking equals rich vowels and imagery in poetic forms. Does the character enjoy speaking? A character could use verse forms but not really speak or love poetry (e.g. Iago). These people are not to be trusted. Poetry is a reflection of the soul. Is the language very pragmatic? Clinical? Exact? This means you may need more vocal control with more articulation.

Range is also linked to emotional freedom or repression. The more freedom, the more range; the more repression, the less the range. Is her thinking clearer or less clear? This will reflect directly in the clarity of speech. Is she more formal or informal? This will be reflected by precision, or not, of speech and presentation. Does she hesitate more or less? This is reflected in breath holds. More flow means freer breath.

Is the character more or less connected to language? Does he display more right to speak? This would mean a much more confident approach to speaking. A free voice with more movement? More relaxed? More tense? A higher or lower voice? More or less pitch? Does the character work through bluff or denial? This might be reflected in how loud or quietly he speaks. Are his thoughts more direct or cluttered? This would reflect in vocal directness or conversely an indirectness.

Does she laugh a lot?

Would your language shock her or does hers shock you in any way? Is there a belief or value system expressed in her words? Does the character use a high moral tone or is she amoral, judging from her language? Different or the same as yours? You will have to believe what she says!

List the words he uses which you would never use. How do you make them sound your own? Don't take the words you would use for granted. Do the words sound dated? Are the words rich in imagery or devoid of it? Does he use clichés? Jargon? Codes? Are his words and consequently his voices affected by fashion? You have to find the experience, history and need for all these words.

Does she listen or not? Does she listen to some characters and ignore others? Does she discuss and debate? Are there any subjects she would not discuss? Is she anecdotal? Does she have favourite topics and particular passions? Does she have specialist knowledge? How does she use it?

How intelligent is he? Does he use language which even he doesn't understand? Is he academic? Streetwise? Innocent? What history is in his language? Does he speak mostly about himself or others?

Does his language alter under heightened circumstances? Does his language transform during the journey of the play? Does he change? Is he changed by what he hears?

Even as you go through this list and try to answer these questions about a character, you are playing, you are starting imaginatively to build your character's voice and the differences or similarities you have with him. As the actor speaks, his or her voice, the text and the character should begin to blend.

Circles Of Concentration

I use what I call 'circles of concentration' to help actors focus and energize their voices and place their imagination directly in service to the characters' words. The various circles the exercises below take you through are tools, placing you in the here and now.

As tools, they are only necessary when you are unsure of either a speech's or a scene's focus. There are three circles of concentration, but the variants are infinite and by no means rigid. As speakers, we exist in one of these circles every moment of our lives. We can shift rapidly between them. All three can be covered in one sentence or even in one word. As you experiment with this approach you will begin to realize that language is usually connected to the focus of where we are at a given moment.

These are the circles of concentration:

- The First Circle is speaking to yourself. The imagination is very internal.
- The Second Circle is speaking very directly to one other person. You might shift rapidly between several people, but your imagination is focused on one person at a time.
- The Third Circle is addressing many people or the universe. The speaking imagination is very generally distributed.

In essence, these circles are connected to how and where we are focused when we speak or listen. Moment to moment, our concentration can shift slowly or rapidly between these areas and we may not even be aware we are doing it. But actors aware of these shifts in concentration can use them to create some powerful and canny moments on-stage.

Using Circles of Concentration

Mostly you will find that your speaking shifts between these three circles very rapidly. Nothing is set in one tone all the time. Someone might be stuck in one circle and consequently be frightening and dramatic. Your character might be prone to one circle more than another. Your relationship with the world will be reflected by the circle in which you speak. In relationships you can find out how intimate you are by working on the circles. A couple who once spoke to each other in Second now only exist with each other in First or Third.

Some characters might be able to use Second with a certain type of language but not with others. Nora in *A Doll's House* can be silly with Torvald in Second but never serious until she shifts into a combination of First and Second at the end of the play. A boring performance could be described as one where the actor plays the whole part in one sphere only. It is neither psychologically real nor exciting to be confined in one circle.

Here are some ways of using the circles of concentration in your work:

- Soliloquy – could be First or Third or a mixture of both. I've even seen 'To be or not to be' addressed to Ophelia in Second.
- Prayer could be any circle, but whichever one you chose reflects your relationship with God and those around you. It might be the difference between a direct relationship with the Creator or a community one. In many of the medieval mystery plays characters have a strong relationship with God and pray in Second. When you hear a good priest pray, he is probably in Second. Third is generally too formal and unexciting.
- Certain professional types fall into a specific circle of speech. In the service industries many professions such as receptionists, air stewardesses or telephonists are required to be friendly, which needs Second, but that would be impossible to maintain with all the contacts they make on a daily basis. So they often sound patronizing because they are using Second language but are actually in Third. 'Have a nice day!' isn't meant at all. To sustain Second all day long would result in a breakdown!
- Shifting circles can be a great comedy tool. Third sliding through Second into First. You are talking to a group around, say, a dinner table. No one is listening, so you talk to the person seated next to you. They do not listen, so you end up talking to yourself. The reverse could be most energizing. You have an idea and address yourself, take the idea to the person next to you in Second and then propel yourself and the idea to the whole group in Third.

- You might discover that a character can only speak in Second to objects. There are plays that explore this theme. Speaking to a toy or a ventriloquist's dummy. Less dramatic but equally revealing are those people who find Second so difficult that they can only make that intimate contact while busying themselves and doing something. Making tea, ironing or washing, even walking over to a window and looking out while addressing someone in Second.

- Swearing starts mainly in First and goes up to Third when the energy builds and explodes. If someone swears at you in Second it is a terrifying experience – it becomes a true curse because it is so directly made, one to one. Brains damaged in any way, by drugs maybe or alcohol, will often shift disarmingly slowly between the circles, taking a few beats between each one or staying locked in one for an unnatural period of time. The Ancient Mariner locks the Wedding Guest so that he can't escape: 'He holds him with his glittering eye.' I've always suspected that he tells his story in a forceful Second, offering no chance of escape – not a flicker of First or Third.

Long before anyone speaks to us we know that they're locked onto us in Second: that awful realization that the homeless person on the street is going to attach herself to you with First circle language addressed to you in Second which you are expected to understand.

Circles can be used as a power tool: the high-status person who never deigns to address us in Second. We have a sneaky feeling everything is happening above and around our heads. To make Second-circle contact with these people humanizes them. When a policeman addresses you, it's generally in Third. If you can make Second contact with him, for instance when he is ticking you off for speeding, you might be able to get away with it!

However, if you are aggressive in Second you might be facing a fight. Watch any argument in a bar progress into a fight and you can observe a terrible moment when Third or even First abuse hits Second. That's when the real trouble begins.

We probably have all spent time at a party when the person we are speaking to is really not interested in us at all and is talking to us in Third and scouring the room for more appealing company. If we are locked into a Second-circle conversation at a party, then we are probably not interrupted. If we are, it's by a very insensitive person. As we enter the party we look for a group of Third-circle communicators in order to ease ourselves in.

I have been told by American friends that the English are experts at not communicating directly by refusing to shift into Second. By being polite and offhand in either First or Third, they confuse the world because the language is polite and seems familiar, but the contact is cool and off-putting. When I was told this, I realized to my embarrassment that I used that technique in order not to speak to the airline passenger next to me on a long-haul journey.

Telephones are always revealing. Some people only manage to make Second-circle contact on the phone, simply because they do not have to deal with someone's physical presence. Others can't make that contact and speak in Third when telephoning.

The theatrical aside can be Second, Third (aside) and back to Second. Or Second, First (aside) and back to Second. The latter is harder to make comprehensible, but can be most effective. In reality, even though the person opposite might hear you, because it is not meant for you, it's harder to hear.

Perhaps the more isolated we become individually and in society, the more we sink into a shell-like First. First can have an internal energy, but one from which it is hard to escape.

We also listen in circles. It is a wonderful experience to be listened to in Second. Hopefully, we all have a memory as a child of an adult really listening to us in Second. The whole ear's attention focuses on us, not in the general listening of Third or a preoccupied one of First. It can be depressing to know that we have poured out our heart to someone listening in First or Third.

When painters talk about really seeing an object I suspect they are looking at it in Second. Every circle can have every emotion. A Second-circle look and utterance can be anything – tender, aggressive, intrusive, loving.

Many of us can only address ourselves with the whole gamut of feelings in First. We might be furious about someone – perhaps for keeping us waiting – and have a spirited First-circle debate and rage against that person but when he does turn up we go into pleasant Second with him without revealing our anger. Others find pouring out everything to the world in Third easy, but the close examination of these feelings in First or Second too painful.

When you look at a text, the language will often tell you where and when the circle changes. Peter Nichols's play, *A Day in the Death of Joe Egg*, has a speech made by the schoolteacher controlling a classroom using all the shifts of circles to do so.

It is easy to recognize First-circle language because when you are addressing yourself you have no need of language that informs the rest of the world of certain details. You don't need to explain or say what you already know.

To be pinned down by a Second-circle speaker telling you in elaborate detail about the best route across London can be very off-putting. On the other hand, if people never go into Second their language is rarely direct.

If only for fun, try speaking a speech and be very conscious of shifting circles. Generally, the clearer the shift, the more dramatic and powerful it will be. However, a slow shift could communicate uncertainty or a slower brain. Cross-references can be fun; that is, trying a circle that doesn't match the text. Shift between all three – within a speech, within a thought, even within a word. Try sustaining Second for a long period of time and you will be exhausted if you can manage to speak a whole speech without moving into First or Third. Any long exploration in First will rapidly make you feel isolated and cut off. If you do the same in Third you will feel confident, if not pompous, and very sure of yourself.

You might not come to an immediate conclusion, but after experimentation you will know more possibilities and perhaps where a speech or scene is unfocused. Along the way, the more variety of focus you have, the greater the range, pitch and pace in the voice.

Over the years I've developed an exercise for second-year students at the Guildhall School. They study language and how language informs us about character by means of the various codes that words signal. This study lasts a year. They also work on circles of concentration. In the second year they write their own one-person exploration of a character that can last between ten and twenty minutes. My brief to them is that they must use all three circles and their character must speak in a code that isn't theirs.

Here is one result, by Justin Salinger:

> *Interior of a betting shop, East London. Steve is seen to lose a race. He screws up his tickets.*

THIRD: My wife's just had a baby, yeah, at last, took her long enough. Zoe, she's a girl, 7lb and 2oz, the perfect weight for a baby.

FIRST: She had six miscarriages, my wife.

THIRD: She's my little lady. She's got tiny little hands and tiny little feet, thick black hair and blue eyes. Zoe Jessica Drabwell. My wife won't put her down, I barely get a look in. No, I think she's gonna be a dancer, Zoe, not my wife, my wife a dancer! She can barely move, great lump. She's let herself go a bit after the baby an' all that. She's not so much fat as puffy, y'know. When the theme tune to *Wheel of Fortune* comes on you should see her, Zoe, waves her arms and jigs about. She's so clever. She's got my eyes and my wife's mouth, her nose is a bit of a mix.

SECOND: Hey Harvinder, I was just sayin' the brat's got my wife's mouth, don't stop screamin'.

THIRD: She's got a gob on her.

SECOND: How's your lot? How many you got now? I lose count, you got a bleedin' football team, haven't y'?

THIRD: We've just got the one. Harvinder's got about seven,

I don't know how he affords it, he must get a fortune out of the Post Office, mind you he does it all in here. I'm not sayin' we've just got the one because we can't afford it.

FIRST: But I'm goin' to give my little lady everything.

THIRD: I got a couple of photos here, d'you want a deck? No? Well here just look at this one. Isn't she clever, etc.

A dog race starts.

SECOND: Kick on Two. Kick on Two. Go on. Two's pissed it. Piss off Five, stay there Five. Shit. See that! See that, Two and Five straight forecast.

THIRD: Why didn't I do it reversed? I knew that was goin' to happen, I knew it.

SECOND: 'Ere, 'ere, watch it again, see how the Five dog comes up on the inside rails, see that, and 'ere it comes now! Watch it, watch it, the Three dog comes from nowhere and treads on the One dog and falls over, it always does that, that dog.

THIRD: I don't know why I bother, I don't know why I bother. It's all a bleedin' fix anyway.

The Imaginative Voice

Part of the great reward that comes from working your voice, speech and text together properly is that you can become very imaginative once you've reached a level of harmony. I'm not saying that your imagination has not been actively engaged before, but you have now reached a stage in the work where you can fly. You can really harness your imagination to a text. Inspiration now replaces perspiration.

Up to this point I have discussed the craft work of voice and speech. But I do want to encourage you now to become more daring as a result of the work we've been doing over three stages. It seems to me there is almost a daily erosion of vocal daring going on around us. Generally, the voices I hear are sorely reduced ones. This reduction is the result of many social factors, but the problem is illustrated most vividly in actors' voices. Plenty of actors are terrified of using their voices imaginatively. This fear of soaring results in vocal hesitancy; experimenting with the voice does not happen and moving towards a character's vocal reality is done with great trepidation. I can push you in a class or workshop, but the point comes when you have to push yourself.

The more our voices are timidly suppressed or squashed, the more work we have to do to extend vocal boundaries. Imaginative vocal transformation is one of the skills an actor must learn and practise if he or she does not want to risk reducing the text to the lowest vocal denominator.

I suppose work on vocal imagination became unfashionable because actors used to stretch and show off their voices without any organic connection to the text. It was like an aria being sung without its context in an operatic score.

To work imaginatively with the voice, I am going to recommend that the work be done in either of two ways:

1. Voice work which is organic to the text by first serving it, then risking additional transformation. This also requires you to trust that truth can be large and extreme.
2. Voice work that experiments with the voice and opens out the actor's imaginative vocal boundaries with, and sometimes even beyond, the text.

Many actors have the technical equipment to use their voices well but lack the courage to take creative risks. Even if you don't choose to go to vocal extremes in performance, your voice will sound fitter and more filled just by playing with those possibilities. Most of this work will probably take place outside a rehearsal. It is work you can do on your own and not in the presence of others. Basically you should have fun with your voice and experiment without fear.

One recommendation which I hope will inspire you to work on changing your voice and making it more imaginative has to do with getting the audience's attention. Actors too often leave the stage angry and irritated during or after a performance if they feel an audience has not been listening. Perhaps the actor hasn't gained enough craft and cannot be heard. We know that we can only listen to a dull voice for a few minutes before our attention wanders. In a society which finds listening increasingly harder to do, the actor has to strive to be more interesting and arresting at every turn.

Ideally, a free and flexible voice will make variety happen organically. Unfortunately many actors don't have the time or the courage to push themselves further. If we had months for rehearsal, this process would probably be more organic. And in some companies who give themselves the luxury of time in order to produce better, clearer work you can hear the difference in the quality of voice.

Stretch both the physical voice and the imaginative one, and during the course of the journey I hope you will discover some secret about the character, yourself and your combined vocal reality.

Stage Four

VOICE AND TEXT MEET
THE REHEARSAL

In the third year of training, a student actor's work on the voice moves out of the studio and into the rehearsal room, where the actor now begins to work on a series of plays and roles. A conservatory actor may work on as many as eight to ten major productions throughout the year, focusing acting skills from all areas of his or her training. The actor continues to work on all the basic techniques we covered in the first three stages of work, only now he or she is applying them in earnest. Rehearsals dominate the timetable in the third year. Now the young actor begins a pattern of work which he or she will follow throughout a career. Over at a place like the Royal National Theatre, rehearsals are also under way for professional actors.

The first three stages of work make rehearsal possible. Without this foundation, work rehearsing can become confused and has the potential of being divisive. Professionally, many actors have constantly to work the first three stages on their own and without guidance, particularly if they are out of work or making a living in TV or films. To use a rehearsal period creatively takes enormous craft. You have to pace yourself and know which tools of the trade you need. Many actors of a certain age may have come through a system of constant work in regional theatres when a repertory system was still in place in Britain and elsewhere. They have worked so much that the proper way of working has become ingrained. Younger actors who haven't had that experience will have to work hard before rehearsals start if they want really to use this testing time for imaginative experimentation and release.

Casting

I know that what I am about to say does not apply to all
directors, but I am sometimes alarmed at some directors'
complete ignorance of acting craft or just how fundamental
it is for a successful show to have actors who know how to
work properly on themselves, with each other and on a text.
Maybe all directors should go through the difficulty of
speaking on a stage themselves to know what the actor
faces out there. Speaking on stage doesn't happen by
magic. When the speaking does sound magical, you can be
certain that it is always being supported by robust
technique. Perhaps directors think they can mould and
create performances without the actor having any experience whatsoever. I've seen enough talented but untrained
actors suffer abysmally at the hands of directors to know
this is true. A less skilfully trained performer might be a
success in film or TV, but not in theatre.

Many directors cast inexperienced actors in major roles,
asking them to speak difficult text in a huge house. Why?
There are enough wonderfully trained actors in the world,
why cast outside that group? It's not fair on the other
actors. The director then ends up spending so much of the
rehearsal time supporting the weak link in the company.
(I have to say that generally actors are incredibly generous
and work to help any inexperienced colleague without a
moan.) It's also unfair on the audience. Inexperience
creates a gaping hole in the production. And it's certainly
not fair on the inexperienced actor who is a victim of this
kind of casting and who will be suffering a baptism of fire
from which he or she may never recover.

Years ago I worked with a company where a young,
beautiful and completely untrained girl was cast in a major
role. At the first read-through my heart sank. She was
clearly in the dark, not only about her voice but about
acting in general. She had been cast because of her naïve

charm and freshness The boy playing opposite her – and it was a big break for him – paled at the realization that his partner could not act. Each day I worked with her on her voice, both inside and outside rehearsals. Each day we were starting from scratch because none of the exercises seemed to have an effect or take hold. Yes, she had a lovely quality but only when you were within three feet of her. The personality which so captivated the director would not transmit further than the distance between the performer and a film lens.

As rehearsals drew to a close and the production was about to open, the director lost patience and became angrier and angrier with the young woman. She spent most of the final week of rehearsal in tears. In fact, she would cry through most of the run, dreading every performance. The rock face of the role was just too sheer and too high for her to climb. She became audible and was vocally free enough not to damage her voice, but she never could occupy organically the words of the text, or comfortably relate to the other actors or to the audience. The reviews were heart-breakingly bad.

One day I found myself alone in the lift with the director. Between floors he turned on me and demanded, 'Why can't you make her sound more interesting and spontaneous?' I replied as only I could, 'Why did you cast an untrained actress?' At which point the lift stopped, the doors opened and he walked out. I never got my answer. Unfortunately the young woman was so destroyed by the experience that she never worked as an actress again. There are dozens of similar tales I could tell about performers who have been cast and thrown into the deep end of rehearsals in the same reckless manner.

Equally disturbing is the casting of a famous film or TV actor – because he or she is a big draw – who has no stage-craft. Usually this sort of actor has difficulty using his or her voice in space and being audible. Actors who have worked exclusively in film and TV not only lack theatre voice technique, they also never have to sustain long scenes – which takes enormous physical and vocal stamina – and have not had to learn massive chunks of text or repeat a performance night after night. These kinds of actors have many talents and skills but most are not applicable to theatre. Few have trained voices.

In a well-balanced theatre training programme the actor gradually moves into a larger space beyond the studio, learning to sustain, by degrees, large scenes in space before taking on the challenge of learning and sustaining a large part in space. This gradual process builds up an almost athletic technique that will last over a long play and run. The actor is also being vitally tested for the career ahead.

Most voice coaches have their favourite stories about rescue efforts to save a floundering film star in a theatre production. Even the most positive stories reveal only a partial success. Those are the rare ones. Most end in disaster.

I was telephoned late one night by a nearly hysterical director a week before the first preview of an important main-stage production. The star in question was playing the lead and had to sustain scene after scene, and wave upon wave of complex text. The show was to tour major theatres before coming into London. All the papers had gossiped at length about the star's escapades in London. (I've always noticed that many film stars spend most of their rehearsal time doing interviews and their evenings being wined and dined. In other words, not working on a text or a performance either in rehearsal or after it.) Not only was this star inaudible, but he had not even learned the text by the opening performance. In desperation he tracked me down. 'Can you do a session?' he asked. I did.

As I walked into the rehearsal room the next day, the star had heard there was to be a voice call and walked out. So I worked with the other actors; all of them wonderful theatre actors and all of them on the point of murdering their star. They simply could not work with someone they couldn't hear and who didn't know the text. On my way out of the rehearsal, I bumped into the star who immediately smiled and turned on the charm. 'I don't do voice work; technique kills me, naturally – and I'm not dressed to work – and anyway, I can be miked.' 'Well,' I said, 'I think you should do the work because it will help the others to act with you and it will help you learn your lines.'

I thought that was the end of it. As far as I was concerned I had failed to make the actor understand his responsibility to himself, the play, cast and audience. That evening the star telephoned me. Would I work privately? One final go, I thought. Three times I turned up to do a session and the star was too busy to work. On the first preview a mike was put on, but the star was still inaudible. The text was still unlearned and the supporting company filled in brilliantly. The lines the star spoke were said without meaning.

After the first week of previews the star fled the country. The show washed up on the rocks of failure. The producer lost thousands of pounds and the actors who had so magnificently saved the lead from drowning were out of work after having signed a long contract; it meant they had turned down other work to do this stint. The theatre is full of similar disaster stories.

Quite simply, if an actor has had craft training there is a reservoir of work he or she can always tap into and reconnect to throughout the career. The work has been done and is there to help him or her. If you have worked in TV or film for some years, you might have to revisit the first three stages of technical work to prepare yourself for the theatre rehearsal period. If an actor has never done that work, then it will always be a struggle to perform night after night in the theatre – not impossible, but extremely difficult.

Rehearsals

Each director and company of actors works very differently, so there is nothing like a 'normal' rehearsal period. There are certain stages of work, however, that have to happen during any rehearsal; certain crucial phases the actor should pass through on his or her way to speaking a role.

A typical rehearsal period can run for anything between one to ten weeks. If you get longer than ten weeks in British or American theatre you are extremely lucky. Obviously, with such wildly fluctuating working periods, the performer must pace himself differently for each length of time. On the basic level you need to have learned the text, probably by midway through the process. You need time with a learned text in order to take your work imaginatively deeper: really to own a text in the way we talked about in Stage Three *and* know it requires some adequate time working 'off book' or without the crutch of the script. Any actor can learn words quickly. However, to be liberated with a text in order to play it through your imagination, you do need time for the learned text to have settled into you deeply and thoroughly. Now this part of the process will carry on through the run and not just stop on opening night. In some ways, acting is about deepening a performance.

Recently I worked with a cast on a new play where the playwright was rewriting the script right up to a few days before the first preview. These rewrites were not small changes but involved whole pages of new speeches and scenes. The actors and the director were in despair. Late one night after a show I had a drink with the writer. He didn't understand the hostility his changes were creating. 'Can't they learn quickly?' he asked. 'Yes, they can learn quickly,' I replied. 'But they can't act it freely. They are frightened that they won't serve your play unless they have time to own your words. They'll do the changes gradually through the previews. Just allow them the time to work their craft.'

In weekly rep, where rehearsal time may amount to only a week (or less), actors appear on the first day of rehearsal with the play fully learned but without sufficient time to work it through to ownership. You have more space and choices about learning and then knowing the text, the longer the rehearsal period. Many actors think that learning a text while rehearsing it makes the whole acting experience more organic. This is certainly true if you have the time to do this work.

The rehearsal is a period during which the director and actors will shape and change the way a play and a part is played. Dynamics and rhythms are searched through and discovered on all kinds of levels, which include performance, *mise en scène*, music, space and acoustics. Hopefully, transformation will occur as you work and encounter all these production elements. You should be discovering something new every day. Actors who arrive knowing exactly how they will play the part on the first day of rehearsal are not going to find any rehearsal or group work productive; nor will the director or other actors have a role in such a pre-planned scheme.

The First Day

During the first day or, in the case of some directors, within the first week, a reading of the play will occur. You will also see a model of the sets and probably a sketch of your costume. Even the most experienced actor will be nervous about the first reading. The most successful readings I've heard are ones where the actors were not trying to perform, but were communicating the text clearly and listening intently.

Directors are now trying to dispel the fear which surrounds first readings by getting actors to read not their own part but taking the various parts and speeches in turn around the circle of actors. In this way you hear and experience the play differently without the actors having the pressure to produce something like a performance on their first attempt at the play. Actors who fear sight-reading will not find this an enjoyable experience. <u>Try to stay centred, breathe and don't rush</u>. Aim to communicate the thought and story clearly, don't feel obliged to produce an emotional piece of work or show off. It's very important that as you read you make the text clear and audible. Some discussion about the play is likely to follow: the social, historic and political context of the play perhaps. A good preparation for the first day is to read some background material which puts the play in context. Do some research. Nerves might make you speak too much and not listen enough to the director and other actors. So try to listen throughout the reading.

When you look at the model for the sets (if they exist), begin to ask whether the set will help or hinder your voice: what material will it be made from (e.g. wood, metal, Plexiglas, etc.)? Does the set contain the acting area or open it out around the actors? Has it sounding boards in the wings and upstage, as with a box set? Is the floor wood? Is it raked (good for projection, bad on the body)? Will it be easy to move around on? Does the set focus the action? Will it focus your voice?

'Yes' to any of these questions will be good. A list of 'no's might make your voice work more pronounced and harder to focus. The hardest set to work within will be very open, without any surrounding surfaces to project the voice out.

As you look at the costume designs, just imagine what could be hindered in your body that will make voice production harder. Corsets, tight clothes, high heels, high collars or wigs, for instance, could all impede you. The sooner you start rehearsing with the bits of costume which approximate to what you will eventually be wearing, the better. In costume fittings negotiate as much physical freedom as possible, particularly around the neck, rib-cage and stomach.

Many directors spend a significant portion of the whole rehearsal period sitting around a table discussing and working through the text. Although it is often a very rich experience, this can drain an actor's energy. The other problem that can occur with this intellectually stimulating but physically passive approach to rehearsal is that the actor can find learning a text much harder and releasing it almost impossible. If this is the case within a rehearsal period, then do more work on bridging the voice into text (see pp. 164–83) so that you compensate for the sitting-around-a-table experience with more vital, energized speaking. Discussing a play places the text in the head, but it rarely places it in the body, breath and emotions. Only working through the text on your feet will accomplish that.

If your director is the sort who gets you on your feet very quickly, you might have to fill in with very gentle work on owning the text so that you can make the language clear and connected. You might have to own the words through very set directions and placing. Your job under these circumstances is to fill in the director's scaffolding.

Most major British companies do not rehearse for any significant amount of time on-stage in the space where the performances will actually take place. They do most of their work in the rehearsal room. If this is the case, you should be aware of two important considerations. Does the rehearsal room have the same acoustic quality as the theatre? It rarely does, so don't be fooled by the quality your voice produces in rehearsal. It will have to change when you work on-stage. At the Royal National Theatre, for instance, the rehearsal rooms are acoustically live and the theatres dead. You must add this factor into your vocal equation. Also, are you playing up against a wall which might be stunting your imagination and breath, closing both down? A rehearsal room rarely produces a true sense of the work you will eventually have to do in a large theatre. It is only an approximation. Try to get into the theatre and experience the size and vocal requirements of the auditorium as soon as possible and bring that knowledge back into the rehearsal room so it can be worked into your performance.

You should start to open up your work beyond the rehearsal room at least a week before your transfer into the theatre. I cannot tell you how many actors feel they have lost their rehearsal-room work and the truth found there in the transfer to the stage space. In order to be heard, they lose something. By acting and imagining beyond the rehearsal room confinement early enough in the rehearsal process, this sensation is minimized.

The First Run

The very first run of a play generally takes place in the rehearsal room. This is often the first time you initially experience the whole journey of your character. The jigsaw puzzle of voice, character and text begins to come together.

The first run is often the first time you learn to pace your performance and discover how much work and energy the play will demand of you and your voice. Great writers will give a major character time off the stage in order to recuperate or to prepare himself for a major exhausting scene. Molière, for example, did this for himself as he had to play so many of his own leading parts. Some new writers don't fully understand this idea of pacing a character for the actor's sake and will have a performer on-stage all the time, without rest periods, for over three hours!

The first run is also a great time to watch the scenes you are not in. This will always, in some crucial way, inform you about your own role. The run will generally be slow and bitty, but that's part of the process. It will become very apparent what works and what doesn't gel.

A major benefit of a run is that the play's inner energy is

revealed. The structure of the play, if it's well written, will suddenly disclose itself through the performing of it. Actors find a new and intense energy just being able to act through the scenes in their proper order. I think it is true to say that certain types of play need more runs than others in order to get either complex physical or staging strategies worked out. Comedies and very energized texts like Restoration plays are obvious examples. With these kinds of plays there is great frustration from the more experienced actors in the cast if runs are not happening. Actors like to run a play. Some directors leave it too late in the process, with the result that actors feel they cannot own their performances until the run happens.

Remember that the last run in the rehearsal room before you transfer to the theatre and the technical rehearsal will be the last time, for some days, that you will have contact with the play and the entire cast. Technical rehearsals are so fragmented that you will feel the play's story is suddenly lost to you. The last run before the technical is a good time to mark the storyline. I call it, 'What happens next?' Throughout each scene, mark in the phrase 'What happens next?' so you don't lose the thread of the action. This will give you stepping stones throughout the technical and help you hold on to the play.

Your Responsibility to Fellow Actors

When it comes to other actors, one fact is undeniable: unless you choose to do solo performances for the rest of your career you will always need to embrace other actors. Acting is a social art form; plays are partnerships. Oftentimes the partnerships can be volatile. Most theatrical events are completely reliant on company, ensemble and human co-operation. If these ingredients are not established from the first moment of rehearsal it will show, and the play and its production will suffer.

Theatre includes many ingredients which are metaphors for the life process: a show is born, an actor grows in the part, an ensemble matures and a production eventually dies (or is killed off by bad reviews). Every step of the way requires nurturing. You have to enter and confront scenes on your own, but always in combination and connection with others; the work requires harmony and union if the play is to seethe with life.

Actors must have professional respect for each other's work and *means* of working. This has nothing to do with being liked or getting on personally, a qualification which young actors in training find confusing and indistinct. What you must engender is a deep honouring of one another's work and the play, along with a graceful approach to each other's acting processes; displaying support for each other but also giving each other the space to manoeuvre as individuals. In a rehearsal room you find equal measures of wariness and generosity, hostility and humility. It is a crucible of all human behaviour.

One of the reasons why the theatre and actors intrigue me so much (the rehearsal process being an important element of this intrigue) is that human skills of communication are heightened into moments of passionate beauty. Rehearsals are the intense explorations and exhibition of all that is both good and bad about human relationships.

The sort of behaviour that will make you unpopular in a rehearsal will be the kind that impedes others' work or distracts from a fellow actor's process. Continue with destructive work habits and eventually you will never work again. The word of mouth about ruinous actors is very potent. The theatre is a surprisingly small village in which gossip and tales travel quickly.

For our more direct purposes in terms of voice, other actors cannot act opposite you if they cannot hear you. You might be having a wonderful experience in the rehearsal room but what kind of a response will inaudibility get on-stage? I remember in one rehearsal watching a knight of the theatre, a very gentle and generous man to other performers, lose patience with a young actor who was mumbling his way through a scene. 'I can't act, I can't hear my cues!' the great actor cried in despair. The poor boy was shattered, but I'm certain he never mumbled again.

At some point in rehearsal it will be essential that you know your lines accurately. Not knowing them will stop the flow and energy of your colleagues, impeding everyone's work.

If you are not working but are in the room with those who are, you must never distract them from their work. As rehearsals intensify, even an actor fidgeting, gossiping or reading a newspaper on the sidelines can block the creative process of others.

Here's another key piece of candid advice. Actors must never talk negatively about each other. Cliques develop quickly in any rehearsal situation so it is easy to fall into traps like this. Yet the atmosphere of most rehearsals is charged with vulnerability. Every nuance in an intense creative process can be picked up and transmitted. And although the performer concerned might not hear or know what has been said about his or her work, he or she will sense negative attitudes with uncommon acuity.

The worst attitudes I find in some actors, though not the best ones, are complaining and bitchiness. Avoid these twin negatives like the plague! Many great actors who have a bad reputation are not difficult people, they are people who seek excellence and who attack the moaning and the mediocre. They will not tolerate sloppiness or negativity. The finest directors I've worked with, like the best actors, never allow destructive attitudes into a rehearsal space. But some, particularly those unclear about the working processes of actors, often fail to call detractors to order or don't know how to create a positive rehearsal atmosphere.

Be clear and dignified about your art and craft and don't be drawn into a web of negativity by fellow actors. You can be pretty certain that the moment an actor becomes defensively negative is the moment he loses his creative spark.

Preparation

Before beginning any rehearsal you must perform the kinds of warm-ups you need. Don't be intimidated into not doing a warm-up because other actors knock you or laugh at you. They are probably doing theirs secretly. It may also be that they are simply untrained or are not vocally very strong or interesting. It may be, too, that they are so experienced from years of speaking in theatres that voice work is embedded in the cells of their body.

Observe the experienced actors, but be careful not to imitate their vocal levels in the rehearsal room. If they know a theatre well, they might only go to their full voice when they hit an audience. I've seen this throw lots of young performers acting alongside some of the pros at the Royal National Theatre.

Share energy and never block another actor's energy. The experienced actors will set clear energy levels and maintain them through a stretch of rehearsal. Watch how many experienced actors will sit still, focus and contain their energy until it is time to work. In so doing they often outlast many actors forty years their junior. Young actors will often dissipate their energy on the sidelines and then get up to act with no reserves left. I've often seen young actors kick balls around in the break and then sag when they return to rehearsing. You must remember that a rehearsal is every bit as fatiguing and enervating as a performance. Conserve energy if you want to last the course.

Take any help offered with grace. Actors are generally frightened of offering advice to one another, thinking, probably, that it is a violation of someone else's process. But if advice comes from an older, more experienced performer there will probably be some gems contained within it. A brilliant actress I know, a skilful commedienne, was reluctant to give a younger actor a note about playing a line which was simply not getting a laugh the way it was being delivered. I encouraged her to give him the note. The younger actor was being too naturalistic and breaking up the line into too many fragments. She told him to try playing the line straight through without a pause. That night he did and the audience exploded with laughter.

It will always be useful for any actor both to give and to take vocal notes from another, particularly at a technical rehearsal. But in order to do this you must be able to listen and take inaudibility notes with ease and gratitude. You also must give them without aggression but always with some positive reinforcement. All performers at this late stage of a rehearsal are nervous and edgy. So you will always have to choose the most opportune time to give a note.

Whenever I discuss actors with directors, most will say that they would rather have a less talented yet flexible and willing actor in the rehearsal room than one who is difficult. No one feels creative with a negative force in the room. No one wants to tour with a destructive actor. To give and take notes well requires a degree of humility. I have to say this same humility exists in all great artists.

The rehearsal room, in a way, should be a protected environment where work can happen safely. Actors should become skilled in leaving their personal lives outside the room. The clearer the boundaries around a space, the more creative the room becomes. Personally, I cannot bear the rehearsal room being used for activities other than rehears-ing. To do otherwise seems to violate the purposes of the work. Recently I was working in a rehearsal room in North America. The space was beautiful but the work atmosphere curiously fragmented. Then I noticed that four of the actors had a poker game on the go in the room during breaks. Only when other actors asked them not to play in the room did the atmosphere become instantly clearer and productive.

Working with Directors

Just as there are no two actors who work in exactly the same way, there are no two directors who direct in a similar way. Add to this infinite variety the different demands of a text. Every new text will require different skills from both actor and director. You will quickly begin to realize the complex nature of the working relationship between both parties. But the marriage is rarely a completely happy one.

Directors often will classify actors as either easy or difficult to work with. The difficult actors are often the ones who will question decisions, who feel their craft is not being fully respected by directors who seem not to understand any of the demands of performing. To be fair to directors, many actors who are labelled difficult are the types who do not take direction well. They can be hostile to different ways of playing a part, not willing to change working methods or try new ideas and are, at worst, lazy.

From the actors' point of view – and I feel always drawn to their view because they are the ones who have to go out on stage night after night to play a part – directors can have too much power. No actor resents a director who is brilliant and who can teach and release an actor's work. Performers often feel powerless in a director–designer theatre. They feel they are only there to serve a series of ideas that have been pre-arranged by a director or a designer so that their own imaginative points of view about a part – the actors' insights – are irrelevant. Therefore they can question the need to rehearse. One actor recently said to me when frustrated about a director's rigidity, 'Why didn't he hire a robot?'

The other fear actors have about a director is directorial secrecy: the notion that the director is thinking things about the actor's work which are not being shared. I have to say the really respected directors do share and do discuss work as equals with the actor. However, many less experienced directors are frightened of actors and cut themselves off from them.

In the directors' defence, their role can be a lonely one. Some members of every company, rightly or wrongly, will complain bitterly about the director's work. In the actors' ideal world the director will bring some inspirational insight to the rehearsal room, encourage them, allowing them to contribute imaginatively, respect their craft and actions, create a safe and happy working environment, light them well, stage them to their best advantage, praise them and then leave them to get on with playing the part after opening night.

The actor–director relationship seems destined to be uneasy and maybe this tension accounts in some way for those unforgettable performances that we always remember. My own observations are that the great directors are often teachers in the purest sense of the word. Not only do they bring into the room a burning passion for the work and the play, but a vision that will not countenance modification. At the same time they give the actor the tools for change. This, like all good teaching, is not necessarily comfortable for the actors who might enjoy trotting along with their usual acting habits. These transformative rehearsals are often spoken about by actors as follows: 'I had a terrible time with so and so, but I did produce the best work I've ever done.'

The truly great directors will get this type of work out of an actor with great care and passion for the play and not by terrorizing the personal side of the performer; the creative side may be shaken, but the personal self is left unscathed. There is a kind of love and a respect that great directors have for actors. Couple that with a passion for a play and they will encourage great acting.

The lesser directors have somehow picked up the myth that you have to be a complete tyrant to be great and that you have to put actors under great pressure in order to get what you want. These directors can be vile without any sense of why they are being vile. Attacks are often personal and without compassion. They are working on the great plays with all the great messages and warnings about the misuse of power and haven't put the two things together – their own behaviour and the moral of the play. In these rehearsal periods nothing is shared; in fact, war has been declared and the director has all the weaponry.

If, and when, these directors get dramatic results it is often because the actors' adrenalin is mixed with pure terror. The audience, in effect, is applauding personal fear – perversely an exciting quality to watch – rather than creative energy. Tyrannical directors are a dying breed as actors are starting no longer to tolerate their own or other company members' abuse. Cruelty is now challenged and is rarely endured by great actors and in the great companies. I have watched increasingly over the years the famous actors defend the younger actors from harsh directors.

How does all this affect the actor's voice, speech and text work? Well, at some point all decisions finally rest with the director and any difficulty the actor is having vocally will be heightened positively or negatively by the director's own working process. Let me give you several recent examples of what I mean. All these I personally witnessed and tried to resolve without any particular blame attached to either actor or director.

A group of actors in a company was having enormous difficulty with a fellow actor who was not learning his lines accurately. The actors rightly felt very exposed and were fearful about missing cues. They approached the director, but he wasn't much interested in the accuracy of the text, nor was he prepared to confront the actor concerned. So the rest of the actors were just left high and dry.

On another occasion a wonderful actor was feeling frustrated and restive as all the weeks of rehearsal passed sitting around a table discussing the text in fastidious detail. The actor simply was not used to working this way. He enjoys being on his feet working the scene through as a series of actions. Consequently he was finding it impossible to learn his lines. For years his process had been to learn lines working on the floor actively, not sitting passively. He was enjoying the director's ideas, but simply could not put them into practice. By the first preview he was unusually shaky with his lines and only managed really to know them by performing and running the play.

Some directors like to rehearse very quietly in order to find the 'truth'. A useful process, but it becomes harrowing for an actor if she is not allowed to open up and explore the text vocally in a big and even loud way. The more experienced actor will just adapt to a director's habits. Once that actor leaves the rehearsal room and hits the stage, she will draw on all her years of experience to enable herself to open out into the theatre. This kind of actor will find an open, vocal way to serve and reveal the director's sense of truth.

However, if the actor is young or not very experienced with his or her own process, the performer can feel very lost and even unable to cope. This recently happened to a young actress who went into the theatre from the rehearsal room and just could not raise her vocal energy without feeling a loss of truth. Just one rehearsal on-stage spent extending and vocally energizing her would have given her the permission to be audible.

All actors find the low-energy presence of certain directors difficult to overcome, particularly when they are having to extend their work into epic areas of a text. It's hard to experiment and weave rich strands of vocal colour with a low-energy figurehead in the room. I am always amused and dismayed when actors complain that they cannot hear what a director is saying in rehearsals. No wonder they are frightened of being inaudible themselves. It constantly saddens me and seems unjustly ironic that in a profession which is based on communication, most of the breakdowns between actor and director are created because the latter doesn't speak!

Actors often feel that secrets are being kept from them. So many directors do not talk to them or give their honest opinions. To an actor's heated imagination this can mean, 'They hate what I'm doing.' It's particularly unnerving when a director gives notes to everyone else but leaves you out. Paranoia easily sets in. And paranoia is just one of the actor's nightmares. Many actors speak of whole rehearsal periods going by without any notes or positive reinforcements from the director. The lack of both normally means that the actor is doing fine, but it doesn't make the performer any less nervous and scared of experimenting. After all, any creative activity in life does need support and approval. If the director doesn't talk to an actor, the actor feels lost and ignored. Actors will say to me again and again, 'Patsy, does he/she like my work?' It is at this stage that even negative feedback would be valuable. At least it would mean the director had noticed something in the actor's work.

Interestingly, some of the most famous actors rarely receive notes from a director. Director are easily frightened of stars. I've spent many hours in dressing-rooms on or just before the first preview with many well-known actors giving them voice notes and suddenly realizing that I am giving them their first notes of the entire rehearsal period. Even stars are hungry for feedback.

A director and designer will often have decided, long before rehearsals have even begun, on the staging and the placing of each scene without ever thinking about the actors being part of that process. I remember an actress rehearsing a very complicated scene around a sofa. She wanted to move off the sofa and the director kept disagreeing with her. She fought him but finally agreed that she would stay seated but needed to experiment by walking around the sofa. Even this request was denied. Only at the dress rehearsal did she eventually realize why. The sofa was on a high pedestal and movement was impossible – to walk around would mean falling eight feet to the floor. Her complaint to me was that she hadn't been told of the set constraints and hadn't been given the opportunity, with that knowledge in mind, to experiment with other forms of movement and voice in order to release the scene.

Then there are those directors of the 'say it like this' school. The actor is told explicitly how each line should be delivered. Even the exact stress is outlined. Often these line readings are given on the first day of rehearsal by such directors and the actor spends the ensuing weeks trying to fill the director's exacting vocal requirements. I remember working with such a director in America some years ago. He had directed several versions of the particular Shakespeare play we were doing. An actor friend who had been in one of the original productions of the same play sat with me at the back of the dress rehearsal and whispered in my ear the precise reading of each line – stress, pace and intonation – the moment before the actor on-stage spoke it. Now, in many instances, the director's interpretation of each line was right, but the only actors who sounded real on stage were the ones who knew how to fill a given reading with organic truth. This is, after all, what a classical dancer must do once she has learned the pre-planned steps of set choreography. She embellishes the rigidity with her own movement personality.

A last thought before I suggest ways of working around different styles of direction. Great actors are very learned and wise people. After having worked on great plays for many years and opened themselves up so completely to them, they have acquired a storehouse of knowledge that is both practical and inspirational. If they have researched many periods of theatre, they are extremely well informed on all kinds of subjects and know how to explore the play on all sorts of levels. Therefore, they will become easily annoyed and anxious when directors are not equally well informed about each aspect of the play's background and foreground. They quickly lose patience with directors who are perceived to be lazy or ignorant.

Working with Styles of Direction

There is no definitive way for an actor to cope with working with each new director but here are a few tips. And directors, if you want to enter the working world of actors, try doing some of their basic routines – movement, voice and acting exercises. You will be amazed at how those simple things will inform you about what craft skills need to be exercised during the course of a rehearsal.

- Some acting teachers I know in drama schools speak about creating 'director-proof' acting. I think that's too cynical, as there are great and enlightened directors in world theatre who will take you on a wonderful acting journey. However, I do think young actors particularly believe that a director will solve all their acting problems. This is partly because some truly wonderful directors are attached to drama schools and do solve many students' acting problems.

- What each and every actor must learn is to take what a director has to give and fill in what he doesn't supply. You must also learn to take any positive direction with joy and somehow deal with the difficult demands – ideas and notes you don't agree with – professionally and without rancour. Try to work any piece of direction with zeal and a good spirit up to the point where it does not work for you. Only that way will the actor and the director know whether any idea is valid or limited. There is nothing that will annoy and alienate a director more than an actor refusing to try out, with energy, the director's note.

- Be grateful for any idea that comes your way. If you find out that it doesn't work, then that is a creative discovery which will help mould your performance. Lists of 'don't's in understanding a character are as important as the 'do's. Assess what you are getting from the director, then what you might not be getting – those aspects of the work you will have to fill in yourself. Whatever you think about any idea of the work, take notes of what is said to you and re-examine the notes at home objectively. This is easy to do when you agree, but harder if you are in doubt or under criticism. It will annoy the director and fellow actors if notes have to be given again and again. You might think you can remember them all, but you can't. Take notes and work on them.

- Try to return to each rehearsal to expand what you found in the last one so that the director can take you a step further and build on the foundations of past work.

- Many directors complain that the actor doesn't do anything on the rehearsal-room floor and is always awaiting direction. One famous director has always said, 'I can't begin to direct until they [the actors] do something.' This can create a stalemate, with the actor awaiting direction in order to start his or her work and the director waiting for something active from the actor which she can then mould. If you are not getting directions, do something (even if you just base the 'something' on what you know about the text) and see what reaction it gets. Generally, if the director hates the 'something' you come up with you'll hear her comments pretty quickly. Don't be alarmed if nothing is said, however: it probably means that what you have done is good or at least possible.

- Abusive directors believe, perhaps, that because the rehearsal period covers only a couple of months of an actor's life it can't possibly hurt for long. What they should realize is that any personal or unprofessional remarks made to an actor at a vulnerable moment in rehearsal can maim the actor's creative centre for years. Poor direction can so shatter an actor's confidence that it may take years of trust away from him. When actors attack directors it is often because they carry a legacy of pain from a previous bad experience.

- The director who can move crowds around in space and unleash a layer of the play through brilliant staging is quite rare today. Maybe this is because many actors are frightened of this approach and few young directors have had the luxury of working with large numbers of actors – which is how you learn the importance of staging. 'When you say that line I want you to be over there and place the wineglass down on the table on that syllable.' The whys of the text are, to the actor, seemingly unexplored. However, the real staging genius will stage you in such a way that the play is being imaginatively explored even though you may not know it.

- When working under a 'staging' director, it will be particularly useful to work very quietly and in tremendous detail on the text at home. Owning the text and connecting the director's outside

staging to an inner life which you are discovering on your own
could make for a wonderful process. If you don't do this work
on your own, you run the risk of sounding uncommitted and
will lose the nuances of the text. Try the staging and if it works,
enjoy it. If it doesn't, and the director insists, you will have to
fill in and make the move work. Whether the staging is good or
bad, you must do a lot of the text work on your own.

- A good staging director will solve a lot of your performance
problems long before you hit the stage, and generally the technical rehearsal will be easier and less troublesome. But if a
director is not so confident about staging, all sorts of problems
will have to be sorted out at the technical and long into the
performance. Crowd scenes are particularly hard to stage and
can create headaches for all concerned if left too late. I suppose
many directors have started and maintained their careers on
small-cast plays in studio theatres and are terrified of the big-
cast scenes.

- Actors in badly staged crowd scenes, often with only one line to
speak, can be rendered inaudible because the audience's eyes
always have to pick out the speaker before they can listen
properly to what's said. We need to see where the voice is
coming from before we are prepared to hear it. Lines are easily
missed as we visually search for the source of the words. I've
seen many experienced actors deal with this focus problem in a
scene by making a physical movement or strong gesture before
they speak to attract the audience's eyes so that they are ready
for the line to be delivered.

- Directors who work hard on the text and the truth of every
scene are loved by actors in the first half of the rehearsals. However, panic can set in if the work doesn't get properly staged or
focused in space towards the end of the rehearsal period. Work
can be genuinely intimate and real, but if it is not staged or
opened out the results can be inaudibility in a theatre, a lack of
momentum and theatrical energy, the form of the play losing
structure and actors not being seen or presented in the most
effective or theatrical way. Entrances and exits can be unclear,
pace unchanging and props or 'business' can distract the
audience from the action. Again, watch what more experienced
actors do. They will start to think out and slightly re-stage
themselves to compensate for the lack of staging direction.
They will gradually work to take the play out to an audience.

- What essentially is happening when a director fails to focus the
work is that the actor has done the inside work, but the outside
is not quite connecting to this inner work. Again, you have to

fill in what is not there. This work might have to happen outside the rehearsal room. You will have to do all the voice-into-
text exercises that release the voice, speak the words clearly and
commit outwardly. In fact, all the work we did on text in Stage
Three will be useful as you move into the final phases
of rehearsal:

● Intone into speaking.
● Breathing and supporting the words.
● Breathing and articulating the text.
● Getting into the theatre and filling it before the technical.
● Any exercise that you can do to open yourself out physically
  and emotionally in order to release the play.
● Where and how will be best in space and on the set to
  communicate most effectively?
● Rehearse with any props or difficult pieces of costume.
● Experiment with pace and vocal rhythms.

The clearer you are as you work, the more any knotty staging
problems will surface. As they appear you can start to deal with
them. You can coax a director gently into clarifying his or her
staging plans by showing him or her physical and vocal options
you have come up with.

● The highly academic director will always inform and intrigue
  the actor with a burst of good ideas but then frustrate you when
  he has no precise plans about how to play these notions. 'How
  do I play a late-Renaissance man intrigued by Machiavellian
  ideas but racked by metaphysical guilt?' you may wonder. Yet
  this is what one actor I worked with was asked go away and
  consider. It is always quite remarkable just how many directors
  are unable to link grand schemes with good practical solutions
  for the actor. You will always gain great insight and knowledge
  from these directors in terms of information on the world and
  the context of the play, but it will be left to you to make the text
  active. You must trust that the abstract and high-minded ideas,
  although not so practically useful to you as an actor, will enrich
  the quality of your work.
● There is also a breed of director who directs primarily through
  actions and not ideas. This makes for very focused moment-to-
  moment work for the actor in search of the play's motion and
  journey, but you might have to do the more academic work on
  the play to mould accurately context with movement and
  speech.
● You will sometimes find yourself in a rehearsal room, working
  on a great epic play, and it will slowly dawn on you that the

director knows nothing about the text – its form, structure, language or verse. In this case you will have to work on the verse line, the iambic, the language of the play yourself. I have heard some directors voice the opinion to a whole company that close text work is not their job but the actors'. If the actors don't know how to do it, they don't know their craft!

- The other side of the coin is the director who is entirely text fixated on every syllable, beat and meaning of a word. These directors will often have very rigid views on how verse should be spoken. They will conduct the actors like players in an orchestra, telling them when to come in, how fast to speak, how long to pause at the end of a line. The director's instincts are often right but many actors feel frustrated that they are not given the time to discover the text and its form on their own and in their own way. You have been given the desired result from the director and have to fill in the organic part of your work. You will have to do work on owning the words and forms of the text so that you can be connected to the play. These kinds of directors will often produce 'well-spoken' productions, but if the actors don't own the text they can sound curiously passionless, bland and, at worst, downright boring! The form of the play is respected, but the emotional drive lost.

Surely one of the most interesting and exhilarating reasons for being an actor is that not only are you dealing with great words and ideas in action, but that each new encounter with a director will demand from you a different way of working, drawing on different aspects of your craft and talent.

Maybe it is the current fashion once again to perceive the director as the all-powerful, all-knowing force in theatre. But actors do have to be mindful of their own power and dignity by accepting with joy any directorial idea but also being aware that much of the work to make a part playable has to be done at home and alone. Directors cannot exist without actors. The actor must carry full responsibility to say the words and communicate the play to an audience. If you can take on that responsibility, no director can entirely scupper your endeavours.

Filling in What the Director Leaves Out

If actors have to fill in the work not provided by the director, I think teachers have to adapt to the needs and fashions of the time. We are no longer a society that uses our voice or regularly enjoys using language, so much of my work is to encourage actors to release the text and communicate it in brave new ways. This is not necessarily the director's job but it is the actor's task always.

I do not believe that you would have needed a voice coach in Shakespeare's time. He lived and worked in a supremely oral society full of verbal flourish and daring. I imagine that Shakespeare and his actors (remember that he himself was one) would have had no problems using their voices and enjoying words. The audience equally would have been more able to listen. Fashion and social conditioning dictate how we work. This sounds simplistic, but I do sense that the trend in our theatre today is to work from the inside out. To fill in, I have to do much work on the outside-in. Both ways of working are valid and both seem necessary.

Inside-out exposes the deep, intimate connection the actor makes with the text. What is sometimes not achieved in this process is the communication of the text across space. And because the text is never fully released, the actor never really experiences the liberating sense of the word helping him or her act. The voice is subtle, but not richly various. Conversely, working only from the outside in – without connecting to the text – can produce a clear, well communicated but cosmetic sound. Both inside and outside must meet and mingle together.

What has always intrigued me about outside-in acting – and this only applies with a well-written oral text – is that as you commit outwardly to the word and form, physically and vocally, a sensation feeds back into you and you consequently discover much more about the psychological and emotional existence of your character.

Outside-in exercises might feel unsubtle and even over the top, but the very nature of launching yourself actively through language can inform you radically about heightened emotion, need and intent.

Whenever I work in non-Western theatre, most of the work is done from the outside in: you say the line in such-and-such a way and as you say it you make this specific movement. There is little or no discussion about thought, psychology or emotional through-line. I am always amazed, though, that the actors are engaging and moving me without seeming to have done any inside work on the text. They appear to be vessels of the text. What of course is happening, however, is that the outside work has filtered down to their inner core where it has mingled with the deepest intent of the actors' being and touched some reality. Otherwise I could not be moved by what is really just the performer's exterior artifice.

What little evidence we have about the training of Shakespeare's Elizabethan actors seems to indicate a similar preoccupation with outside-in acting. The boys playing those incredible Shakespearean women (e.g. Rosalind, Cleopatra, Lady Macbeth) must have engaged and moved the audience by the mere outward delivery of the lines. But in doing so, they must have caught the reality of those ladies and become them as they spoke. When all elements of craft are securely under control, any transformation is possible for the actor.

Truth Can be Big

One other preoccupation of mine, which is directly connected to fashion and ways of working, is the notion that truth can be big. I know I've mentioned this idea before, but it is worth underlining it during the rehearsal phase of work. For many young actors this notion is almost anathema. They believe that if they are big on stage they won't be truthful. They will be like some old-fashioned, hammy actor and, probably the worst crime of all, they will be uncool! Consider the following:

- There is nothing cool about heightened emotion. There is nothing cool about Shakespeare and the release of the great scenes. So to be cool, small and inner about huge ideas and feelings bursting to be expressed is inauthentic. Truth, revealing moments of life, is a huge process. Passion is not expressed reductively in our major plays. The trend in our society is to deny passion, but that is not the actor's job. If the idea that truth is small prevails, we instantly lose contact with all our great, passionate plays.
- If the trend that small is beautiful prevails, all the large theatres will become redundant because no actor will be able to fill them. We might be able to place a microphone on the actor in order for him to be audible, but reaching out over space is more than a matter of amplification. It is about believing that your feelings and dilemmas are big enough to be shared over space.
- Any move or vocal expression, however large or extreme, will be truthful if you are connected to the word and the acting moment. Perhaps our turning away from truth and size in acting has been bred by us all watching hammy actors who have not done their work on the text, coupled with our predilection for film and television acting. Remember, you can always bring a performance down by notches once you have found the larger truth. But to enlarge yourself on stage when you have been working small is technically much more problematic.

The Audience's Reality

It is the actor's job to communicate reality to an audience. This reality might be difficult for an audience to believe, particularly when the text is about heightened experience and the audience is, for want of a better word, provincial.

Here's a harrowing story that happened two years ago. I was lecturing on voice and text to an audience of mostly theatre practitioners. I was discussing release, sound purging us, all the issues involved with seizing the right to speak, the words we need and the sounds that free us. I noticed in the audience a man who was evidently not an actor. He was sitting very rigidly, looking down. His body language was tight and held. He wore a business suit. He was very out of place. It crossed my mind, 'Why is he here?'

At the end of my lecture I was answering questions and I noticed he was hovering, waiting to speak to me. Somehow I knew this conversation would be difficult, but I was sure I would have to face him. When everyone had gone, he moved slowly towards me. Throughout most of our conversation he refused to look at me. He said, 'My wife and I once went to a play. A Greek play. About women in Troy.' '*The Trojan Women*?' I offered. 'Yes, that's it.' Pause. 'There was a woman in the play who lost her son. He was thrown from a wall. The actress made a sound. She made this awful, embarrassing sound.' Pause. 'When we left the theatre my wife and I said that sound wasn't real. It wasn't real.' Silence. In the silence I thought, is he saying that to release sound with passion is unreal? I didn't speak because he was struggling with something. After maybe two minutes he continued, his voice now flat and over-controlled: 'Two years ago a policeman came into my office at work and told me that my daughter's body had been found. She had been raped and murdered.' Pause. 'I made that sound. I made the same sound the actress had made. I've never told my wife that I made that sound.' Suddenly he looked me in the eyes. 'That actress was real and we didn't understand reality at the time because it hadn't touched us yet.' He smiled. 'Not a good way finally to understand truth in art. Thank you.' He turned and walked away.

The great lesson for actors is surely that the truth they are communicating is not only for the now but for the future. An audience might not understand yet but perhaps one day they will. Equally true, you have to remember that there is every likelihood that at every performance there is a member of the audience who understands more about a given situation than you do. Again, the responsibility is to endeavour to communicate truth without in any way patronizing those who really have lived situations and know.

The Design

There is a young theatre designer I know who constantly designs wonderful sets for the human voice. Everything about the design, from the materials he uses to the proportion of his sets, helps the actor to communicate across space. His work is a rare instance in which good design can set off the speaking actor to grand advantage. Why isn't more theatre design like his, I wonder?

I remember standing on stage with this designer, telling him what a great set he had produced for speaking. He smiled and said 'I learned the hard way.' He then told me this story. One of his first big breaks was to design a set for an opera in which a great tenor was to star. When the set was constructed and the on-stage rehearsal began, the tenor took the designer onto the stage with him and said publicly that he would not sing on the set. The singer then humiliated the designer further by telling him how to design a set for the human voice. Designers never argue with the likes of famous opera singers. They have much more power and commercial worth than actors. What a terrible and unforgettable way to learn a lesson. But at least the designer now knows how to display speaking actors to the best advantage.

The brutal truth is that actors often walk onto a set which not only doesn't help, but actually hinders them vocally. Sets that a highly trained singer wouldn't sing on, actors, who mostly feel powerless, dutifully struggle with against all odds. It is a cliché that we are in a period of Designer Theatre with extravagant designs overwhelming the actor and sometimes even the play. But I have never heard an actor publicly complain about one of these sets. They simply walk out night after night, knowing that they have to work ten times harder to be heard and seen properly, and that whatever they do the set design, however artistic, will make it impossible for some scenes to be completely audible.

At the risk of sounding harsh, it seems that many designers are not only ignorant about sets in relation to the acoustics of a theatre but also as to how a set will affect the actor's performance. Some don't even seem to care about these essential details. The look is more important than anything that might facilitate actors and a text. It sometimes feels to me like the final negation of theatre when a set takes precedence over the play and the performers. I have observed actors in deep distress over sets which defeat them vocally.

The audience will always blame the actor for inaudibility, not the fact that he is being asked to work in a wide, empty space with no sounding boards to bounce the voice out, with lighting that doesn't light his face (however atmospheric the lighting, if we cannot see the face it's a hundred per cent harder to hear the voice), amplified sound effects that either drown the voice or compete with it and, perhaps even more wearing, costumes that impede the body and consequently the voice.

I have worked on shows when all these elements have clashed together so dramatically that the actors could not even hear themselves on stage and were reduced to lip-reading in order to figure out when their cue came and when they should start speaking! Or an occasion when actors were acting on a stage full of mud and water. Not only were they unable safely to support their voices because they were skidding over all the time, but they got mud in their ears, eyes and noses and spent most of the performance wet and cold. To combat these obstacles and still be expected to give your soul is a tall order.

The Set

To match a set acoustically with a theatre's specific acoustic quality is a complex scientific equation. Engineers are more qualified than me to figure this out. However, there are certain basic facts you can note when you first look at a set's model in rehearsal. To be forewarned is to be forearmed. I doubt your opinion (if not shared by the director) will ever change the set design, but you can be clearly conscious of how it can or cannot support your voice in acting. This knowledge might help you decide how or where to play certain scenes.

The now old-fashioned box set, made of wood, is still the ideal container for the actor's voice. In this set you can play scenes in any direction and be heard any place in the house. Your voice is reinforced from every angle. It's like standing in a guitar box from which sound resonates. Clearly this is the kind of set which has served actors for centuries.

At the other end of the spectrum is the actor's vocal nightmare: a completely open set which has carpet on the floor. The only possible way you will be heard, without amplification, is by playing each scene down front and out to the audience. Playing up or across the stage will be vocally pointless. We have all seen sets which make rich and colourful use of carpeting (or similar material) that actually muffles the actor.

These are the two extremes and of course there are infinite variants in between. The open set might help you vocally with the aid of a wooden raked floor or a ceiling. You might be able to speak into the wings if there is a solid structure there to throw the voice out. A flat, solid piece of scenery might be flown in and if you can stand downstage of that you will have a much easier time. Experienced actors will gravitate automatically towards such flats. Even a piece of heavy, hard furniture will help echo the voice as you get closer to it.

If, however, there is nothing to use as an aid to project the voice you just have to face using athletic support, staying on voice, sustaining every word and sentence out and articulating every syllable with enormous energy, like a sprinter running uphill.

I recently worked on a show with an open set and scenes were played across such a wide gulf that the first row of the audience was 45 feet away. It was the equivalent of acting in a field without even a cow to bounce the voice off!

As soon as a set is constructed walk around it, but also try any doors or windows you might have to use. Doors can suddenly not open the way you expected, or door handles turn differently and windows not slide effectively. The aim is to open everything that needs opening without wobbling the rest of the set, speaking lines you may have in order to complete an action.

Every set has to be thought about in combination with the acoustic of the theatre. I never really know what vocal obstacles or aids a set will deliver until it is built in the theatre; although I can often make calculated guesses. Before the set is built, if you don't know the space, get into it and try to figure its acoustic. Is it alive or dead, and what lies between? When you do this exercise you will probably be working on a set for another show that certainly differs from the one you will be using later. Try to calculate whether this set is grander or more minimal than yours. Then, as soon as the set is built, get onto it and play. It is often easier to do this at lunch-time when no one is about.

Also, be aware that you might have several scene changes and some might be better or more complicated than others. What will this do to your vocal and acting energy? Try to rehearse the hardest change and in the technical never relax if the first set changes are easier. The final set might be open and you will have to pace yourself for the hardest vocal challenges at the end of the show. Note the texture of the floor. Does it makes sounds as you walk or run? Is it gravel crunching underfoot? How will your costume shoes sound on the set? Remember to find some physical centre in order to speak your words.

It's always very useful to sit and listen to other actors on the set. Their audibility will educate you about the space. Equally, the inaudible performers will show you how not to play a scene or where not to stand. For some reason, all actors want to bring down their voices to the quietest position. I understand this need for subtlety, but don't do that until you understand not only the theatre but the acoustic help or hindrances of the set. Intimate scenes from the rehearsal room might not work on the set and in the space.

The Costume

Never underestimate how a costume can affect your body, voice, speech and performance. The effects can be positive. As soon as you get the costume on, you feel the part. Many actors talk about how their first vivid impressions of a character come through knowing what the character would wear on her feet, her head, her hands, etc. These moments forge a creative marriage between the actor and the designer.

What worries me are the negative effects when some element of costume design can impede the breath, the voice and the actor's movement, making the performer's communication to the audience more difficult than anticipated. Anything that constricts your neck, jaw, rib-cage, stomach, or stops you making a strong contact with the floor could be problematic: hats that hide your face, wigs that are top-heavy or too tight around your head, armour that not only weighs down your whole body but creaks when you move or walk; collars that choke, corsets that suffocate, masks that squash your face; clothes that weigh down your shoulders, heavy jewellery that freezes your neck . . . well, the list goes on and on.

Not only do you have to consider your costume from the point of view of speaking, but also as to how it will work on the set. You might not be able to cope with high heels on a steep rake. A long train might be easy to wear in an open rehearsal room, but what if you have to make an entrance down a long winding staircase or move around a cluttered Victorian parlour?

Here are some basic tips to consider as soon as you know what you are wearing:

- Never be measured by a designer or wardrobe mistress off your breath support. That is, only let them take your measurements when you have a full rib swing. Do not let your vanity get in the way. So don't hold in your stomach but let the breath go down. Do not think you will lose weight before the opening night and get too tight a costume. I've known designers take a costume in (generally when they are trying to get a stronger line on the costume) but they rarely agree to let one out. When your neck measurements are taken, go for the loosest position they'll allow so the throat is not constricted.

- Rehearse as soon as you can in clothes that resemble the eventual costume. Have a word with the designer if you can. Of particular importance are shoes, long skirts, suits, ties, hats and corsets. Try to reproduce the weight of the clothes. Heavy clothes will not only impede the voice but carrying them will exhaust you and you will need more energy to play with the added weight on your body. I recently worked with a petite actress who was asked to wear a costume so heavy that she could hardly stand.

- Be honest about what you are happiest wearing. Your habitual clothes might have encouraged you to be very awkward in, say, a formal-looking costume. An actress used to wearing trousers and flat shoes might not consider it such a big deal to go into non-period costume of heels and a skirt, but then get an enormous shock at the first dress rehearsal as she staggers around the set losing her voice, her performance and some of her dignity!

- Designers typically complain that many young actresses can't wear feminine clothes any more. They also moan that young actors don't wear smart suits enough to be able to look elegant and move easily in certain period designs. If you predict a big problem, wear equivalent clothes at home and in rehearsal.

- If you feel the problem is so great that it will make your life a complete misery, talk to the director and the designer as tactfully but as soon as possible. I've watched many actors fester silently about a costume and finally explode at the last dress rehearsal when it's often too late: they suddenly shout at everyone that the colour is wrong, the fit is wrong and nothing about it suits the character they have been creating. Be reasonable, but explain firmly why it constricts you. No designer with even an ounce of human compassion will fail to listen when an actor explains that he can't breathe, swallow or use his voice.

Every actor has a good costume story to tell, either funny or frightening. Here are a few I have heard and, in some cases, helped trouble-shoot. There was the famous actress who was asked to play her most dramatic scene in a pair of stiletto heels on a wooden, raked floor. Her normally strong breath technique failed her and she was in danger of losing her voice. We had to place the breath deliberately low and find, within the scene, spots where she could lean against furniture and a door frame in order literally to support her voice. The leaning enabled her to get a low breath that the shoes and the rake denied her.

There was a young actor who, for some reason, refused to rehearse a fight with his armour on. On the first preview he fell over backwards and couldn't get up. He was left on stage on his back like a dying cockroach, his legs and arms waving in the air. This was particularly unfortunate, since he was playing the victorious hero who had to take the play to its triumphant conclusion.

There was the movie star making her stage début in a period play. She insisted on rehearsing in trousers and not wearing her long trained dress. On the first performance her train got caught on the set and she couldn't leave the stage.

There was a whole clutch of masked actors, unaccustomed to wearing masks under hot lighting, not only being completely inaudible but having suddenly to leave the stage in panic when they realized they were suffocating. Neither the masks nor reasonable facsimiles had been ready for rehearsal and they only appeared at the first performance.

I also remember the actress who tore up her tight costume in front of the designer because she couldn't breathe in it. On another occasion the same powerful actress threw a large-brimmed hat at the designer as it hid her face in such a way that the audience in the circle could not see or hear her. Most actors would not have the power or status to react like this, but it doesn't mean they don't want to from time to time.

Props

I once sat mesmerized in a theatre canteen as an old, famous knight of the theatre sat on his own, pouring water from a bottle into a glass. He uncorked the bottle, poured the water, then re-corked the bottle. He repeated this action – when the glass was full he replenished the bottle – for over an hour. As I left the canteen he caught my eye. 'What are you doing?' I inquired. 'I have to speak a line and pour a drink at the same time and I'm worried that I won't be able to handle my props without shaking.'

This was a great lesson for me because it highlighted two very important aspects about props. One is that if you don't handle them well, they can prevent you from speaking a line with ease – the prop becomes more important than the line and gets in the way. The other is that if you are frightened, you must work with a prop until it ceases to cause you worry. Props and their co-ordination with speaking and moving must become second nature to the actor in performance.

A pretty consistent note when doing Shakespeare is that if a prop is mentioned you need it, and if it isn't it will only get in the way. Having said that, I have watched actors rehearse speeches that demand, say, a letter or a ring and not have one at hand. As soon as they do the speech, their whole voice becomes disconnected until they work the essential prop into the scene. The earlier you work with a prop, the better you can easily disown it and cut it if necessary. But to add a prop late in the rehearsal does create problems.

Work with accurate props. It is no good rehearsing lighting a cigarette with a lighter if you will eventually have to use matches. And make sure the lighter works. There are many types of wineglass, each with a different weight and stem. Props can easily upstage you and throw off your rhythm

There are whole acting lessons given in how to use a telephone, but remember that styles, workings and weights of telephones have changed rapidly over time. An old dialling phone, accurate for many period plays, is a very different prop from a modern digital phone. I recently realized how old I was when I was the only person in a rehearsal room who knew how to operate the old public telephones in which you deposited a coin after the pips.

Swords, guns and other armoury are always problematic; handling them is a craft in itself. How many times have I sat in the theatre watching an actor stumble over his sword or get it out and not be able to put it back. Spears in the wrong hands nearly decapitate fellow actors. If you are going to fire a gun you will need expert advice. A blank does have dynamite in it and the charge can burn and seriously hurt anyone close enough to it. All these weapons must be used under the strict guidance of a good, skilful fight coach.

Whatever the prop, rehearse as early as possible with it or with an accurate replica. Even the smallest prop can become the most embarrassing barrier between you and your text. If it makes you feel awkward, take it away and work with it until you can speak and handle it without clumsiness.

Wigs

These can be a problem if they are too heavy and give you a 'pain in the neck'. If you have one of these on, you must continually free the shoulders and jaw and when it's removed at night you should massage your neck and do exercises to open out the chest, swing the head and lift and drop the shoulders.

An old tip to keep the face free when the wig is put on is to stretch the face out with a wide-open mouth, widened eyes and lifted cheeks. Many wigs pull the facial muscles into the hairline and this can affect the speech muscles. By pulling this grimaced face you can keep the muscles free as the wig is placed and consequently have no problems or discomfort with your speech. The same applies with false beards or moustaches. When glued, move your face around to re-engage the speech muscles.

Another trick I've noticed actresses do is always to know where the hairpins are, how many are holding the hair and which ones, if removed, would make the hair fall. Hairpins can catch onto other actors, particularly in intimate scenes, and it is good to know how to release yourself and the consequence of that release!

Make-Up

If you are not used to heavy make-up, its application can stiffen your face. As you or the make-up person apply it, take time out to move your face to find maximum flexibility. Remember that the audience may at first notice your costume and make-up, but as the curtain falls what they will remember best is your performance.

The Lighting

All actors who have worked over the past twenty years view with some suspicion the now highly developed and technologically supreme role of the lighting designer. Who doesn't admire the extraordinary skill and art it takes to light a show well, but actors can feel that the lighting effect is sometimes more important than they are. In some scenes the atmospheric lighting may not light the actors sufficiently. Therefore they are playing scenes without being properly seen by the audience and, on some occasions, hardly able to see their fellow actors. This will certainly throw off the rhythm of communication.

There are some basic truths about light and the human voice. If you can't see a face, it is much harder to hear what is being said. If you have to play in a dimly lit scene you will have to speak with more articulation and care, and perhaps with more support. The more light there is on a scene the faster you can speak, so if there is not much light you have to slow down slightly.

I think this phenomenon is linked to the old saying that comedy needs a lot of light. A full wash of light not only lifts the spirit but enables clarity of pace. I have watched comic scenes that are dimly lit being played without the audience laughing, then the scene being played in exactly the same way under much fuller light and suddenly the actors get laughs.

There is an old theatrical saying: 'Find your light before you speak. Don't speak until you feel the light on your face.' However, often the light from many newer instruments is harder to feel on the face. You need practice to feel light on you, so do practise. I've seen actors in a technical rehearsal help each other. The actors in the stalls tell the actors on stage when and where they are lit from and if they can't adequately feel it they remember by their exact position. Some lighting is so concentrated that even shifting two inches can put you in darkness.

Bear in mind that many contemporary lighting designs will build up or focus down their light in stages, so the first preview will probably be the darkest and, rather like a

Rembrandt painting, light is built up gradually through the preview performances. The light might also gradually change – from night to dawn, dusk to night – throughout a single scene. These changes in mood also affect the way the voice is used in a new mood.

Sound

Sound systems are now so advanced that weird and wonderful things can be done in most theatres. If you are acting with very heavy sound effects you should be aware of certain tricks the audience's ear has to perform. It takes time for the ear to adapt from a loud, amplified sound to an unamplified human voice. Also for the ear to hear a normal level of speech after suffering incredible noise. So if you are speaking after a loud sound effect you will have to compensate and help the audience to hear you by using, initially, more volume and dropping down to the volume you want to use gradually. This applies also to using your voice after an amplified sound. If you are asked to speak with a sound effect, think of going over the top of the sound not through it. Arc up and out, don't try to compete head on. You won't win. The same note applies to speaking after or through amplified music. Unamplified music rarely creates a problem.

If the whole task seems impossible and you are straining or hurting your voice, request a body mike so that you are competing on an even level. If you haven't got a body mike the technicians will simply have to bring down the sound level. It is your right to request this help in order not to strain your voice.

The Hi-Tech Theatre

I have often taken actors into a theatre to have a voice class on-stage and at the point they are easily filling the space

I've asked for more power. They naturally understand that an empty theatre without an audience is easier to project in acoustically than a full one. But what many fail to realize is that in a performance of a highly technical show the noise around them interfering with their voice can be huge. The problem with the decibels created by hi-tech movements on stage is that they are of a note so low that the human ear can't consciously pick out the sound, although it is directly affecting the focus and clarity of the actor's speech. Hydraulics, for instance, hum away at a very high decibel rate. Likewise the drum revolve or the whirl of hi-tech lights changing position all make for a very noisy space. When you are speaking or are being turned on a revolve, think about this. It will help if you are clearer and use more head resonators to cut through the lower droning notes of the machinery.

Some hi-tech sets nowadays are quite dangerous. At a flick of a switch scenes are moved about and scenery flown in quite rapidly and silently. If the actor is in the wrong place at the wrong moment he might be squashed. Gapping traps, thirty-feet deep for instance, can suddenly appear on the stage. The ground sometimes shifts very quickly and the actor's world is moving at an alarming rate. Any fear of falling, physical harm or disorientation will mean it is hard to support and play a line clearly.

Most theatres are safe and have rigorous technical standards. But even though the actor knows this intellectually, he can live in a state of panic for the first few performances because the environment is so new and unexpected. Negotiating yourself around a hi-tech world is not easy. There is a saying in the business that the cruellest critics of theatre are first-year drama students. They 'know' about theatre without ever knowing the cost and the risks of performance. They will often enter class having seen the first preview of a hi-tech show and in a sarcastic way criticize the performances as being very careful and without passion.

What they are probably seeing are cautious actors finding their bearings.

They are mostly humbled when I tell them what is happening on the set: what devices are whirling around the actor and how frightful it can be not only with the moving sets but with, perhaps, smoke and pyrotechnics exploding around the performer. Even if these effects are not in some of your scenes you know that they are coming up and awaiting you!

The Rake

A rake is a sloped stage and the stage can slope from upstage, furthest from the audience, to downstage (the gradient ranging from 1 in 15 to the steepest, 1 in 7). The rake helps both design and viewing perspective. Metaphorically the rake thrusts the actors into the audience. However, this thrust can also be literal because stories abound of actors rolling in wheelchairs or simply falling or tumbling into the orchestra pit or audience as a result of a steep, sloping rake.

The Vocal Problem

The most immediate problem that affects the actor is one of physically communicating with the whole house. Standing on the rake, keeping your balance and looking upright, can throw the actor's vision to the back of the stalls. When on a rake you must often consciously tilt your head upwards and make eye contact with the circle rather than the stalls. Audiences in the circle viewing a raked stage will frequently complain of only seeing the top of the actor's head.

However, there is a more subtle and potent problem with a raked stage and this involves the freedom and health of the voice. Many times I have been asked to solve a rash of voice problems in a show that have been directly linked to actors working on a rake. These particular problems only surface, it seems, six to eight weeks after the actor has started performing on the rake. What happens is that in an attempt to appear upright and secure on the slope, actors often lock their knees. This tension slowly creeps into the hips, lower breath, spine, upper chest and shoulders: all areas that are susceptible to vocal tension. In time, the breath support system gets higher in the chest, the actor loses vocal power, begins to push vocally and ends up tiring and, at worst, damaging his voice. The rake is never blamed because the process is so gradual.

Solving the Problem

Experienced actors will often cope by standing on the rake slightly off-centre, thus diminishing the rake's forward thrust and, by way of release, keeping their knees and their body more aligned. In the technical rehearsal, stand facing upstage as much as you can to take the strain off your legs. The tensions created by a rake insidiously accumulate, but will only affect you if you don't realign your body and re-centre the breath after working on a rake.

The best solution is to warm down, getting the breath freely into the body after the show so that you don't take the tension to bed and therefore compound it. A series of measures to counteract the force of the rake would be to re-centre, unlock the knees, release the shoulders and reopen the breath into the back and stomach area. Spend perhaps ten minutes lying on your back with your feet up on a chair before going to bed.

Corsets

Many different articles of clothing make it difficult to breathe and vocalize on stage. But one such is particularly fiendish. A corset can destroy a voice. Unsuspecting actors are bound into these torturous contraptions that actually stop their breath and ultimately can damage their voices.

Many directors and designers will argue that corsets are necessary for certain period plays and 'looks'. All well and good, for the sake of authenticity. But in order to save a voice, compromises should be made. On more than one occasion I have seen famous actresses (the less famous would be too timid to assert their rights in this way) rip up a too rigidly tight corset in front of the designer announcing, 'My voice and career are more important than your design!' Bravo!

Am I being too fervent? Can a corset really damage a voice and a career? The answer is, yes they can. Many performers will testify that their only vocal problems arose from wearing a corset.

So how does a corset affect the voice? It depresses the rib-cage. After a few minutes of wearing one, the breath can only get into the upper chest area which might be all right if you are not speaking on stage and in need of breath support and power. The stomach muscles can, in response to the restriction, become taut. Not only does the voice lose power but there is a great temptation to push it. This pushing will lead to a very tired, if not bruised, voice. The other effect of a corset is that the voice becomes thinner and less resonant. The range will be less flexible and trapped in the higher notes of the voice.

But there are things you can do to counteract the above and still wear a corset without dire results. Never be fitted for a corset off full breath support. That is, be measured with your full rib swing and your spine up, allowing the stomach freedom. The old wardrobe mistresses used always to insist on this but there are not many left who understand the need for breathing in a costume.

Even if you are landed with a very tight costume, try to keep the breath as low as possible. If you can't get full rib swing, concentrate on the lower abdominal area for support. Try to keep the upper chest as still and relaxed as possible and you might really have to concentrate on getting the breath into the back.

As important, when you remove the corset re-centre the breath and work the rib swing so that you don't carry any residual tension into the rest of your life. Rehearse as much as possible with the corset.

The Transfer from Rehearsal Room to Large Theatre

Bridging these two spaces can be problematic, particularly for actors who don't regularly play a large space. The comments I constantly hear from performers are 'I feel I have to push', or 'I lose the performance I found in the rehearsal room', or 'I lose the truth'. The important point to remember is that to play a large space you have to believe that truth can be large. Many younger actors have been brought up on television and film truth and, until they get experience and confidence in playing a large space, this concept is one that they fight.

The problem is compounded by the fact that most companies don't rehearse on-stage but in a room with a wall where the auditorium starts so that the actual rehearsal process is intimate. I know that the huge demands of technical theatre make it nearly impossible for the actor to get on-stage but if you are playing a new theatre try to get onto the stage and familiarize yourself with the space.

Stand centre stage and breathe the space; that is, breathe to the perimeters of the space, not where the audience ends. Figure out the eye focus of the space – where do you need to look in order to make full contact with the whole house? Where are the strongest positions on stage and where are the weakest ones? Are the house acoustics alive or dead? Most modern theatres, because they are so padded, are dead. You will need to take certain things into account.

Human bodies absorb sound, so generally, when an audience is in the house, the house deadens further. Very often the rehearsal room acoustic is different from the house. Generally speaking, the deader the space the more the actor is tempted to push.

If you can get on stage during your rehearsal period it probably won't be on the set of your production, so you will have to take that into consideration. A vocally useful set would be made of wood. Metals are powerful amplifiers of the human voice and can sharpen it. A set that has substance in the wings or upstage will help project the voice. An unuseful set is open or made of material like carpet, curtains or gauze that absorb the voice.

Is there a fly tower and is it full or empty? The more scenery in the tower, the better. Where is the main action staged? Most actors and directors love to pull the action closer to the audience. This isn't always the best tactic for sight lines and audibility. Often, as the action moves forward downstage the house metaphorically collapses around you and it becomes more problematic to reach the whole of it.

Remember the old and true saying; 'If you can't see an actor's face it is much harder to hear him.' The more you can venture out into the performance space the more you will, imaginatively and actually, feel the space in your breath, support and vocal release. Not only will you begin to own the space, but you will physically remember its demands and the energy required to communicate easily across it.

Take this memory back into the rehearsal room and gradually feed it into your work. Begin to think and experience the text beyond the rehearsal-room wall. I know many actors like to rehearse initially in an intimate way so that they can connect very personally to the text, but try to open this out within the last two weeks of rehearsal-room work. If you only have two weeks' rehearsal, start opening out in the second week. In this way transferring to the theatre will not be physically or artistically shocking.

It is worth noting again that a pause in a small space can be easily filled and interesting, but as the space expands long pauses can bring a play to a grinding halt. How to fill a pause in space is an art form in itself. Most experienced actors talk about earning that kind of pause.

Also consider that the bigger the space, the more focus you need vocally and physically. A large space is often more frightening, so you have to stay calmer; breathe and exhale fully in order to calm yourself. Articulation, defining ends of words, the definition of each syllable in a multi-syllabic word, sustaining the line and not just falling off, all become essential. It might feel exaggerated and odd to you but the bigger the space, the more your mouth, support and energy through a line have to work. What might sound unreal to you will sound natural to the audience. You have to commit in space, otherwise you deny the space and become inaudible and unfocused.

The same note applies to the body. In a small space you can shuffle and fidget without distancing an audience, but as soon as there is distance between the actor and the audience, every move reads. Undefined movement confuses the audience and dissipates your energy. Define, think, feel and breathe out to the extremes of the space even when you are not facing the audience. The actor who does this can act with the back of the body facing the audience.

Don't be tempted to push but use support, stay on voice, release each word into the space, define every syllable and sustain each line. This might sound very technical and physical, and on one level it is, which is why it is essential that you work your technique early enough so that it becomes organic and you can then concentrate on acting.

There is no doubt in my mind that to play a large house is athletic and requires energy and craft. Don't be fooled by the experienced actors in the rehearsal room who don't do these techniques before they transfer. They probably know the space and have served a long enough apprenticeship to transfer with ease.

The Technical Rehearsal

Technicals (especially for a complicated play or musical) can go on for days and the actor is always in danger of not only getting exhausted and lost among the technical needs of a production, but he can often lose contact with the play and his performance.

Technicals normally come at the moment when the actor has just unlocked the energy of a play as it is being run in the rehearsal room. Suddenly the technical fragments of the play impede progress at a critical juncture. But, if used imaginatively, the technical can be a great discovery period and can be used to learn about the theatre, the set and, by opening up the play, also to uncover more textual riches.

Try to work in the theatre before the technical. Find out its perspective, acoustic and sight-line problems. The greatest learning task you can perform is to watch the experienced actors work in a technical.

It's going to be a long process, so conserve your energy. When you have to speak or act, do so with clarity and precision. Rest when you can. Acquaint yourself with the set, but also, when you are not working, sit in the auditorium and listen to the play from the audience's point of view. Sit in the worst seats and look and listen.

Note the voices which carry with ease and figure out why. Do the same with the actors who are harder to hear, either because they are using too little energy or too much. Always remember that an empty auditorium is acoustically different from a full one. An audience gives you energy, but their body mass deadens the voice. A well-designed theatre will be slightly live when it's empty. Remember also that some voices are harmonically more suited to certain theatres. They carry better. Analyse why this might give you an insight about how to use your own voice.

You are allowed to mark the voice in a technical to save your energy and not tire yourself, but never mark when you are speaking with or alongside a sound cue. In order to balance the voice you need to be at the level you intend to play that moment. I have heard so many actors moan about levels of sound and blame a technician when they have marked their way through the technical.

This also applies to body mikes. No one can set a level for you until you play it at performance level.

Note how each set might change the voice in space and make adjustments accordingly. For instance, one scene might be in a box set that projects the voice and another on an open stage that doesn't. You will have to supply different energies to get through both types of scenes.

Note whether there are sound effects you will need to speak over or whether the stage machinery is in action when you speak. A turning revolve will produce high decibel levels even if those decibels are not discernible because they are lower than our ears can pick up. They will still distort your voice.

What is the lighting like? Are you visible? If not, then you need more vocal energy. The equation to remember is that the less we can see, the harder it is to hear. If you are required to speak in gloom you need to work on extra vocal energy and definition.

This is the time to check the vocal effects of costume, make-up, wigs or masks and the physical cost of a rake. Don't be frightened about being too thorough. If something is worrying you, go back over it. Some hi-tech sets are very dangerous and you will feel vulnerable and unable easily to act or speak if you are not absolutely sure of where you are and what you are doing. In my experience actors, as compared with other artists, are very well behaved and patient during a tedious technical, but this sometimes leads them into not preparing adequately. What you must never do is be unavailable when needed. Don't just wander off!

Remember that when light, sound and several tons of scenery are swirling around, you can become so terrified that you might forget to breathe and support. Try to give yourself a constant note to keep all your physical and vocal technique going. Quick changes can leave you breathless and disconnected so be prepared to re-centre as quickly as possible after a quick change. Standing under lights will dehydrate you, so keep drinking water. Relax before going to bed because sleep, with all the tensions of the tech locked into your body, will not be refreshing. Rest and be still and silent whenever you can. I watch many young actors scamper around the first day of a tech and exhaust themselves. The voice will tire if you have to repeat a song or a scream again and again, so you must mark when appropriate.

First Dress Rehearsal

Use this not only to re-connect yourself to the whole play and the storyline but to sound out the house vocally. I know you will be thinking about all the technical problems, but if you can really reach out into the space the next few runs, or even the first public performance, will not be so problematic.

For some reason it is easier to bring down a performance vocally than to hoist it up. I always encourage the actor to extend slightly more and pull back. This particularly applies in the modern spaces which are vocally dead. The dead acoustic means you cannot hear or feel your voice in the space. By overreaching the space – though *not* pushing – you begin to sense the work and energy the theatre needs. Then you can pull it back without reducing your work. You should never aim to meet your first audience wondering whether you are audible. What a handicap to suffer while you are trying to give your best performance. Get that worry out of the way in the tech and the first dress rehearsal.

Marking the Voice

The chances are that at some point within a rehearsal period you will need to be able to mark your voice. The likelihood of this need will double when you move into the technical production period in the theatre. To mark the voice simply means to save it. Even the strongest and healthiest voice will tire if used constantly on full support and a fully energized position. There are occasions when it is useful and occasions when marking is ungracious to the acting and technical company.

It is infuriating when an actor marks in a full-throttled rehearsal because it unsettles the other actors' energy. It is equally maddening if a technician is trying to set the level of a sound cue against a marked voice. So when you use marking, use it with sensitivity to others. Tell the director if you are going to mark a run. There are times when it really is going to help save your voice.

Repeating a vocally charged scene again and again might require some marking. If the repetition is not to help your performance but to settle a technical problem, then mark. Technical rehearsals can take their toll on you as you might have to repeat a particularly demanding section of a play to get a cue right; again, you can mark. To learn a song, you can mark. You can mark during a line run, anywhere where it doesn't impede others.

How to Mark and Save the Voice

The word gives you a good idea of how to do it. You mark the air with the voice, but don't overstretch yourself. Place the voice lightly into the head resonator. Hum into the skull. You will immediately feel pressure relieved from the throat. A tired voice will feel much easier in this place – clear and light.

Always stay 'on voice', don't save it by either whispering or devoicing as this will only tire the voice more. Use support. It's easy to try and save the voice by not supporting – but this will not help in the long run. The support must be there, although not too much. To ease the voice you are not going to use much volume. Use instead more articulation. Using the word's energy will take pressure off the voice, but still give it energy and clarity. Stay up and physically centred. You will tire more if you slump or over-relax.

A few key things to avoid when trying to save the voice:

- Whispering. Always bad for the voice and it will tire you quickly.
- Not Supporting. Many do this thinking it will save energy; it doesn't.
- Mumbling. This might feel more relaxed but will only annoy everyone and make you tense.
- Over-relaxing. It's harder to keep energy alive over a long day's rehearsal if you keep over-relaxing and slumping. To hoist yourself back into a place of energy is much more exhausting than to stay energized all the time.

If you sense your voice is overworked and might tire, save it at every opportunity and the best way to do that is to be quiet. Take any time off to relax, breathe deeply and stay silent. Avoid smoke, alcohol and conversations in smoky and noisy rooms.

Cue Lights, or I Can't Hear the Play So How Do I Get On?

The cue light is a relatively new device. As theatre has become more hi-tech, a combination of huge sets and sound systems, the use of the cue light has become essential. Actors could not hear their verbal cues above the din of on-stage action. Their entrance was out of their control.

Actors in many productions now enter a scene by standing in the wings, waiting for a green light to signal them to go on.

All very necessary, but I do feel this has not helped theatre. Cue lights do not assist the actor to listen or stay connected to the play. Such devices can encourage, in the lazier actor, a rather blasé entrance and, in the nervous or over-anxious actor, a frenzy of activity which creates a sudden vacuum in the play.

Many of the best shows work because they are fashioned from an ensemble of actors sitting in the performance space and, when not acting, listening to the play and staying connected to the story. The audience can experience a seamless and sustained piece of work from the group performance. Energy is shared among the actors and the momentum of the play is released. Cue lights can disrupt this momentum, but as they seem to be a fact of theatrical life the actor must learn to use them.

I've always noticed the better and more experienced actors are reluctant to have the light, only conceding when it is absolutely essential. Don't stop listening to the play and even if you are straining or it is impossible to hear, you can stay in character and you may even have to do more work on basic acting notes (i.e. where am I going, where have I come from?) and concentrate more on your entrance.

If the cue light frightens you, it can stop you breathing. I've watched actors hold their breath waiting for the light to go on. Try to keep breathing, to avoid tensions and holds. Think of the light as being only part of your entrance, not the whole of it. Your coming on-stage is the important part of the play, the light is an aid to that and not the key.

With talk about cue lights and entrances we have now reached the end of the fourth stage. Rehearsals are over, as is the technical. The actor now prepares to play on-stage in front of an audience. After all the preparation, the real test of vocal skill is about to begin.

Stage Five
VOICE, TEXT AND REHEARSAL
MEET THE STAGE

One day after rehearsals at the Royal National Theatre I was lunching with two celebrated British actresses waiting to open that night on the Lyttelton Theatre stage. One said to us, 'I can't wait to get on tonight.' After she left, the other actress turned to me and said, 'I hate going on every night, I'm so scared. I only act because I enjoy working on good plays.'

The fact is, there are many actors who love to rehearse but hate the moment when their work has to meet the stage and the audience. They are performers who get their purest enjoyment through the imaginative process of the rehearsal period. Equally, there are actors who hate rehearsals and just can't wait to get on stage 'to do the production' and meet the audience.

Whatever the need to act – and for every actor the need comes from a different source – most actors feel very nervous about leaving the rehearsal room and presenting their work on-stage. It can be the moment when they lose the play. Their work can be cluttered or muddled by the production.

Yet the intimate, detailed, subtle and private rehearsal room work has to meet space at some point.

Space

One of the fundamental transformations any actor has to face is working in different spaces. Every space demands a different energy. Every space has a different acoustic. Every space has a different point of focus. We spoke about this in the last stage during rehearsals. Space changes quality with the kind of set in place as well as an audience. An audience might well give the actor an energy but the sheer body volume that people bring into a space will deaden the human voice and create new stress and tensions.

One of the most painful processes an actor can go through is having to share her work in a large space like the Olivier stage at the Royal National Theatre. However wonderful she is in a part, it has to be shared and seen by an audience. It cannot be kept hidden unless it means to be pure laboratory theatre. However truthful a performer might be, or indeed creative, it means nothing if she cannot communicate over space. An audience sitting in space cannot move like a camera towards the actor. The actor consequently has to move towards the audience.

There are some inescapable facts regarding performing in space. Actors who do not appreciate these facts will find a space crushes and consequently defeats them. Here is a list that has to be considered if an actor wants to be heard and effective in space. The level of work required is absolutely connected to the size of the performance space. So, the bigger the space:

- The more breath and support you will need. You can feel its requirements if you breathe the space. As you imagine the space and face it, you will take in the breath required.
- The more you have to reach out across the space, the more articulation is needed. You must begin to heighten speech, particularly the ends of words. Every syllable of every word must be clearly defined. This can feel very false to the actor but will not sound so to the audience.
- Lines must be held and sustained. Any falling line will be eaten up in a large space. Tremendous energy to work through a thought will also be required.
- As the space increases, any off-voice position will sound like vocal fuzz. You will need the whole of your voice to reach the back.
- The bigger the space, the more physical definition is required. In space the actor's body becomes clearer when set against the

static perspective of a set. Every movement reads. So, like the word, the body also will require extra definition. Vocal or physical muddle will confuse the audience. To speak and move without this definition will mean many lost lines.

- In a small theatre a pause can be thrilling, but long pauses in a big space are very difficult to hold or fill. Only a highly skilled performer can risk silence in a big space and actually sustain the silence.
- The bigger the space, the more energy is required from the whole company. An actor entering a space and dropping the speaking energy can very quickly drag the whole company and play down with him. This is equally true of the one actor who is inaudible. The other actors then suffer and all risk inaudibility as the audience strains to hear their unclear colleague. The confusion and time lag this causes means that the audience misses the lines of the next speaker.
- The bigger the space, the more the audience needs to see the actor's face to help understanding. If you hide or face away you risk not being heard and losing audience attention.
- Words need more space around them in a big area. Audiences will disengage if you continually rush the lines.
- The head resonators carry best in large spaces, so rather than push for audibility, 'think' the sound from the head.
- It is always easier to fill a space and bring your voice down than to work from a position of inaudibility. Many actors forget to place the audience's bodies into their equation and will be 'under' the space rather than on top of it.
- Some accents might need extra definition if the space is large. Genuine familiarity and mastery of the accent is a real benefit and necessity.
- Words need to be released, so the further forward you place the voice, the better.

Common Misconceptions About Space

- Pushing vocally or shouting never helps. The audience might hear your voice, but they won't be able to understand what you say. It's rather like being hit over the head with a hammer. Also, you will rapidly lose your voice if not damage it in the long run.
- Many actors push when they can't be heard and push their voices into their chests. This might feel strong to the actor, but the sound won't be defined in space, only muffled.

- It is possible to speak quietly in a large space but this position requires exquisite control of the breath, fantastic voice placing and super-clear articulation. Actors earn this position with wonderful technique and superb emotional and intellectual intensity. To speak quietly in a huge space and be heard is considered the hardest vocal challenge an actor faces.
- At the moment when an actor needs more breath in a large space he is often rendered breathless and is frightened of taking a large breath. The bigger the space, the less likely the audience will see you breathe, so take what you need.
- The small theatre also has its traps. The advantage of a large space is that most actors know they must work it. In a smaller space you can forget that need. However, an audience will be more angry at not hearing you if they can almost touch you. They will not forgive laziness.

Testing the Space

- Does the play match the space? Some plays work better in a particular space. I suppose this is directly linked to the writer's landscape and imagination. Epic plays work very well in huge theatres. The subject matter, and probably the form and language, are opened up and released by space. A domestic play might need more actual help from the actor if it has to be communicated in a vast theatre. Verse lines can often breathe better in a large theatre, whereas Chekhov becomes lost and less subtle. From experience, I know that if a play in its form, energy and language matches a space, the communication of the play is a hundred per cent easier.
- Spend as much time as possible in the performance space. I've said this throughout the section on rehearsal and I don't mind saying it again. Breathe the space. Find the space's focus – where you have to look in order to communicate with the whole audience. Lock the space into your breath memory. Walk the space. Look around the whole of it. Imagine you can catch the eye of every member of the audience. Take those sensations into the rehearsal room. Imagine the audience and its energy with your back to them. Feel the space through your whole body so that you are three-dimensional and not merely two-dimensional.
- Understand how the set will help or hinder your voice. The worst scenario is a completely open performance space or a very padded one – curtains, drapes and carpets soak up the

voice. The best will be a set with surfaces, preferably wood, that can throw out your voice. Metal might make the space too live, creating an echo. As you do this, take note of the space above the stage: for instance, whether it's a fly space and full or empty. An empty fly will not be useful in throwing out your voice.

- Test the space to find out whether it's acoustically alive or dead. Always remember that the mass of an audience will deaden the space. In a live space, if you call out or send a strong 'mah' into the audience area you will get the sense of your voice returning to you, like a mini-echo. The deader the space, the less feedback. Most modern theatres are dead. The materials used in construction are generally cement, brick and padding, which don't support the human voice. A good auditorium is constructed of wood and plaster, with many reflective surfaces to support the voice. Carvings are more than just decoration! A well-designed theatre is slightly too live until the audience enters and balances the space. A dead space requires more support, definition and voice. A live one needs more space between words – less volume, careful articulation, a finer-balanced voice.

- Find the focus of the space. This will include sight lines so you can always be seen, but check in what places your face cannot be seen. Where do you need to 'think' to in order for your body and breath to connect to the space? For instance, the Olivier Theatre at the Royal National Theatre visually pulls you to the back of the stalls. The actor must consequently concentrate on thinking the whole circle, otherwise the audiences will feel left out and the actor won't breathe and imagine the space.

- Test the space with other actors dotted around the auditorium. Be supportive of each other but pick any lost word, pulling line, devoicing or pushing. Play a scene, a duologue with one on stage, the other in the auditorium. Immediately after the scene, swap over, then both return to the stage and play the scene.

- Try to do as much of your thinking and feeling out to the audience.

- Does the space embrace you or push you away? If the latter, you'll have to think out more to befriend it. Some modern theatres feel as though they are flat and stark.

The more you do these simple tests, the more you will own the space and believe you have a right to be there and tell a story.

Next, a few hints about tackling different configurations of theatre based on some specific theatres I have worked in most frequently.

The Proscenium Arch

The arch around these boxed-in stages creates a picture frame and, like any frame, it highlights the contained picture. Everything you say and do in this frame is immediately heightened and defined. Any unwanted vocal sound, movement or acting intention is clearly communicated. The arch magnifies everything.

Wherever the audience is sitting, the proscenium arch will render even the smallest physical fidget or vocal grunt into an important event. So definition and clear intention is the name of the game here. Certain acting positions or vocal habits that seem interesting in a rehearsal room become silly to the audience in this framed space. Equally true is that what can feel artificial to the actors is communicated as truth to the audience. For instance, an intense interaction across a small space with the actors facing each other, which seemed fine in the rehearsal room, will appear slightly ridiculous in a proscenium arch. They will look like little stick figures. For the scene to work in the theatre, the actors will have to think, and physically turn, out. It is at this point that the inexperienced actor can feel artificial. Actors need space around them in the proscenium arch; getting too close to each other will again look like strange clumps of people in space. The proscenium space clutters easily. It is possible to play the most intimate of scenes across a large space and still look real and close to the audience.

You cannot speak into the wings in the proscenium arch because it will render you inaudible unless the wings are boxed in with wood. But if there is a decent set around you to pitch your voice out to the audience, you can speak upstage and be heard.

The notion of upstaging other actors really comes into its own on this type of stage. The term comes from getting upstage of an actor so that they have to turn their backs to the audience to speak to you. On top of this obvious attention-grabbing trick is the more subtle one that works within the heightened quality of the arch. An actor can easily distract from another player by fidgeting or doing some business too relentlessly.

Precision, definition and very active sharing with the audience are the clues to playing the proscenium arch and winning.

The Thrust Stage

The main point of this design is to throw or thrust the actors, and consequently the action of the play, out into the audience. This kind of stage revolutionized the theatre by breaking through the proscenium arch and defying the distance an audience might feel when the actors are isolated from them. The thrust hurls the acting at you and also exposes the actor to the audience. Some actors hate the thrust for this reason. The audience is too much a part of the play.

In a perverse way, the fact that the actor feels closer to the audience is where the vocal pitfalls lie. The performer getting too near the front row of the public can fall into a number of traps, both vocally and physically.

Stand upstage on a thrust stage, the furthest you can get from the audience. Look out and breathe. You might feel at a distance from the audience, but you will feel you can own the whole space. Now start walking, slowing down as you reach the thrust part of the stage. You will feel immediately the moment you lose some of the audience physically. You will have lost eye contact with the right and left of the auditorium and the audience above. As you are drawn and propelled further forward towards just a part of the audience, you will be losing more and more of the house.

The thrust can lull you into a false sense of connection to the audience. The further forward you are, the more you actually have to work for audibility and clarity. Yet because a portion of the audience is so close you can be duped into working less.

When working in the thrust part of a stage, a proportion of the audience will not be able to see your face. I've worked on many plays in thrust and charted the reactions of an audience. The side that can see an actor's face will hear the actor's voice. The side that can't see the face will listen for a few minutes, then switch off. This is probably a note to directors, but be aware that there is a direct link between seeing a face and hearing a voice. We won't listen after a few minutes if you don't show us, in the staging, an actor's face. There is little an actor can do technically. What generally happens is, she senses an audience switching off and will begin to push, which will only alienate them more. The experienced actor will just look out and the problem is resolved.

Continue breathing the whole space. The temptation is that as you get closer to the audience you close down the breath. Breathe into the whole body, if the audience has to look at your back it should still be alive. In fact, an engaged actor can communicate very well through his back.

It is so easy to drop the energy, moving forward towards an audience, but you need to heighten it. You need to define ends of words, sustain lines and be on voice. You will not blow the near members of the audience out of their seats – a common fear of actors when they get close to an audience – with definition and clarity, but you will lose a large proportion of the house if you go flat.

Studio Theatres

There are many vocal traps in a small and seemingly cosy studio space. The main one is that you feel you don't have to work because the audience is so near. In fact, the work required is very specific and in some ways technically harder than in a larger space.

When performers step into a large space they know that vocal work will be demanded in order to be heard. As soon as they fill the space the vocal equipment can snowball and gather momentum. This sensation doesn't apply in a small theatre. The smallness of the space can reduce, stifle and suffocate the actor, particularly if the play doesn't match the space. Shakespeare in a small space might be very exciting in its intimacy but the text might lose its line power and epic quality as the actors pull back from releasing in the intimate space. A balance of power has to be found.

The domestic drama will obviously work best in these theatres, but there is a new trend of placing large-scale and large-cast classics in very tiny spaces. The ingenuity of actors and directors can make this experience quite exciting. This trend has exposed epic plays to new scrutiny but not necessarily helped the form of the language which, by necessity, is often made more humble than it is.

Let's think of the problem from the audience's point of view. The closer I am to the actors, the more angry I will get if I can't hear them. After all, it seems I'm in the room with them. I can maybe even touch them. At home I would hear them across my own living-room, but suddenly that basic reality is shattered. Meanwhile the actors are thinking that they can't speak out because they are afraid of bellowing at the audience and along with that notion will often go the fear of clarity, so words are not ended. Emotions are bottled up and constipated, and the text swallowed and not released.

When working in a small space:

- Go back to the breath! Breathe the space. This might not be as straightforward as in larger theatres, as the audience might be so close that you don't feel able really to engage to the perimeters of the space. Also, the audience might not fill the whole space.

There might be an area behind where the audience sits that must also be breathed if the space is to be filled. So breathe to the perimeters of the theatre, not to where the audience ends.

● You might not need much volume, but that doesn't mean that definition is not required. I often say that the hardest vocal technical achievement is to speak with tremendous clarity but quietly – finishing words, holding lines, staying on voice and using very subtle support. All these qualities are required in a small space. You might have the sensation of truth being small and intimate but for audibility that mustn't mean you lose the vocal work and tension of release and sharing. It's hard.

Theatre in the Round

With the audience surrounding you, it is an inevitable fact that you will spend most of the play facing away from a proportion of it. Standing on the edge of the space and opposite an aisle there are possibilities in the round where you can be seen by the whole audience, but as soon as you enter the main action space someone will be looking at your back. More than ever in the round you have to be active throughout your whole body.

All the above rules apply. Breathe the space, definition of words, staying on voice, as well as moving around in the space so that your face is seen by the whole audience at some time. The vocal hints given to me by actors who work in the round a great deal are about using their voices out of the tops of their heads. I take this to mean that they used their head resonances to pierce the space around them. This makes sense as the head resonances travel further. Again, the instinct could be to push the voice, which is not at all useful. Heightened articulation is needed and very strongly held lines are required.

Acting in the round is visually intense so useless movements, like undefined speech or sound, will distract. Everything you do reads to the audience. This kind of space exposes you the most though it can be very thrilling to work in the round.

The Traverse Theatre

The audience is on two sides of the acting space and this placing creates an acting corridor. The traverse has the same problems and needs as the in-the-round space. You have two great advantage points. At both ends of the corridor you have a place that commands the whole space vocally and physically. Never forget the audience behind you. Again, it is a question of thinking and almost vocalizing throughout your entire body.

Often the layout of both traverse and in-the-round theatre means that the audiences bank up steeply above you so be aware, if this is the case, that you mustn't forget the height of the space. Remember occasionally to look up and communicate to the higher reaches of the audience.

The Open Air

This kind of space is always a tricky one for many reasons and it will always demand enormous technical athleticism. The problems with open-air theatres are often compounded by the weather (a slight wind will whisk away your voice), the rustling of trees, aircraft overhead, traffic or river noise. The theatres, sometimes makeshift, are not always defined with a solid perimeter behind the audience that will contain and reinforce the voice.

The seating is often flimsy so there is no acoustic help from that quarter. Audiences will also lose attention rapidly out of pure discomfort. The best open-air theatres are nestled into rock, have water behind the audience (water is a good medium for the voice because it reflects sound), or have stone seats: the ancient Greek theatres, for example (see theatre at Epidaurus, below). All these factors are beyond your immediate control, so what can you do to help yourself?

Open-air acting will require a support system on full recovery rather like a singer's. Stillness as you speak will aid focus. Moving your head quickly and speaking rapidly will merely dissipate the sound. You will have to play out. Subtle exchanges across the stage will not read or be audible.

Try to find a place of focus behind and around the audience so that you have some place to look, breathe and think. You must stay on voice. An off voice won't travel anywhere in the open air. The higher head resonances will be more effective than the bellowed chest ones. Any dropped syllable or line will disappear into space – definition, definition, definition! All this means is that your concentration has to be intense.

I find it interesting that the new Globe Theatre on London's south bank of the Thames – reconstructed as closely as possible to be a replica of Shakespeare's original – had acoustic problems in the run-up to its opening season. Actors and directors who tested the space discovered that the only way to be heard was to deliver the text out to the audience. The intimate forms of theatre we are now used to won't read or be useful in this open space. It seems that actors stood still and spoke out to the audience, not across the stage to each other. Maximum stillness and vocal focus is required, the bigger the space, the more focus you need.

The Greek Theatre

The Greek theatre was and remains the best kind of epic space. Great and important ideas and stories were performed there. It was not designed for domestic drama, but for stories that would transform and heal a whole populace. This really was theatre as a temple to performance. The audience arranged itself in a fanned semicircle around the stage and was banked up above it.

I've only ever worked at Epidaurus and the Theatre of Dionysus at Athens, but I think it is true to say that the architects of these spaces got it all right. The first astonishing experience you have as you walk out onto the stage – or playing circle – is that the space not only embraces and welcomes you, but is designed for the human body. You cannot help but breathe the space. The configuration of the theatre invites you to do it. The space also centres and focuses you. The perspective pulls you up and out, you have to reach out in your imagination to the back and you feel every inch of the auditorium in your body. You become very aware of when you have physically and visually lost the audience. The space immediately touches and heightens your imagination. This type of space releases and liberates the actor. The Olivier stage at the Royal National Theatre was fashioned on a Greek model, though I'm not sure the space is of quite the same quality.

It appears to be true that the acoustics of a theatre like Epidaurus are superb. The auditorium is built of stone that reflects the voice. Although I've never worked in Epidaurus with its full audience capacity, I believe it would still resonate the voice and reinforce the speaker.

These are open-air theatres and need that physical and vocal focus as well as the sense of playing out, but because the relationship with the audience is so easily felt the actor doesn't get beguiled, but works with the space.

Breath is required, but again the space tells you that. Lines and words have to be finished. But an actor working in such a space understands why the word and its release were so sacred to the Greeks. They designed space to encourage this connection between speaker and listener. I suspect we don't have the patience, money or knowledge to build theatres in this way any more. Theatres today are often multi-purpose civic centres, not places for special and unique theatrical happenings. It is interesting that we have taken the Greek shape, but have forgotten that it was an open-air space and that a ceiling would probably squash the whole imaginative notion of the theatre and, as that is squashed, the acoustics are impaired.

Non-Theatre Spaces

Much theatre today, particularly small-scale tours and educational projects, take place in spaces not originally designed for either performance or the human voice. My second-year students at the Guildhall School do a week of school tours each year. In seven days they perform in ten different spaces. They always report that the major lesson of the tour is how to perform in a hostile space.

Most of the spaces they encounter are designed for one-way communication, that is, an authority figure speaking out to a gathered, silent and, perhaps at worst, submissive audience via a public address system. The amplified lectern is the appropriate symbol of this type of space since there is only one vantage point from which to speak.

Many school halls and churches are very live, so the delivery has to be slow and deliberate. The speaker will get a very high energy feedback from the space, if not an echo. You might not need much vocal power, but you will need to pace and articulate each word carefully. On the occasions I have taught members of the church – priests and vicars – they all joke that the rather caricature vicar's delivery – slow, precise, with rising inflections – comes from years of giving sermons in stone churches that echo. Who knows, but I rather like the theory. All those qualities are indeed required in a 'too-live' acoustic.

In these school halls it is very hard to humanize the space. If you try to break down the formality by either re-arranging the chairs or performing off the platform, you can end up with many students not being able to see. Any scene with actors sitting on the floor definitely becomes pointless.

The echo can produce a rather hard or aggressive sound to the voice so as much modulation as possible and opening of the vowels will help. Throwing drapes or curtains can help to balance the echo but don't be tempted to push. The gentle vocal approach is best.

Newer halls are often too acoustically dead. In an attempt to humanize the space it may have been padded with carpets, polystyrene ceiling tiles, cushions and curtains. This will often make you feel as though you are speaking into cotton wool. Again, don't push, but define words and lines carefully. Really motor through to the ends of thoughts and don't let the energy drop. The dead space will sponge any undefined sound and smother it. Head resonances will be useful.

To find focus in all these spaces is difficult. The space, unlike the theatre, will probably not have a place to play to and work can get too spread out. Physical economy will help contain the space and you might really have to think about making contact with the audience. It will feel as though the audience is pushing away from you or that there is a barrier separating you. Reach out to them to pass through these sensations.

Once you understand that the space is rarely used as a performance space – in fact its normal use has little to do with theatre – you will begin to realize that your performance concentration has to be heightened. Most actors who have experience playing in these spaces tell of skidding on squashed peas left over from school dinners, visitors wandering in to look for lost jumpers, school bells, telephones ringing in the hallway or the caretaker emptying the rubbish bins throughout your performance. Take courage! This is often where theatre starts nowadays and where young audiences get their first taste for live performance. The chances are that the audience is used to such distractions and won't notice them, so just keep telling the story.

There are several simple exercises you can do to enhance your work in these non-theatre spaces:

- Even if you have only a few minutes, walk the space.
- Sit in the audience seats so you can see what they see.
- Breathe the whole space.

- Do a few minutes of warming up the voice in the space. This will very quickly tell you about its acoustic properties.
- Scatter the company throughout the space and one by one speak a few lines of the work and get some feedback from your colleagues and apply that knowledge accordingly.
- Check the sight lines of the space.
- Check how quiet you can go and don't go below that level.
- Check how loud you can go before there is too big an echo and don't go up above that level.
- Be aware of where the audience will begin so that you feel you can reach them all.
- Few of these venues have adequate lighting, so you have to focus the action and also be aware that this means you will see your audience. Use this potential eye contact as an advantage, not a terror.
- Don't be distressed if by filling the space you feel you lose subtlety. Any actor filling an unknown space will feel this. As the performance continues you might feel you can begin to explore nuances, but the initial concern is that you are heard and are telling a story clearly.

Other Spaces

I've been lucky enough to work in a variety of theatres around the world. What I will attempt to do is discuss a few that fit the categories I've already written about.

I think you will have gathered that in general the design and building of theatres since World War Two have lost the understanding that we had for centuries. Modern theatres, with the exception of recent creations like the Swan Theatre in Stratford-upon-Avon (all wood and handsomely engineered), are often acoustically dead and not designed for the human dimension. The theatres of the eighteenth, nineteenth and early twentieth century are compatible with the human body, voice and experience. They help the actor to share the word.

All over Europe and South America you can stumble across theatrical gems, small opera houses all lovingly designed for the human voice and audience contact with the performer. This is not so true of houses built recently; padded seats and flat concrete walls conspire to alienate the voice and the word. The architects of these theatres will often ignore actors' needs in order to design a state-of-the-art structure, then call the performers malcontents when they complain. This misunderstanding frequently goes so far that the dressing-rooms are lift rides away from the stage, as they are at London's Barbican Theatre.

I remember standing in a stalled lift at the Barbican full of actors dressed in armour. They were due on stage to fight a Shakespearean battle. We could hear the tannoy announcing that they were all off but we stood there powerless. That night the battle scene was merely a skirmish due to a stalled lift!

Some modern theatres are so unlike a theatre that older actors have stories about wandering around backstage trying to unearth their dressing-rooms, only to find themselves accidentally on stage during another performance. The once-sacred space has no definable perimeters, just acres of technical equipment.

THE BARBICAN THEATRE (THE LONDON HOME OF THE RSC)

I started working with the Royal Shakespeare Company as a voice coach when they moved to their new London home in 1982. Many actors enjoy this space because it has a more intimate feel than the RSC's official home at the Stratford Memorial Theatre. The most immediate problem with the Barbican stage is that in order to make contact with the top circle you have to pull your head right back to look up to the circle. Apart from that, the perspectives are good.

Unlike the RSC's old London home at the Aldwych Theatre in the Strand, the Barbican is a padded, dead space which needs much definition and sustained vocal energy to the ends of lines. This deadness can be helped by a good wooden set, but this doesn't often happen so the actors never fully feel their voices return to them. It is therefore a hard space in which to monitor the voice.

I remember being very shocked at how far away an actor could be when positioned upstage from the first row of the audience. With increasing technical demands, the actual staging area is expanding so actors can find themselves playing a scene 30 feet away from their first audience member. This expanse also means you have to play out and avoid speaking into the wings.

This was first modern theatre I worked in which needed conquering. It was at the Barbican that I discovered what most experienced actors instinctively know, that there are three basic vocal demands a dead space requires:

- Support.
- Being on voice.
- Fantastic articulation – the full definition of the word and thought.

At least the Barbican mostly houses heightened plays that can release the space and encompass the strong technical attention needed to the word.

THE OLIVIER – ROYAL NATIONAL THEATRE

The Olivier is an epic space. Its design, as I have mentioned already, is based on the ancient Greek theatres. At best it is a liberating space for the actor's voice, imagination and spirit. At worst it can terrify and suffocate the actor because of its very specific vocal demands.

The first thing I noticed when beginning to work on the Olivier stage was that there is a feeling of intimacy created for the actor which doesn't exist for the audience. Standing on stage you feel closer to the audience than the audience feels to you. A potentially dangerous misconception, this forced sense of intimacy can lead an actor into not sustaining enough or being specific enough.

The second strange design feature of the Olivier is that when you stand centre stage the space pulls the actor's imagination down to the back of the stalls, making the actor constantly work to think up to the back of the circle to include over half the audience. You can sit in the circle and feel left out as the actor has seemingly forgotten you. In the original Greek theatre, and in many well-designed ones, the space's perspective pulls the actor up to make full contact with the whole house. The design is based on what the human body needs and sees. The design of the Greek theatre centres the actor's body rather then suppressing it.

You also notice immediately that the Olivier is dead. That is, you can't sense your voice in the theatre. It's like speaking into cotton wool. This further deadens as the audience sits in the space, body volume absorbing the voice even more. When you work in the empty theatre you must always make allowances for the audience. You will need more volume and energy when they are seated. This deadness can severely panic the actor who can be tempted to push vocally or over-support and bellow. Not useful, but an understandable instinct.

As with all epic space, the centre point of the stage commands the whole house. From this point you can hold the audience visually, vocally and without much effort. As you move off this place, portions of the house are lost to you, so you are stronger further from the audience. However, many actors and directors feel an overwhelming temptation to pull the action closer to the audience. The closer you get, the more of the audience you lose and the harder it is to be heard by those seated on the sides of the theatre.

To test this out, all you have to do is walk downstage from the centre point. As you walk you will feel that you lose contact with more and more of the audience. Right downstage, the middle block of the stalls will be having an intimate experience with the actors, but the side and circle have been completely forgotten. Of course, actors with huge technical skill can play the house from this downstage position, but it's hard work.

Like all stages, the acoustic potential of the Olivier is very dependent on the set. The empty stage is enormous and offers no vocal aid for the human voice. It is impossible for even the most experienced actor to be clear without some sort of solid enclosing set. My heart breaks when I watch an actor vocally fight an empty space on the Olivier stage.

Even with a good modern set that can help amplify the voice, there are certain needs and things you can't do. You can't speak into the wings. Half the audience behind you will not hear. You have to look and think out. You can't speak and move your head across the arc of the audience – words will just disappear. You can speak, then move, or move, then speak, but any lack of physical definition will make you inaudible.

As is the case with any dead acoustic, you can't be off voice. If you devoice, the space erodes the voice and the sound becomes fluffy. You can speak quietly on full voice. This is the most difficult technical position: on voice, supported, defined, placed and yet quiet. Speech definition has to be heightened; every syllable and end of word spoken. Many actors at first feel that they are overworking, yet from the audience's point of view the speech sounds clear and truthful. We can't experience much truth if we can't hear or understand the word. Nothing will read or carry if it is swallowed.

Lines and thoughts have to be sustained and held. Any falling line will disappear. Many actors are audible but are rendered inaudible by their scene partners on the Olivier stage who are dropping lines and words. The audience struggles to understand the fallen line and misses the next audible one. As in all dead space, the head resonances travel better than the chest ones.

The Olivier will demand a strong breath and support system. The space must be consciously breathed. The strange perspective that pulls you down to the back of the stalls will often tempt you not to breathe the whole space. Recently there was a show that wasn't filling the entire house. The audience only occupied the stalls. With a full house the show was perfectly audible, but when only the stalls were occupied complaints rolled in. What was happening was that the actors only sensed an audience below them, so failed to breathe the whole house and became under-energized with their support. Whatever the capacity or numbers in a theatre you must always imagine and breathe the whole space.

Because the Olivier is so wide, being clear and heard in crowd scenes requires particular skills. You have to grab the audience because their eyes will wander and although they might actually hear the line, their eyes are so busy trying to find the speaker their ears miss it!

Many actors love the Olivier. As I mentioned before, it feels epic and that energy can really liberate the actors, but only if they are prepared to use their voices with enormous precision, support, energy, freedom and definition. Anything either physically or vocally sloppy will make you inaudible. You need to play and think out to the whole house. Initially, this might feel as though you have lost intimacy, but that is not how it will read to the audience. You don't need to bellow, but you do need to be on voice and sustained. It's no wonder that great theatrical actors who successfully play the Olivier are like athletes.

The Olivier will really come into its own with plays that are heightened and use language actively and specifically. These sorts of plays marry ideally with the space; space and play mutually support each other. There is nothing 'cool' about the Olivier.

THE OLD VIC

After five years of dealing with the modern stages of the Royal National Theatre, I recently went back to work with actors at the National's first home, the venerable Old Vic Theatre. As I started a voice work-out on stage, I became very emotional. I had forgotten just how wonderful a space this kind of theatre can be. In every aspect of its design it helps the actor speak. It's not a hi-tech theatre, but one that houses a history of language and stories being told from its stage through the scale of the human body and voice.

Stand on a stage like the Old Vic and you feel the whole house embrace you and take you up to the gods (the highest balcony seats). Almost automatically, you breathe the whole space. It creates a natural relationship between actor and audience. The materials and the carvings – wood and plaster – of the auditorium reinforce the human voice. When empty, the house acoustic is live, so you can feel immediately when your voice fills the space. It instantly feeds back to you. You know what is vocally required. When full, the audience balances the space and the live quality disappears, though you still have a sense of how your voice touches every part of the space.

All the voice principles which apply to proscenium arch theatres apply to the Old Vic. You cannot speak into the wings and you do need to play out to the audience. But in this kind of theatre you can get away with a lot which would be impossible in a modern space like the Olivier. You can whisper or go off voice, for instance, and still be heard. Because a space like the Old Vic is more contained and focused, you still need energy to the ends of words and lines, but not nearly as much as the Olivier requires. The Old Vic acoustic aids the energy of the word, so of course you need to be clear. But the space doesn't drain a word of its clarity as ruthlessly as the Olivier does.

The Old Vic is an actor-friendly space and one that supports the spoken word before anything else. I last worked in the space before going to the RNT, but my return there made me think of all the voice-related criticisms actors level at the National, and with their criticisms came the inevitable comparisons with theatres like the Old Vic. Despite the fact that young actors are not as vocally skilled with language as those of thirty years ago, it must be remembered that they are fighting regularly with modern theatre design and begin their careers with the odds stacked against them.

THE LYTTELTON – ROYAL NATIONAL THEATRE

This is the Royal National Theatre's proscenium arch space. It has many of the Olivier's design and acoustic problems. A lot of actors tell me that speaking from the Lyttelton stage is like sending energy into a padded room. The auditorium absorbs sound as soon as it is spoken. Other actors talk about it as if it were a cinema. They find it hard to monitor their voices or the audience. These are all signs of a very dead acoustic.

These obstacles can be overcome by a wooden set and a wooden raked floor. The physical disadvantages (for the actor) of the rake (see p. 280) are made up for by the advantage of the voice being flung out. An open stage will require huge amounts of sustained and on-voice energy. Like all proscenium arch stages, speaking into the wings is fruitless. You have to play out if you expect to be heard. Like the Olivier, the physical focus of the Lyttelton pulls you down to the back of the stalls, so you have to look and breathe consciously to the back of the circle, otherwise the audience in the circle will experience the play through the top of your head.

This problem is emphasized when you are working on a rake because your energy is thrust further into the stalls.

After getting on voice and using sustained support through-out every line, the biggest shock you will experience in this kind of theatre is the amount of articulation required. The padded space needs so much clear energy on every syllable of every word that many younger performers believe they are overdoing it in order to achieve the most minimum levels of clarity. Without this articulation, any muffled words get soaked up by the space. Avoid pushing vocally (always a temptation in this kind of space) when confronted by a space that doesn't give you feedback. Also, use head resonance to pierce the space.

Many shows that play in the Lyttelton tour nationally and internationally to other vast regional theatres. This is because the Lyttelton most resembles the configuration of modern proscenium theatres outside London, though auditoriums elsewhere can be double and triple its size. On their return from working in these other spaces, actors are often able to fill the Lyttelton with much more ease. They discover on tour that the Lyttelton requires the same kind of intense and concentrated vocal energy as a theatre twice its size.

THE COTTESLOE – ROYAL NATIONAL THEATRE

This is the RNT's smallest theatre (essentially a black box studio space which was squeezed into the design of the National as an afterthought) and it has the potential to transform itself into various shapes, from small proscenium arch to traverse to thrust stage. In many ways this kind of theatre is the most straightforward acoustically. It has the traps of all small theatres: the audience is so close to the performer that the actor tends to forget to work vocally and may easily drop lines and words.

Although the Cottesloe only houses a few hundred people, its actual size and volume are bigger than many theatres with double the audience capacity. A good many of the seats are in fixed, steep tiers that surround the space on three and occasionally four sides. When breathing the space, actors sometimes forget this capacity and the vertical arrangements of the seats. So you must connect to the whole space.

Here is the important note about working in a space like the Cottesloe. Since the auditorium is so unusually high, most complaints about audibility come from this part of the seating. The actor has to make a connection *above* his head, therefore well above eyeline. In a strange way you can do this without looking up, simply by 'thinking up'. Breathing in that direction, you will include this part of the audience even in your body gestures. Sensing energy in this way, you will send up the word and not drop or pull back on lines. Here again, the actor has to test out the vocal demands of this unusually configured space which looks, at first glance, quite straightforward.

You can be intimate and speak very quietly in the Cottesloe, as long you adhere to three basic rules: being on voice; supporting through the line; and finishing every word. This all requires intense emotional and intellectual concentration.

Finally, one of the great features of the Cottesloe is that epic plays work here as well as more intimate and domestic ones. I think this is partly due to the theatre's enormous volume. It can easily transform from a cottage to the interior of a cathedral and feels natural in both configurations. The main difference will be in how the actor vocally handles this change in volume.

THE STRATFORD FESTIVAL THEATRE, ONTARIO, CANADA

The Stratford Festival Theatre in Canada, founded by Sir Tyrone Guthrie in the 1950s, is one of the wonderful thrust stages designed by Tanya Moiseiwitsch. As a set designer, she knew what the actor needed in terms of a performance space. The Chichester Festival Theatre in Britain is of a similar design. These theatres are often called 'processional stages'. The spaces encourage movement and epic processions. Neither theatre is a hi-tech space and both are completely reliant on action through the word. Language and thought are the drama on display and often both theatres use a minimum of scenery.

The stage configuration does encourage the actor to move physically and it can take an entering actor some time to walk onto the stage before the audience can see him. This physical movement should be used to propel the voice and text out to the audience. Most actors feel very exposed on this type of stage. There is nowhere to hide, and although you need to be vocally and physically bold, any fidget or fluff will be very obvious to the whole audience. Clarity and focus in all your work is absolutely necessary and if it is not there, it will be frighteningly clear to one and all.

Despite these challenges, the Stratford space is actor-friendly. It is made of wood and from the stage you feel an intimacy with the whole audience and they with you. The physical perspectives feel fine and the space actually encourages you to play out, which is good because this is exactly how you need to play the words. Because the relationship with the audience can feel intimate, there is a tendency to lose formality in speaking. So be aware that it is easy to be less articulate or not have enough support.

For many years there was one annoying additional feature added to the Stratford space, which Tanya Moiseiwitsch did not design: an extra bank of seats on the back end of the auditorium. It has recently been removed. Reaching this section of seats drew the actor's focus away from other parts of the house and it was impossible for the actor, in any staged position, to communicate to these seats. Inaudibility complaints came from these areas and there was little an actor could do to rectify the situation.

When I asked one experienced actress about the seats and why they were there, destroying the whole focus of the space, she just raised her eyes to the ceiling and said 'Greed'.

Random Thoughts on Other Theatres and Space

The following thoughts will be so obvious to many experienced actors that I almost hesitate to include them here. But in my daily dealings with student and professional actors, I find that many are so limited in their experience that they are unaware of the basic principles of space and the effects of staging. Many performers seem terrified of playing out and making contact with an audience. The feeling they give is that by doing so they lose truth and some, perhaps through work in television and film, don't want to share their work so directly. But the actor's job is to speak directly to the audience even if the artifice of the script is indirection. Speaking to another actor on stage must always be sent to the audience.

Sightlines and Aisles   If you cannot see or feel the audience, you will not be seen or easily heard by them. Understanding sight lines is vital not only for your relationship with audiences but for your work with other actors. It is easy to mask one another on stage, complicating the communication.

You can simply stand downstage of or in line with fellow actors if you stand opposite an aisle (i.e. where no audience member is seated). If you are not placed in this way you could be masking someone, so check your sight line. Always stay in touch with the whole audience. You can do this even through your back. This check is generally the downstage actor's task; however, if you are upstage and you wander into the blocking corridor of downstage actors, then you have masked yourself.

A lot of this blocking awareness is the director's responsibility, but many directors without training or enough staging experience leave it to the actors to work out. The more space you have between each other, the easier it is to alter this masking. The real problems come when actors are clumped very close together on the stage.

Older actors tend to be uneasy when younger actors get too close to them, particulalrly on wide or proscenium stages. I think younger performers believe that physical closeness reflects truth and intimacy, but this doesn't necessarily read well in larger theatres. An audience will tolerate not seeing an actor for a minute or so, but any longer and they will get restless.

Light   Light can focus a scene and an actor, but can also encourage the actor to cut off from the audience. It's always useful to remember that Shakespeare's players at the Globe, acting in daylight and without artificial illumination, could look into the eyes of their audience; really feel and know what was going on out there. Lighting today makes the audience a darkened mass, initially without individuality or reactions. Of course, many actors can feel and read an audience through the lighting barrier but you can blank out the audience, if you desire, and almost forget them in a way which would not be possible without lights.

If the lighting is not clear on your face then it is actually harder for an audience to hear you. Vocal and facial expression really do need to marry for the most successful performance. Many actors don't 'find their light', they speak without light on them even if it's there, and consequently lose the audience. It seems that the brighter the light, the more intense and focused the speaking. Dim light dims the voice. There are wonderful traditions that older actors frequently mention which I think are true. One is that comedy needs light. Recently an actor in a technical rehearsal was complaining that he couldn't play his comic scene in the dim light provided. At preview after preview he didn't get his way and didn't get many laughs. Eventually the director conceded and increased the level of light on the scene. Only then did the scene get waves of laughter.

Dead Spots Most theatres have so called 'dead spots', patches of the stage or the auditorium where sound does not carry because of some weird acoustical dysfunction. Actors arriving at an unknown theatre for the first time will instantly ask, 'Where are the dead spots?' No matter what you do vocally, it is usually impossible to overcome a dead spot. It's like a black hole sucking in the sound and energy and deadening both.

Many dead spots also occur in seemingly good seats: usually in the stalls under the overhanging circle. Odd acoustic circumstances conspire to ping the sound over a couple of seats but arrive smoothly to the surrounding ones. Patrons can sit bemused as they believe themselves deaf because everyone around them can hear the play but they can't. Why do theatre managements sell seats that are known to be dead? Well, some will acknowledge that certain seats are impossible acoustically and refund any complaints from those seats.

Some seats have reflective surfaces close by that can either absorb or throw a voice too violently away from the seat. Some dead spots are intensified by certain types of sets or configurations of the space which deflect the sound further. You can get a crop of them if the stage is extended over the orchestra pit.

Certain qualities of voice will be dead in a theatre, while other will pierce into it. It's always intriguing how various qualities of voice will react to different spaces. No science can predict this result. Some performers have told me that to play more directly to those seats in a dead area can help, but those seated in the dead spot will feel like the royal presence if they are specially played to and the remaining house is ignored.

The Orchestra Pit   An orchestra pit can feel like a barrier and gulf to a speaking actor. The first row of the audience seems a long way off and it is tempting to move your acting position downstage to help close the gap. Ironically, in those theatres with an orchestra pit this movement downstage will confound the acoustic and as you move past the proscenium arch you will begin to lose the acoustic properties of upstage. Generally, staying just up from the arch will give you maximum acoustic power. You have to work across the pit and use that energy to fill the house. Don't be tempted to move forward towards the first row of the auditorium. This will only distort you.

Interestingly, some orchestra pits can be covered over and the action staged over the pit. The hollow resonance underfoot can be very useful, but actors are often lulled into a sense of ease because they are closer to the audience and not only lose the acoustic benefit of the stage but don't work to the whole house.

One final point about an orchestra pit: it can be dampened with drapes around the sides to balance the orchestra and the speaker or singer. If this is the case, be aware it is also dampening your voice and you will have to use more support, definition and head resonances.

Vertical Placing of the Audience   Lastly, a small point about the actual placing of the audience. Always be aware of how the audience is arranged in seating. The most ideal position is rising up and away from you. This is straightforward seating for proscenium houses like the Old Vic, but many theatres go down, then up, or flat and then up. The only problem with these spaces might be that you are drawn down and forget the vast numbers of the audience rising above you.

The Promenade Performance Promenade means to walk and that's what the audience does, they walk around a space or into different spaces following the moving action of the play. Acoustically this can be a nightmare as each location can be different and at each stop the audience will take time to settle and listen, requiring the actor to generate a different energy for each new scene and place. Walk the route and test each place separately during rehearsal. This is obvious if you are actually moving from room to room, but not so apparent if you are just changing place within the same space. However, be very aware that one part of the space might have very different problems. To play a scene in front of drapes is very different from a brick wall drop. To play a scene under an overhang is very different from the main playing space. Test each space and don't be alarmed if you have to make radical shifts in vocal energy in order to be heard.

Transfer to the Theatre If you have been on stage during the rehearsal period (even walking around on the stage during lunch breaks if that is the only chance you have), know and have played the theatre before or have consciously imagined the theatre space in rehearsals, this transfer won't be too traumatic. It can be traumatic, however, if by entering the theatre you have to open up and extend your performance – and the voice plays a large part in this process – in such a way that you feel you lose intimacy and contact with the text. Any transfer from a small space to a larger one (a common enough change for successful productions) will require more breath and support, more vocal energy with a higher level of sustaining and more defined articulation. All these needs can lead an actor to feel he has lost subtlety and the performance has become crass. You may feel you have lost truth. You must bear in mind that truth can be as large as the space you are filling and that if part of the audience can't hear, then no truth exists for them! On the positive side, a heightened text might suddenly find a new lease of life and clarity with a bigger space. Verse, epic and powerful language suddenly come into their own in space. Whatever happens, you have to resolve the situation and be heard by all in the new, large theatre.

Special Effects   Will there be any stage effects such as smoke or dry ice which may prove troublesome to the voice? Remember that if smoking herbal cigarettes, they can dry out the voice more than tobacco, as they burn at a greater heat. Dust or Fuller's Earth powder, sawdust, earth – all these will mean you have to drink more water and perhaps steam to clear the throat.

Fog, peat, dust, earth, sawdust, smoke, incense – anything floating in the air – can dry the voice or irritate the throat. In everyday life these particles might be a mild nuisance to your voice and breath, but if you are acting, breathing in huge amounts of them under hot lights, sweating and dehydrating, these irritants can be most troublesome. If you are clearing your throat constantly, this will aggravate your vocal folds, making speaking a harder chore, performance after performance.

Stage managers can help by damping down any substance that will float around. This process will have to be repeated in the interval because the stage lights will quickly dry up the water.

If you are acting in this kind of environment, it will be useful to:

- Drink more water.
- Use steam after a show. Even a hot shower will help.

- When the action permits, breathe in through your nose to help filter the air.
- Persuade the designer or technical director to use a minimum of the material.

I find it is counterproductive to warm up in the performance space when dusty matter is present, particularly if technicians and stage hands have been resetting before a show. Dust will take time to settle.

It is very easy for your complaints not to be taken seriously. I recently worked on a production with peat on the floor. A vocally strong cast, after a week of shows, started to complain about sore and tired voices. One of them tentatively mentioned the peat. Because they had been overworked and understudies sent on, I did not instantly believe that the small amount of peat could be responsible. That is, until I gave a two-hour class on the same stage and began suffering myself. Simply by constantly dampening the peat, the problem evaporated. I've noticed that when substances are in the air the section of the audience closest to the stage will cough more and suffer too.

Masks　Masks can be visually stunning. Some masks might even help amplify your voice,[*] but most actors find them hell. As one prominent actor said to me, 'It's like speaking with a bucket on your head.'

Whatever the mask you are using and whatever its material, you have to make friends with it and use it as soon as possible in rehearsal. Find out immediately whether the rehearsal mask is the same as the performance one – in my experience, it rarely is. If it is not, ask whether the material and moulding are similar to the one you will be using in performance. Check the mask for anything that may hinder your throat or mouth.

[*] There are some convincing theories that the mouth aperture of the mask used in the ancient Greek and Roman theatres was engineered to work like a small megaphone, enhancing the speaker's voice.

However you look at it, be aware that the physical and psychological problems that attend wearing a mask will be immense and constant. Many people find wearing a mask claustrophobic and frightening. Half-masks might be easier, but if your whole head is covered panic can occur. Some actors find that wearing a mask neutralizes their personalities and make it difficult to produce a character. But there are other actors who find the wearing of a mask liberating, vocally and psychologically.

Obviously the lips, jaw, tongue and face can be impeded by a mask, which is the chief difficulty of wearing them. You will have to work on constantly freeing these areas, but the tensions are often much more complex. In a mask, seeing can be hard, hearing can be hard (if it is a full-head mask) and breathing can be hard (a real danger). You might have to negotiate very strongly with the designer to have the relevant orifices enlarged in order to see, hear and breathe better.

Masks can also freeze critical parts of the body which help you produce sound. Neck muscles can tighten from working to keep the mask steady on the face. The jaw can freeze as it works to hold the mask in place. Most actors find that their breath becomes short and panicked behind a mask. Dehydration can occur if you are in the masks for long periods of time and the material from which they are made is not transparent enough. Sweat can roll into eyes and sting you. Shoulders have a habit of lifting and bracing themselves.

Each mask will have a resonant quality. This quality might enhance or hinder your voice. The rehearsal mask might produce a different resonance from the performance mask. As you speak, the sensation coming back on you can be disconcerting and give you a very inadequate sense of how clearly you are speaking.

I hope I haven't put you off wearing masks. As with most problematic obstacles which affect the voice, there are things you can do vocally to survive a mask:

- As soon as you get the mask on, breathe as calmly as you can and as low as you can.
- When you are not speaking, try to breathe through the nose; this will help you not to dehydrate.
- Release the shoulders and try to keep the back of the neck as free as possible.
- Release the jaw and systematically move the lips, tongue and face muscles.
- Move the head around to discover what you can see and hear.
- Warm up your voice in the mask and if you have no one to monitor you, tape the process. This will help you discover what pitch, placing of the voice and articulation works and what is muffled.
- Work to speak long speeches with the mask as you will probably find that what seems to be over-articulation (e.g. ends of words) is barely enough.
- Too much volume in a mask might muffle the whole voice.
- The mask will probably respond to certain pitches and some resonances better than others. Generally speaking, placing the voice into the head resonators works better than the chest. Having said that, there is always a mask that does the reverse.
- Whoever is making the mask must understand that the stiller it is on your head and face, the better. The freer your facial muscles are, the easier it will be to speak.
- Sweat bands built into the mask will stop sweat stinging the eyes.
- After you have removed the mask, release all the articulation muscles, the neck, the shoulders and any tightness of breath.
- Drink water or take steam to rehydrate yourself.

Flying and Abseiling   In the quest for more visually exciting theatre, actors of all ages and shapes are being asked to perform more daring and demanding physical feats on-stage. Abseiling and flying, to mention just two, are now quite common.

Never underestimate the fear you might encounter the first time you attempt one of these feats. The eager actor volunteering to fly in the rehearsal room could easily be shaking in the fly towers overlooking the drop to the stage. Safety harnesses used to support and fly you can be a particular problem for the voice.

Here are some basic tips to remember:

- Keep breathing; the constant and always appropriate advice when you are working with added support is, the lower and slower the breath, the better.
- The harness attached to the ropes must be secure, but this security can stop you breathing. Whenever you can find movement in the breath system, find it. Stomach, back and sides of the rib-cage might have to be worked more. The more support you feel, the safer you will be.
- If you have to speak while being flown, do realize that because your feet are not making contact with any ground the support will have to be more conscious. You might need more articulation to propel the voice. The hardest bit about flying and speaking is not feeling anchored.
- The advantages of flying and speaking often lie in the fact that you have the audience's full attention and focus, so they will strain in order to listen. You can also find that above the stage there is a better acoustic supporting your voice and sending it out.
- It is worthwhile re-centring after you have finished your stunt in the air; this will help relieve any tensions created by both the harness and the sudden lack of floor contact you experienced while in the air.

Stage Fights and Speaking Stage combat is one area of work that few performers will be able to avoid in their work. Any extended physical activity that also involves speaking will probably have to be carefully thought through and choreographed beforehand, then thoroughly worked through in the technical rehearsal. Every time you rehearse the fight, keep contacting the breath and leave room for any words as and when you require them. Always rehearse knowing fully the area and dynamics of the set in which you will be performing: will it be a flat, open area or one cluttered with stairs, a crowd or furniture? A smoke-filled, shadowy space littered with bodies? How and where will you be falling? What protective gear will you need to wear and how will it impede your speaking?

It is likely you will have consciously to place and point where you are to breathe. As soon as you are out of breath, you must concentrate on getting your breath down in order to speak and support. Because of the aggressive nature of fighting, it is very tempting to push the voice in a too athletic way and forget about support. Another hazard is that you can get stuck on one volume level and range during and after the fight. If you are not careful, these vocal trends can linger inappropriately for the rest of a scene.

In combat, jaws can tighten and you will have to be more careful and precise about articulation. This will not only stop you from biting lips, tongue and cheeks, but will have the added benefit of keeping you in control of the word and your breath. If the voice feels tight or pushed, think of a yawn to open it.

Slow all the movement down and mark it as you speak your lines. If you speak when you move, you run the risk of throwing away words and not making sense. The lines will be more effective if they happen in moments of stillness rather than when you are in motion. This can be very dramatic and also allows you to retain the shape of the line and avoids you having to compete over noise.

During the fight, non-verbal sounds can be effective. The organic note for this advice would be that as you fight for survival you wouldn't waste your breath on words. The breath is needed for blows.

You should warm up for the fight before a show *after* a voice warm-up and then always try to re-centre after the fight scene or the show.

When possible, do any and all warm-ups in the space in which you will be performing.

Stage Six
THE PRODUCTION MEETS
AN AUDIENCE

By this point, the actor has been speaking the text largely to fellow actors and a technical crew. Appreciation for what you have been achieving on-stage has largely been from the director – an audience of one.

One of the strange features about the organization of most theatre work is that the actor meets an audience for the first time at the most exhausted moment in the whole work process; after a gruelling and sometimes enervating rehearsal period followed by a sometimes disorienting technical fit-up. By the time an audience comes in for the first preview, the actor has probably been working a twelve-hour day for over a week. It's hard to find the real kind of energy to perform which is not just pure adrenalin.

The first night or press night is even worse. Most actors have to show their work to the critics at their lowest physical and emotional ebb. You have probably not had proper rest for some weeks, depending on how the work has been progressing. In this state of fatigue, accidents easily happen. The growing fear of the press night adds to this. I have known many actors to *change* their voices in the run-up to this all important show, which can sometimes lead to confusion in their playing.

A bad press night can obviously destroy a production, so there is uncommon pressure to get tonight's opening right. Actors sometimes feel so tired that they neglect to warm up properly. Warning: *above all else, please avoid this temptation.* A tired body and voice desperately need a good warm-up.

Pace yourself throughout the day. Eat healthily and avoid too much alcohol. Rest in your dressing-room at every opportunity; legs up on a chair is a very good release. If you are having trouble sleeping – a tense sleep is potentially more exhausting than no sleep – relax before you go to bed. A hot bath helps, as does the legs-on-chair release (see p. 27). Remember that nervousness is dehydrating, so drink plenty of water.

Most domestic affairs in an actor's life come to a grinding halt around technicals and previews. Partners who fail to recognize this will find this period particularly frustrating. It's no accident that marriages break down around the press night of a show. Many actors always get their 'press night cold', or 'the old injury' resurfaces. Stress and psychosomatic aches and pains are common afflictions. The only way to get through this period is to be as gentle with yourself as possible and not to neglect your body and voice.

Basic Voice Warm-Up

The actor assesses the physical demands and technical needs of any show, space, set, text and audience far in advance of performance. As you calculate these needs, you will have to adapt your warm-up accordingly. There is, however, a basic warm-up which I think will keep a voice ticking over in most performance situations. Starting with this basic foundation, you can build into it any extra routines to meet specific challenges.

A very experienced actor said to me before a warm-up session, 'Once upon a time the work kept us fit, now we have to work extra in order to stand still.' What he meant was that there was a time in theatre when a constant repertoire of work kept you ready and warm, from week to week, rehearsing all day and speaking athletic texts each night. The voice was constantly used. Few actors have that regime nowadays. Their vocal work is fragmented and therefore a warm-up before a show is not only necessary but essential. Never go on stage to speak without first warming up.

A warm-up should make you ready but never tire you out. It should prepare the body, breath, voice and speech muscles and also concentrate the mind and heart on the performance ahead. The work is very future-oriented to your first appearance on-stage. All it takes is one actor not concentrating in a company warm-up to destroy the focus and commitment of the whole group. The performers themselves must take charge of the warm-up in order to derive full benefit from this time together.

Many actors like to do a routine they know by rote, so they can put all their energy into the mental and emotional preparation needed to perform. The routine is also a much-needed safety net that they can use to support them through nerves and fear. It's no good doing a warm-up if it doesn't work or becomes an experimental or hit-or-miss affair. Once an exercise achieves its objective, move on to the next. There is no need to do two exercises which achieve the same result.

An ideal time to do a warm-up is one hour before the show; but any warm-up at any time is better than none. You should also be doing this work in the space in which you will be performing. You should allow at least twenty minutes for a proper warm-up. If the warm-up is too relaxed (e.g. too much floor work) or too energized (e.g. like a physical work-out), the actor can lose vital performance energy. Speech work is important during a warm-up but too much of it when an actor is nervous can produce the wrong tension. I always encourage a vocal release after warming up the speech muscles in order to release tension.

The Body

- Centre the body, be very aware of the physical state of readiness we covered in the first stage of our work.
- Weight on balls of the feet.

- Spine up.
- Head balanced on the spine.
- Work any tension out of the shoulders.
- Swing the arms.
- Stretch up and flop over from the waist.
- When you are flopped over, shake the shoulders free and release the back of the neck and the knees.
- Massage the face and release the jaw.
- Smile and open the jaw.
- If you are under-energized, walk or run with focus, stop and feel that moving energy in you.
- If you are very nervous, concentrate on keeping the breath low and your shoulders and upper chest released.
- Move or snake gently through the spine to release the whole body.

The Breath and Support

- Stretch the ribs.
- Side stretches and open the back.
- Do at least three full recoveries on a voiced sound, maybe 'z'.
- Locate the support as low as possible.
- At this point, breathing and pushing against a wall might immediately locate support.
- Spend a few seconds breathing and feeling ready to speak.
- Sustain the support by counting up to 10. Be very aware of feeling the support connect to the voice and that the counting is sustained: the numbers leaving you, sending your voice to a point above eyeline in the room or, if you are in the theatre, to the back of the circle.
- You can use the text of the play for these exercises if you wish, but some actors would rather not and only use neutral words.
- If you are not warming up in the theatre itself, spend a few seconds imagining the space in which you will be performing and breathing the scope of it.

Warm up the Voice

- Start humming gently with support. Don't rush this process and don't try to place the voice forward until you feel it is warm. Actors will invariably push to get the voice forward before it's properly warmed up.

- Pitching a bit higher than your normal speaking voice often warms up the voice faster.
- Stretch and move all your facial muscles.
- Speak on the edge of a yawn with full support.
- Smile, open the jaw, breathe.
- When the voice feels warm, it starts without stickiness.
- Now place the voice forward.
- 'Oo' into 'ah' to a point in the space above eyeline.
- Continue this until you can sustain a release with energy and support over 7–10 seconds.
- At this point it might be good to work the speech muscles with any sequence of sounds that produces agility in the face:
    - Strong 'b', 'd', 'l', 'ng' (add words).
    - 'Th's, 'v' ('many men', 'lily', 'red lorry').
- Overdo vowel sounds, placing them forward in the mouth.
- Mouth a text, making sure you contact every sound written.
- Deliberately get to the ends of words (e.g. wor<u>d</u>, lov<u>e</u>, brin<u>g</u>, ca<u>ll</u>, ho<u>t</u>, ear<u>th</u>).
- Shake and stretch out the whole body.
- Centre the breath and release any shoulder, neck, jaw tension.
- Return to a gentle hum and 'oo' into 'ah'.

Stretch the Range

- Come down from the top of your range to the bottom on 'ah', always thinking up to a point. Keep your head centred.
- Repeat this descent several times before going up through your range, which is always more problematic.
- Speak up and down through your range. Use counting or a text and stay connected to the breath.

Warm up the Resonances

- Hum into the head, nose, face, throat and chest resonances.
- Then speak from each area.
- Intone words, then speak them.
- Feel the full release of the voice.
- Intone and speak.
- Return to centre.
- Stand fully focused and breathe calmly for a minute.
- Enjoy the show!

Adapting the Basic Warm-up

For a Large Theatre:

- Do more sustained breath exercises (e.g. six or seven recoveries).
- For strong support (e.g. over twenty on the breath).
- Make sure you are fully on voice.
- More intoning into speaking.
- Stronger speech definition.
- The same adaptations will apply for an epic or a highly charged emotional text, whatever the space.

For a Dead Acoustic:

- Concentrate on more sustained speaking.
- Work on not pulling off a line or a word.
- Crisper articulation.
- More head resonances.

For a Live Acoustic:

- Support but use it with subtlety.
- Clear and focused placing of the voice.
- Clear articulation but with space around the words.

For a Wordy Text (e.g. Restoration or Oscar Wilde):

- Very athletic articulation.
- Sustained breath for longer thoughts.

For Musicals:

- Physical warm-up with dance.
- Voice warm-up followed by a singing warm-up.

First Preview or First Public Performance

I always say that the most critical audience member you can have is a first-year drama student. Someone who wants to be up there, yet probably knows very little about the cost or the technical snags in playing a tense, opening-night house. So often my students come back from a first preview full of criticism about the actors, mostly to do with their hesitancy, too much care and lack of exuberance. Let's put this critical stage of meeting the audience into perspective.

On the most extreme and alarming level actors can be terrified, not only of meeting an audience and showing their work for the first time, but simply in fear for their lives. Some sets are so dangerous that until you have played them many times you are naturally frightened that if you are in the wrong place at the wrong time your life and limbs are under threat. No wonder the actors appear circumspect.

You can only abandon yourself to a play when you feel safe and familiar with the stage environment. Some performers never play enough public performances in a space to feel fully at ease. It is always a shock when an audience reacts, either positively, negatively, or not at all, to whatever you are doing. The reaction might come in a place you least expect it, causing you to re-examine a line reading or piece of business. Lines can be lost in laughter and focus lost in crowd scenes. Lighting, sound and set cues can go wrong (often do in previews) and throw you off. The pace of the play may drag on far longer than it did in rehearsals and runs. Fellow actors are often tired because of the long tech. What you can do is hold onto the story. Tell the story even if you can't act as freely as you were doing in the rehearsal room because of getting the technical things in place. Communicate the words and the story.

In an ideal situation, a 'word run' in which you focus on the moment-to-moment story is a great warm-up; but if this is not possible, plot your character's story in your head. Suggested warm-ups could include low breathing to combat nerves and energize the voice and focus work.

After a performance, note what has gone right as well as wrong, particularly the technical things you need to clear up and where you could have been more audible. Was it your fault or not, and what can you do about it?

Press Night

A medical study which once monitored actors going on stage on a press night reported that performers experience stress equivalent to that of a major car accident victim! Your fear of critics passing judgement on your work on the basis of one traumatic night out of a long process of work is indeed an awful ordeal to have to submit to.

Tradition has it that a press-night audience is always subdued, as each critic holds his cards to his chest. Actors know that weeks of work can be praised or condemned in the space of a few column inches the next morning. No wonder most actors never read the reviews! Many express doubts that even the very good critics understand anything about the process of theatre, rehearsals, performance or the play. These doubts add tinges of anger to the normal fear of a press night. But it is an ordeal which you have to endure. You will come through it.

Try to rest during the day. Extra adrenalin surging through you will tire you more than you realize. If you are called to rehearse during the day, give yourself time after rehearsal to rest and lie down. Nerves will dry you out more than you know. You will probably need to drink more water than usual. You might not feel like eating, but try to eat in the afternoon, something light, you will need the strength.

Some obvious technical notes for the performance ahead are:

- Breathe as low and as calmly as possible.
- Keep the shoulders as free as you can.
- Keep unclenching the jaw.
- Warm up, calmly doing a lot of centring exercises.
- Avoid very energized exercises as they might unite with the extra nerves and produce the wrong kind of tensions.
- Too energized articulation exercises can over-tense an actor.
- Try to have at least ten minutes or so in silence and just reflect on your character and the journey he or she makes, along with the purpose of the play and why it should be performed.

I've heard many actors discussing nerves before an opening speak about the importance of the play. At the moments of high anxiety we often pull focus onto ourselves; by transferring it to the play you can relieve yourself of all the pressure of the fear connected to ego. As one great actress said to me, 'I always remember that the play and its communication are more important than my fears.'

After the Press Night

This is the moment many actors adore, when they can finally take the play and own it, without a director 'interfering' or a critic to judge it. The moment you really start to find out about a play is working it in front of an audience.

To keep your work fresh, always try to discover more and more about your character and try to enter each show as fresh and as open as possible. Obviously a rich text makes this easier. You can play Shakespeare for years and still discover something new every night. If you do not work on this level and are not prepared to work night after night in the moment with a spirit of discovery, your acting will become stale, your audience patronized and bored, and the job rendered as tedious as work on an assembly line.

The Audience

Audiences will get especially bored and angry if they cannot hear, or in any way feel excluded or attacked. They surely want to be engaged, included, touched and informed. The actor must start with that premise whenever he works before them. After all, your work is ultimately for an audience.

Here are some vocal notes to bear in mind:

- Bodies absorb or deaden the acoustics of a space. Remember this when working in an empty theatre. If your voice just fills an empty space, it will need more energy with an audience.

- An audience should give you the energy to compensate for any deadness, but if they are not listening don't get angry with them. Annoyance will only lead to vocal pushing, which will alienate an audience further. You might consider lifting the volume, energy and commitment of your performance and heightening your vocal variety.

- The audience does not necessarily have to like your character. Don't take this personally. How many plays have been thrown off-balance because an actor fears displeasing an audience. It is a truism that actors want to be liked and many have trouble playing heinous villains.

- Depending on the audience make-up, some accents may be alienating for them. So although the actor is audible, the audience may 'switch off'. Every year I receive a number of complaints about inaudibility which really read, 'I don't wish to sit and listen to that accent.' If the play is dependent on an accent you will have to weather this type of comment.

  Some plays take time to tune an audience's ear to the language and accent (e.g. the stage version of *Trainspotting*). The more obscure the text or extreme the accent, the more it will sound like a foreign language. If this is happening, your instinct might be to rush, but try the opposite: slow down to give the audience a chance to catch up with you. The audience will need time to adjust to the text's difficulties. Changing the range and tone might also prove successful as an audience cannot listen for long to a voice which sounds dull or lifeless.

  It is hard for an audience to switch aurally from loud music or sound effects to the spoken word, from amplified sound to unamplified voice. Different accents within a play can also throw an audience. Varied lighting effects, too, can impinge on hearing and extra clarity and energy will be required to bridge the differences between effects for the audience.

- When you perform very passionate plays, it is possible for an audience to become embarrassed and consequently switch off or laugh in inappropriate places. I suppose it is tempting to lower the tone of a play and work on a less passionate level, but perhaps you should try to stay true to what you are communicating and plough on. Having watched actors stay courageous and true, the audience is generally ennobled and raised to a higher level of listening and acceptance.

- Different types of audience can also be problematic. A play or a production that works in front of a London audience might produce a very different reaction on tour. Young audiences will receive in a different way from adults. A political statement might be well received by a sympathetic audience, then jeered by another. And audiences do jeer.

Actors tell wonderful stories about performing in a highly acclaimed show that suddenly flounders on a corporate evening when the stalls are filled with a completely unsympathetic audience. When Caryl Churchill's *Serious Money*, a sharp, satirical attack on the financial world, transferred from the Royal Court to a West End theatre the actors suddenly found themselves playing to the very yuppies they were attacking. The West End audience – by and large – thought the play was a celebration of them, not an attack, and laughed and enjoyed the play in a new way. For some of the actors, it was very hard to stick to the original intentions of the play because they were enjoying being so well received.

- The important thing to remember is that every audience is potentially different and worthy. One brilliant actor I know always says he never underestimates any audience, because within it could be the producer who will give him his next big break – a note that should be remembered by any actor who might give a tired performance at a matinée in order to save energy for the more 'important' evening show.

It is always astounding to realize how powerful live theatre is and how a performance can profoundly affect members of an audience. Most actors have stories of being stopped in the street, on a bus or train by someone who remembers their performance in a show years ago. Whoever is out there, it is worth your giving your best.

The meeting between actors and an audience is the final marriage of the actor's process. As this marriage occurs, you will have to adopt and play scenes and lines differently. If a pause doesn't work for the audience, you might have to move through it faster. If the audience needs more time to experience a moment, you must be prepared to give it. If they seem to be laughing in the middle of a line and not where you want them to, you will have to push the pace through the line until they laugh where you want it. All comic actors will tell you that timing is actually about *stopping* a laugh and getting on with the play. This requires an energy that drives you on, that will compel the audience to stop laughing and listen to the story. After any audience reaction, you will have to pick up energy anew in order to drive the action forward. Many experienced actors are so pleased with getting a reaction that they let the play sag and sit back. Through any anticipated or unexpected reaction, you need to stay full of energy, then pick up the play with new vigour.

It takes incredible skill and experience to invite an audience to come right down to you. All actors work to achieve that magic moment when everyone in the theatre hangs on every word they speak; but it does take huge technical expertise as well as a fabulous connection to the play and audience to be able to create such a moment.

Finally, a word or two to the audience. You do matter. A receptive, listening audience member is almost as creative as the actor. That reception will be felt and creatively used by the performer who, without any doubt, will feel your response even if it is just rapt attention. Without an audience, theatre does not exist. Shakespeare's audience walked past taverns, brothels and blood sports to get to the theatre. They made a kind of pilgrimage and wanted to be there to listen, to think, to feel, to be changed.

I remember working in an American theatre where on matinées a high percentage of schoolchildren were in the audience. Before the show began, the education officer would talk to the audience and say, 'This show is live. The actors are real and what you are about to see is unique. It will never be repeated in exactly the same form again.' This speech was necessary because actors were leaving the stage having been wounded by missiles from the audience members who were checking out whether they were real.

An audience has a responsibility to be active, alert and aware of the uniqueness of the work they are seeing and hearing. There should be no barrier between the shared experience of watching and performing a play. Shakespeare's actors could see their audience and speak directly to them. Today, with sophisticated lighting, the actor can only feel the audience's state of receptiveness. The more receptive an audience, the better the acting. The correlation is that simple.

Combating Fear

This section could, and maybe should, appear at every stage of the actor's journey. For the actor, fear arises every working day:

- On the first day of training.
- The first reading of a play.
- The first poem spoken.
- The first song sung.
- At auditions.
- At previews.
- At press nights.

Fear is a minefield which every performer has to tread his or her way through and you all have to cope to a lesser or greater degree with it in order to get through a career. It's doubtful that fear ever leaves you. In fact, many actors would feel incomplete, uninspired and under-energized without it. Drugs that deaden fear will deaden the performance. Musicians seem to be able to play with, say, beta blockers, but actors lose their edge.

I think it's true to say that the actor gets used to this constant state of nerves and some even look forward to it – and need it. Mostly, actors cope. However, there are some occasions when the fear and nerves can overwhelm the actor and result in true stage fright. Press night is such an occasion – all that work that has been done is being judged in a single performance – or an understudy going on, or the audition that could change your professional life, or the audience with a particular member, or the first day of rehearsal. These and other events can produce a fear that it seems will swamp and overwhelm you physically and emotionally. The body will shake, the line can get lost, the voice wobbles and the head spins.

I am not an expert on stage fright or a therapist who can counsel a performer who has hit bottom out of fear, but as a voice coach I do have to help actors cope, get on and perform through agonizing and paralysing worries. There are techniques you can apply, either physically or intellectually, which might help get you through a bout of stage fright.

The Physical Techniques

- Fear literally seems to lift us up off the ground. The shoulders go up, the chest rises and the breath gets higher and higher, faster and faster. We are, of course, walking on the earth but it is all too easy not to feel grounded. The heart speeds up, the brain races, the sweat pours and panic can set in. The body dehydrates rapidly, the more we sweat. Fear can make us feel nauseous and unable to perform any task. We are weakened by it. Physically we are on the verge of hysteria.

- When this occurs, drink more water and try to eat something light as you will need the strength. Doing a set routine warm-up is both comforting and a form of security; it will shift your energy into a less blocked position. It also will stop you concentrating on yourself in a negative way. I always find warm-up a way of instilling positive thoughts in the actor.

- If it really feels too awful for you to do even a warm-up, lie on your back in the dressing-room with your legs up, supported by a chair under the calf muscles. In this position, the shoulders will release, as will the jaw, the spine, the pelvic area. Work on getting the breath down into the body – breathe as slowly as possible, low, unrushed breaths. Slow the whole system down. Really breathe out, wait for the breath and let it come back in its own time.

- When you warm up, concentrate particularly on centring the body and releasing the shoulder. Get the spine up and the jaw, lips and tongue free. Open up the lower breath, the back of the rib-cage and the abdominal area. Breathe slowly and try to do most recoveries through the nose, which will calm you. Spend time feeling the support and the readiness to speak.

- One of the most destructive aspects of nerves is that they force the actor to speak before he or she is ready. You find yourself snatching breaths, speeding up and consequently losing control. Really invest in feeling the right to breathe and the readiness of the breath position.

- Work the first few lines that you have to speak with that security of breath and support. It might be useful to build up the words with the breath, one by one.
- Most importantly, take your time.
- Do some articulation exercises before warming the voice. If you are very nervous and you do articulation after the vocal release exercise, the speech work can freeze you again, panic you.
- One of the manifestations of fear is gabbling, or allowing a text to push down on you, run ahead of you and reduce you. It is like a huge weight on your head. With this in mind, the more you can define and sustain every word and thought, the more you will fight through nerves. Hold on to the physical nature of the word. By holding on to the physical make-up of each syllable and thought, you can cling onto the rock-face, not fall off, climbing up and over your fear. Define, define, define as you speak. Breathe and use the text as the physical handholds that will get you through. You will only lose control when you fail to breathe and physically to speak the word.

Before the Show

- If you can, walk around the performance space and own it. Think of it as your space and that you have a right to be there. The audience is visiting you.
- Walk through the auditorium, sit on the seats and experience where the audiences will be seated and viewing you.
- Stand in the wings, breathe and walk on. Do this with all your entrance points.
- Handle the set and the props.
- Acquaint yourself with the physical space that houses the fear. Walk through the fear, breathing all the time.

Here are some additional 'tricks' which other actors have suggested as their ways of coping with fear:

- Believe that the story of the play is more important than your nerves.
- Try to conjure up a real passion to tell the story and a desperation to get on with it. Feel excited to tell a story as you are waiting to go on.

- Think of the audience not as an enemy, but as a friend who wishes you well and wants you to give a great performance.

- Imagine all those actors before you throughout history who were also nervous and fearful. See ahead to all those to come and allow those thoughts, like a wave, to carry you on. You are part of a chain. You are not the first to feel this fear, nor are you the last.

- Concentrate on the first moment in the performance, don't worry about the whole. Really take yourself only as far as that first thought, breath, word and just deal with these in isolation from the rest of the play.

- Many actors talk about visualizing a space and, with that picture, imagining walking into it.

- In other religious cultures, actors will say grace or a prayer to a space as part of a ritual that embraces, among other things, fear. I've known many actors and dancers who perform a ritual of grace to the space to bless the space before they work it. The ritual helps dispel fear.

- Finally, and most potently, when engulfed by fear stop and ask yourself the question, 'Do I really want to do this?' Mostly, your answer will be 'yes'. Even saying 'yes' to yourself will empower you and help you find a corridor through the fear. I've known many retired actors who finally surrendered to fear and said 'no' to that question. They found themselves pursuing careers far away from the stage.

Stage Seven
RE-CREATING THE WORK AGAIN AND AGAIN

Opening in a production probably feels like the hardest hurdle the actor faces, but you could find the possibility of a long run equally difficult. Recreating your work and finding it fresh and interesting each time you perform is a craft of its own.

Reviews, particularly poor ones, might be hard to work through. But even a good review might tempt you to play the *review* rather than the play. You must constantly return to the text for inspiration and guidance. A bad text, a text lacking dimension, will always be harder to keep fresh, so you'll have to do more work on it. A fine, well-written play with lots of depth will always offer new finds in terms of the language even after years of acquaintance. You will be certain to find new gems every night if you have worked deeply enough on owning the words.

The Long Run

Because there is a frantic dash through technicals, previews and the press performance, many problems only become apparent after the play settles into a run. Here are some of them. Check these points to see if you are working in the moment:

- Try to discover something fresh in each scene every show.
- If something doesn't work, take note and try to rectify it.
- Constantly chip away, honing the play and your part night after night.
- If you don't get a laugh where you have had one for most

performances, feel disconnected, or start to lose contact with other actors, work on it to explore where the energy is severing contact.
- Stay interested in the play and the process of work.
- Always remember the audience. There is somebody out there who doesn't know the story and who will be changed by the work.
- Use repetition as a refining energy, always moving towards the most apt and effortless performance.
- If the text no longer inspires you, use all your technique to make it as believable as possible.

If you become cynical about what you are doing during a run, it will be murder to your soul. Always use the experience of playing as an exercise to improve all facets of your craft. Timing, pace and audience communication can forever stand improvement. Think of it as a way of testing yourself rather as a good chef can make a passable meal from poor ingredients.

The Patchy Run

Some theatre companies have several shows working in a rep system at any given time. This is the way the Royal National Theatre operates its shows. This scheduling can mean you have a patchy run, playing the show in short bursts of, say, two weeks with days or even weeks out. Most actors hate this system. They lose momentum and connection to the text. In the same way it is easier to speak many lines as opposed to two lines in a show – the instrument is being used and exercised – it is hard to have time off and come back to a part. It seems to be more exhausting and is always harder to pace yourself. In the time off, keep working out your voice. The day before you return to the play, work the text. Visualize your moves. Plot your intellectual and emotional journey. Remember the original energy needed to play the part. There should be a line-run with the whole cast the afternoon of the come back, but if there isn't, speak your text aloud at least once all the way through and do a thorough warm-up before the performance.

The Short Run

It is relatively easy to pace yourself through a short run. There is only one potential difficulty in the short run, which probably affects a young, inexperienced performer more than the seasoned actor: you can get through a short run on a false and uneconomic amount of energy. You could, during a short run, do things to your voice, body and emotional energy which would be damaging and destructive to you through a long run. Knowing a show is coming to an end after just a few weeks, you might be tempted to risk things you shouldn't be risking. For example, you might push too far emotionally and vocally, or risk your voice with screams without support. Amateur actors will sometimes wreck themselves in a week, knowing that they have a year to recover. You cannot do that as a professional and hope to survive.

When tempted to be reckless, always ask yourself :

- Could I do this short-cut – normally a technical short-cut – and survive for a year?
- How much emotional drain of this kind could I take?
- Should my voice feel like this after three days?

Be honest and try to right anything technical that feels wrong or exerts pressure on you.

I think most trainers in drama schools know that their training – mostly for economic reasons – cannot give students a real sense of pacing themselves through a long run. But it is important to impress on young actors that a long run will draw on many skills and techniques that only regular practice will instill.

Take-overs – Can I Be Creative?

In taking over someone else's part, particularly someone who may have made that part his or her own, is there room for a fresh actor to be creative? The answer is yes, although your creativity might be pinned down and you might have to be extra imaginative to feel fulfilled.

When you take over in a show for someone, you will be required to act a part in a manner similar to the performer who originated it. You might get two weeks, one week or two days of rehearsal. The director might help you or the assistant director will rehearse you. You can be pretty sure you'll be getting lots of suggestions from the cast as to how to play it!

You might be the only take-over, or it could be part of or the whole cast, which will be a more creative and exciting prospect. You will have to fit into sets, costumes, moves, pace and often timing created by someone else. You will have to fill someone else's decisions, work within another actor's shadow. Even if the moves are set, you can do a lot of work on ownership of the words. Rehearse at home on the moment-to-moment experience of the text. Because the rehearsal period will be short, the text might be harder to learn because you won't be working the text gradually and organically. Intone, mouth, breathe it, generally play with the text. Rehearsals will be very practical and to the point, so all experimentation will have to happen on your own, probably at home.

At best, a take-over can revitalize a production, pump new blood into it. At worst, you might suspect that the old company resents anything new you might be offering to the part because it affects the way they play their roles. Compromise might be necessary. Try to stay true to the text and serve the play, but respect the work of your fellow artists.

Understudying

Understudies do go on. In a big company you can expect at least one actor 'going on' for another every two weeks. No actor likes being off but it seems that with the increase of air-conditioned buildings, hi-tech shows and large companies sharing dressing-rooms and their viruses, as an understudy you may frequently go on.

Perversely, audiences love it. Perhaps it is the scent of blood, an actor being thrown to the lions, or a sense that the theatre is really live and something unusual might happen. The first performance by an understudy is often very good as a new shot of adrenalin surges through the whole company. Everyone is on guard and out to help the understudy. The test is when and if you go on again. The theatrical joke is that a successful performance by an understudy will be the boost for the ailing actor to get back on stage!

The brief of an understudy is to play the part as closely as possible to the performance of the original cast member. Wondrous flights of fancy and imagination will not be appreciated by other cast members or the technical crew. Besides, any deviation might result in a close encounter with the scenery!

The hard, unpleasant fact could be that you have not had an understudy rehearsal, let alone a dress run. Invariably you might get a day's notice that you are going on, you might even only get an hour's notice or five minutes, or you might have to go on half-way through a show.

What understudies need to bear in mind:

- Know your lines.
- Know the staging.
- Watch as many rehearsals as possible.
- Watch the technical.
- Watch all dress rehearsals.
- Try to see the show, as often as possible from out front.

- If you are not in the show, work on stage vocally and physically to walk and test the space whenever you can.
- Become familiar with the set, props, costumes, wigs, etc.
- Be thoroughly immersed in the show.
- When you are given an understudy role, assume you will go on.

The fear I've seen grip an understudy about to go on is astonishing to behold. There are certain exercises you can do to calm yourself, centre the adrenalin and survive:

- Breathe as low as you can. Take as much time as you need for the breath to get in.
- If you are shaking, re-centre by lying on your back with your legs up. Don't do this immediately prior to your entrance as it can drain your energy; do it half an hour before.
- Warm up thoroughly and with the company if you can.
- Constantly release shoulders, neck and jaw tensions.
- Open your back; this can be done in the wings. That is, hug yourself and breathe into the back. This is the most efficient and immediately calming activity.
- Control the text. Always feel the support before speaking and the word in the mouth. These two points of tension will keep you in control.
- On stage, play each moment, don't conceptualize the whole scene or play. Working moment to moment will help you to focus.
- If something goes wrong, don't brood on it; cancel it out and move on.
- Think the space, be clear and tell the story. You might not give a great performance but if you are reaching the audience, are audible and communicate the plot, you've served your function.

After the show you can be sure that nothing in the theatre will be so nerve-racking again and you can be pleased that you've survived.

Waiting to Speak

'I have to wait on stage for two hours before speaking my one line. How do I do this?' asks an actor whose first speech is not until the second half of the play. To speak one line or be on-stage throughout a show, seemingly doing nothing, is harder than playing a central role. At least if you have a lot to say, your voice stays active and free, it gathers momentum rather than freezing or locking.

If you only have one line to speak or are waiting for two hours before going on, or worse, are on throughout but silent for a long period, you can easily forget to breathe. The expectation of the line or the entrance can grow in magnitude and feed your nerves. After all, it's easy to think that you only have one chance and it had better be good. The long wait can lead you to deliver the line or mark the entrance with too much vigour. You push your way into the play rather than become a part of it.

There are things you can do to help eliminate this. Keep breathing and stay as centred as possible. Try and stay in contact with the play by listening to it rather than worrying about your own specific role. Effectively, this takes the pressure off you and places you into the play. Keep consciously active by staying in contact with your support. If you find yourself drifting off, reconnect yourself to the breath. Avoid getting misty in the eyes, middle-distance focus. Look and listen. You will look and stay active as you partake in the play. If you are waiting to go on for hours, stop whatever you are doing at least fifteen minutes before your entrance and centre. Shake out and listen to the play. You don't want to drift into a daze.

'How Do I Take a Prompt?'

At some time in your career you will dry or forget a line and maybe have to take a prompt. I am always relieved when a terrible dry happens in training an actor, so he can experience the horror early enough to learn to deal with it. When you dry, take note as to what happened to you physically and mentally at that moment. This knowledge will protect you when it happens again. Perhaps your mind was on something else other than the play. Perhaps something happened to you that day which put you off. There may be a very good reason why you suddenly forgot. There may be something, too, about this part of the text which you have never fully resolved.

There are now directors who discourage the taking of a prompt. Their argument is that if the actor has really worked, understood and owned the text, even if she dries she will be able to find her way back into a speech or scene. I think this is true, but there are always occasions when the actor will not find his or her way back to the script. It is true that if you know a text well and suddenly forget it, if you breathe, let the breath drop low into your body, giving your thoughts and feelings oxygen, then generally you will recall the line. You might have to go back to the beginning of the thought. You might have to wait, keeping the breath fluid.

Dries normally happen during previews or the first performance. In certain plays it is impossible to wait and reconnect to a text. The action has to move on and cannot wait: farce, musicals, a scene when a cue is urgently needed to set a technical one in motion. In these and other situations, to wait would be detrimental to the progression of the story. If you dry, ask for your cue and go on.

Actors take prompts differently. Some will say 'line', others wait for the stage manager to recognize the pause as a dry and give a prompt. The latter method can be problematic as you might be pausing and waiting for a moment, only to receive an unwelcome prompt. The best policy is to negotiate with the stage manager on how you might be prompted. For instance, if you are confident that your pauses will be regulated, the prompt can be on any unnaturally long pause. Otherwise, opt for requesting the line.

Throwing Away Lines

Many actors talk about throwing away a line. In essence, this means that you underplay a line, often for comedy, and consequently change the energy of your voice. It is not as easy as it sounds. Many unskilled speakers will throw away a line and be merely inaudible.

If you listen to a wonderful technician throw away a line, you will hear every word. In fact, it will require more energy, definition and placing than the text around the line still to be audible. The effect you are going for is to go under the speaking energy of the scene. This is very hard to do in a theatre that has a dead acoustic. In these kinds of spaces, to throw away a line will need a different approach. You will have to use a very perverse technique to gain the same effect. Instead of going under the scene you will have to lift your vocal energy above it, then return to the original level of the scene.

Whichever option you choose – to go vocally under or over a scene – you must always leave and return to the original vocal energy cleanly. If you don't, the effect will be lost. You will know you've failed if the audience fails to react. If going under fails, go over and vice versa.

Pulling Focus in a Crowd Scene

Crowd scenes are potentially problematic for audibility because there is so much going on. If you have to speak with activity all around you, the audience might miss your line because they are trying to find the speaker in the throng. It could take several words before they locate you and in the process they may miss the lines. So you have to pull focus in your direction.

There are stagecraft techniques that might sound unreal and 'hammy', but could prove useful. A definite movement before you speak attracts the eye. A noise before you speak attracts the ear. The image I give – which could be more organic to the scene – is to charge up your vocal energy as if you were taking a baton in a relay race. You've got to catch the moment securely. More support, voice and articulation will be needed, if only for the first few words, to give the audience time to adjust to you.

I recently worked on a play that is so busy with acting traffic that until the actors grasped each line with conviction and energy, twenty per cent of the text was destined to be lost. Some of the actors found adding action in order to pull focus was difficult because they were all audible. The production was set in a very wide traverse and the audience was made to follow the play rather like spectators at a Wimbledon tennis final. At times, there were eighteen separate actors on stage at any one time, each with some business or line to speak. Pulling focus was the only way to draw attention and also serve the play. The actors had to learn to pass and catch the vocal ball with enormous vigour and clarity if they wanted their work to be heard.

Overcoming Noise When Speaking

Paradoxically I've left this problem until last because it was my encounter of noise on-stage which led to an understanding of how useful stagecraft and the voice could be. I remember playing a scene as a student where I had to bang the table and speak at the same time. The acting teacher told me I was inaudible. I thought he was trying to stop me being 'real' and 'emotional' and I became enraged. He then told me that he was making a point. I should bang the table but time it so that the audience could also hear the words.

For some reason that simple tip, delaying the noise on either side of the line, taught me my first major lesson about stagecraft. It merely enables the audience to be included in all your acting decisions. It focuses the work and allows ideas to be read physically.

When I banged the table over my speaking it merely confused the audience. Nothing but generalized emotion was being communicated. You can apply the same note to speaking, walking or running noisily. You will either have to walk more quietly, use a clearer voice or time yourself differently. Sometimes a set is so noisy from competing effects or the texture of the floor (e.g. gravelled ground) that you will have to find moments of stillness in which to speak.

After the Job has Finished Growing

At a closing night party, as the wine flowed, a director started to give an actor notes. There was much hilarity as the actor turned and said, 'I don't want the notes, it's over.' Well, it was and it wasn't. I worked with that same actor some weeks after the party. He was rueful: 'I wish I had listened to those notes. I could've learned something.'

In order to build on your work, for it to mature, you must assess each job after it has finished. The job of acting never stops, learning about the craft of performing never ceases. You are always looking for ways to fill in the gaps in your physical, vocal and imaginative technique. Time will give you a perspective on the experience. You need to erase the work, yet return to it. Move on, yet take the experience with you. Ask yourself what went right. Also ask what went wrong.

It seems true to say that the good experiences are harder to analyse, but they do keep you wanting to do more and to keep working. Perversely, the bad experiences can teach you more solid lessons about your technique, your ability to survive and your relationships with other actors and the director.

At the end of a production, give yourself a break, then reread the play. How did the production serve the play? What was released, what was missed? How did the director serve the play, the actors, the space? How did the design aid or deter the production? How did *you* serve the production, the play, the character? These questions can become very specific and for me a great window into your voice and speech work. Did my body, voice and speech serve the play, the space and my creative and imaginative input? If you answer 'no' to any of these questions, then it's time to look at your technique. It could mean you have to return to the early stages of work in order to find answers. Any area of your work which left you unsatisfied should be examined in detail for flaws in technique.

The Experience of Actors

Here are a few brief case histories relating to the above; each one a recent work-related story I have experienced in my work with actors:

An actress working with me now does so because in her last show she felt she didn't have the breath to serve either the text, her own emotional connection to her character or the space. 'Every breath was a struggle. There was never any ease. I just fought with the part every day.' As we work, it is becoming apparent that she has never done any basic breath work. Her role was the first theatre job after leaving drama school. She has had to start from the very beginning of the technical voice work, the opening pages of this book. As her breath and support improve, she is also finding her natural voice. She had no foundation upon which to build her work and only by being honest about her failure is she repairing that fundamental drawback in it.

Then there is the actor who had one section of a play he was doing every night which constantly hurt his voice. 'I dreaded the approaching line.' Basically his technique was good, except he needed to open his throat fully and work on the extended voice exercises. As is the case with many well-trained actors, he had a fine technique but a small tension which had never surfaced before raising its head on one emotionally charged line. Interestingly he had mostly played very cool, laid-back characters. This was the first time in the theatre he was challenged to be emotionally disturbed. A small throat tension that had been allowed to exist without a problem because he had never had to stretch himself to those charged moments was suddenly exposed. He had a tight back of tongue. He needs now really to experiment with extended voice exercises finally to put his fear at rest. Any hurting voice is more worrying than other technical failings as it could damage the actor's voice and career.

One actor I worked with was described by his wife as dull (family criticism is always worse than the critics'). A TV actor who was returning to the stage for the first time in years and having to speak a heightened text, he just could not do it. He possessed good basic technique but no sense of vocal range. All he needs to do is work on range exercises, then experiment with using range and dispelling his own notion that he's going too far!

There was the actress who realized she was very vocally unsubtle in her last show. 'I just didn't trust myself and pushed and pushed and pushed.' Friends said that they were pinned to their seats by her voice. Basically she had a good technique and a very strong voice – if she hadn't had this strength, all the pushing could have destroyed it. She simply didn't trust her own technique enough. As we work, I realize that she has done very little text work. She had no concept of owning words, sensing their weight or physical power. Connecting the word to the breath is something she is not sensitive to doing. The director never gave her a note during the rehearsal so she had no sense of what to do. At drama school she was always praised for the power of her voice, so when in doubt she pushes and uses her voice as a weapon and a defence. The lack of subtlety was her panic about being ignored by the director and disconnected from the word. Stage Three work was all she needed.

Recently I worked with an actor who had had a long career as a radio actor. He had what he termed 'a beautiful voice'. He came for lessons because in a foray onto the stage he realized that his body was unfocused. 'I pointed a lot, fidgeted and flapped my arms.' His voice was good, but his body was out of shape; flabby, uncentred and lacking any sense of readiness. He had to go back to all those early body exercises – centring, readiness and support. He didn't need voice, range or speech work, but he built up his physical confidence with work on physical transformation and the free voice. To be physically clear on-stage, you need to be in your body, aware of it and centred with low support. None of the above is necessarily required in radio where you are invisible to the audience.

I am reminded of the young actor with a strong, clear, well-placed voice, but who was called inaudible in a review. Actually he was incoherent (critics often confuse the two). His diction – the articulation and definition of the work – was non-existent. Speech work was all he needed.

How about the actor whose agent said his voice had damaged his career? He had been playing an upper-class boy but his 'London sounds' had scuppered him. His voice was fine, his RP non-existent and because he had tried to get RP quickly through the rehearsal period it had sounded cosmetic and false. Not only did he learn RP, but he had to connect it to his breath and voice and to live in it emotionally before it sounded real rather than acquired.

Lastly, there was an actor who had been savaged by the press for his lack of verse-speaking skills. Within a few minutes it became apparent that no one had ever worked with him on verse. Not only had the director not spoken about it, but he had gone through drama school without ever hearing 'iambic pentameter' mentioned or the difference between verse or prose. Hard to believe but, I think, true. We worked on the iambic, the line, the length of thought. He was delighted to learn the rules if only consciously to break them.

Back to Basics

Every time you go back to the basic exercises described in Stages One to Three the work becomes more known and more profound, yet simple and more a part of you. Returning to basics after each job adds layer after layer to your craft and your voice. Life is enhancing your voice and your artistry, and the basic work you continue to do will enable you to understand the textures of your voice.

'Resting'

Only a few, highly successful actors welcome a rest. Even after performing in the most critically lauded roles, actors still fear that they will never work again – and some don't! When I audition young students for Guildhall straight from school, I often advise them to 'take a year off – travel'. The advice is relevant on many counts not least of all for some life experience, but it is important to realize that the year off travelling might be a young actor's last holiday for years. Even when not working, actors are terrified of going away in case they miss that phone call, that audition. No wonder an actor's family life suffers!

There is mounting evidence that one of the reasons actors suffer depression when not working is they are off a drug – adrenalin. Every time an actor performs, he or she is boosted by a shot of this most powerful drug. Out of work, their bodies crave it. It seems the same is true of soldiers who leave the army and the excitement of action. However you look at it, 'resting' is depressing and an inappropriate word. Waiting and anticipating are more accurate words.

Working on your own – body, voice and text work – is hard. By nature, actors are social animals. You work in an art form that requires people and interaction. It's hard not to be jealous of friends who are working and doing well, especially when they are your contemporaries. The most well-balanced actors I know have interests and passions outside the theatre. Any creative animal is curious; other knowledge can only enhance the work. They also have non-theatre friends so that there are social niches where they do not feel threatened or can resort to carping on about their agents – a common 'resting' topic of conversation.

Try to do some physical working-out on a regular basis. This seems to lessen the adrenalin-withdrawal symptoms. Work out the voice at least three times a week. Keep it fit so that it's ready for immediate action. Read out aloud every day. Remember that you have many skills that benefit society as well as keeping you working on yourself and safeguarding a sense of self-worth.

Be aware that although a regular vocal work-out will keep the voice ticking over, you will need at least ten days of a strong work-out to get the voice up to performance standard if you haven't worked for several months. So when you get to your next theatre job, build in some preparation time before rehearsals begin. Attend classes when you can.

If actors are ridiculed by laymen as not being artists, it is because some do treat their work casually and never really improve. The advice I'm giving would be given to any dancer or musician. Actors have a reputation of being lazy and there is a part of the business that can survive with the 'I just go on and do it' attitude. There are a small number of actors who have reached a degree of success without ever working on themselves. But these kinds of actors are in the minority. Good actors work because they love it. They care enough really to push themselves to their limits and it is at the 'resting' period of their lives that they have to face the real problems in their work, and that is the moment to choose to go on through into a richer landscape. It is the time when you can learn new skills, read plays, question how you use your voice, question your acting habits, your commercial viability, get fit . . . give up smoking.

I remember one student who was very talented but never worked: a very charming, amiable man. Even as a student, he wanted to be in theatre for the glamour (although there is very little glamour in theatre) and the parties. He managed to get invited to all the most important parties. He flitted everywhere and was so busy investing in the party circuit that he never improved. He didn't survive as an actor. The work was too hard. I still meet him at parties and he's become a very successful agent.

Auditions

Auditions can be more frightening than a press night. One audition can transform an actor's career for ever. They can be even more problematic because the actor hasn't been working for a period of time and has become not only physically and technically rusty but has not had to deal with the onset of nerves and fears.

It used to be that most jobs were gained by means of an audition piece. Actors would have a repertoire of speeches which could be trotted out whenever needed. The audition piece or pieces are still required for certain jobs and the initial break into the profession from drama school, but they are losing their importance.

Auditions used to be a 'me' versus 'them' situation: the audition panel nestling in the dark and the actor on stage, exposed and yet perhaps strangely safe in the formality of distance and a known audition piece. It's more likely now that auditions take the form of reading the part to be cast, working it with the director and discussing the play and ways of working. The latter method could involve the actor in sight-reading, a discussion of processes or work that will test the actor's potential flexibility and his or her knowledge of the play.

Technical Preparation for an Audition

Warm up! If you haven't worked for a period of time, this might have to be very thorough. If you have a few days' warning of an audition, work out every day. If you have been given a play and a part to look at, work it all thoroughly and remember to read the text out loud. You can't prepare silently. Read around the subject of the play and investigate any other work by the playwright. Acquaint yourself with any important themes that are broached in the play.

Recently I heard a wonderful director bemoaning an audition day when he was looking at actors for a Shaw play. Not one of the actors had heard of the Fabians. The director felt it was impossible to work with such ignorance.

If the audition doesn't specify a play, you will probably be asked to do an audition piece or sight-read. I can't emphasize enough the importance of sight-reading as a skill. You should have a wide selection of audition pieces, covering not only different aspects of your talent but different styles of writing (e.g. verse, prose, dialect, ancient, modern, etc.). I suppose it's always difficult to know what a director or a casting director is looking for, so the more choice you give them in your pieces the greater the chance that you will fit the bill. One kind of performer whom directors really search for is someone who is flexible.

I have recently had a spate of comments from directors that should concern younger actors. Directors speak more than ever about how hard it is to talk to younger actors; that the latter are sometimes indifferent or unable to discuss work with any joy or flexibility. It is as though basic communication skills in an audition are not fully appreciated by the younger generation of actors. You must remember that the easier and more open you are to work with, then the more likely it is a director will feel able to work with you. This is a first key to success as an actor.

Be imaginative as you approach auditions. Work up any accent that might be required and be prepared to use the accent in the audition. Tune up your body or your singing voice if either will be needed. Keep breathing and stay as centred as possible before the audition. Aim to arrive in plenty of time at the location so you have time to settle yourself. Carry water, as dehydration is often an issue.

Remember that any director worth working for will be wanting you to do well. No one wants to see you fail. If the audition is a brutal, cattle-market affair, they are looking for a very specific type, which doesn't require proper artistic talent; product instead of talent is being assessed. So it's not a reflection on you if you get cut. In any case, if the audition is that brutal the job will probably be equally soul-destroying. One of the least appealing aspects of being an actor is constantly having to deal with rejection. Even famous actors go through this regularly. It can be a weekly dose which you'll have to swallow. Rejection is a fact of theatrical life. Actors are not in short supply. All you can do is prepare as well as you can, be open, willing and care about the text. If you are rejected you have to get up again, shake off the rejection and carry on working on your technique. 'Get back on your feet' is always the best advice.

Learn from any audition. On the simplest level, take note where any physical tensions have gripped you – where your weaknesses lie – and afterwards work on those tensions to banish them. Was your sight-reading fluent enough? Were you relaxed enough to have a conversation with the director? High levels of stress and tension will expose all your weaknesses. Take note and deal with any that you discover.

Lastly, try to transfer your energy from you – the 'I' – to the text. If stress makes you collapse around yourself and become too self-obsessed, you can produce an ugly energy that is not an attractive prospect to work with or explore. Many talented actors never work because they appear aggressive and aloof at auditions. This aggression is generally a product of fear but can really turn off a director who will instantly wonder: 'Can I work with this actor?'

The Multi-media Actor

At the risk of sounding prejudiced, I do think that a trained stage actor is the real thing. Even if the actor rarely 'treads the boards' and is whisked off to fame in Hollywood, the fact that she has stage work in her background means she will have faced the ultimate test of a performer: played a play, from beginning to end, in front of a live audience. The actor will have acquired the skills and energy to sustain a part in space.

It also seems to me that the skills needed to do the above can easily be honed to work in front of a camera or microphone. But an actor untrained or unfamiliar with theatre cannot easily make the transition from the film set to the stage. Sadly, many of us work by taking short cuts and it is important to understand that the full, harder and more profound training that stage actors receive cannot be done quickly or cheaply. The craft is developed over time and through many different kinds of roles. Train for the theatre and you can apply and focus these skills in any direction.

At a time when solid craft work is disappearing, when society is not only becoming less supportive of training artists but also offering fewer opportunity in any field of self-expression, and provincial theatres and rep companies – for two centuries the breeding ground of fine, technically tuned actors – are fast disappearing, actors are ironically pressured to be more skilled and diverse in more media. Actors must now have multi-media skills.

A working day for many actors might consist of a voice-over in the morning and rehearsal in the afternoon of a naturalistic play to be played in a small theatre. In the evening, he could be playing a classic in a huge house like the Olivier, then shooting a scene early the next day in

Scotland for a television series. It might sound far-fetched, but this kind of pattern is very common for many working actors. And you have to take the work when it comes your way so you must stay open to this kind of variety. You merely have to list the skills required over that forty-eight hour period to realize how much a good actor needs to understand and have proper techniques in order to perform.

Placing the voice and timing a voice during rehearsal with sub-text, then in the evening playing at full belt with full technique blazing and with a completely different connection to the word, then finally getting a take right after doing it again and again while technicians light you, exerts huge pressure on you. Add to this all the skills of body miking, working in different clothes, spaces, with different styles of language, using dancing and singing, tumbling, fighting and learning acres of text year in and year out, and you have a fair idea of the sorts of skills and work required to allow even the best-known actors to live and earn a decent wage.

For the actor who doesn't have regular work, to keep oiled and ready for it is even harder. The voice loves to be used and if it is not used regularly it can quickly rust over. Ideally, an actor should be trained vocally for the theatre using classical texts. I and others work this way because we intend to keep a tradition alive, and we know it is the best experience for an actor.

Even if you never want to act in theatre or perform the great texts, test yourself in this area. It can only enrich your whole technique. It seems obvious to me, but many young American actors are amazed to learn that all of Britain's best film actors trained in theatre. The large truth required for theatre demands technical strength, skill and imagination. To reduce is easy, to expand much more problematic.

I recently had the enormous pleasure of doing voice work with an American film director who was acting in London. He was intrigued to discover how actors fill a large theatre without the aid of a microphone. As we worked in space he became more and more excited as he started to feel a connection with the theatre, a connection not only to do with the voice and breath but with imagination, thought and feeling. He immediately started to relate this to working on camera. We then started to play a very simple game. First he spoke a section of text to be communicated to the whole theatre and then brought it down to communicate to an imaginary camera. We both got excited because what the exercise proved was that when one brought the energy down to the intimacy of the camera, but retained the imaginative energy of the stage performance, the work for camera became a focused distillation unobtainable without prior understanding of what the theatre had required.

After playing this game for a while, the director looked at me and said, 'This is very interesting. I'm beginning to understand why great theatre actors are so clear and complete.' The game gave me a new exercise for my students: fill the space with a speech, then immediately do the same piece for the camera.

Working any of the great texts will not only stretch you physically but will stretch your passions, your brain and your humanity – all good stretches for the artist. We are rapidly becoming a society that communicates better through the Internet, television and radio rather than one on one through the word. You cannot be without too many newly learned skills today. These skills can become part of a craft that will liberate your talent and give you more chances to work in a rapidly developing multi-skilled media world.

Microphones

Most actors now train and use microphones constantly. An actor's everyday experience will involve miking. The incredible technological sophistication of even inexpensive miking equipment makes this area of technological sophistication something every actor should know about. Generally, theatre, film and television sound technicians are so skilled that most of an actor's old worries about, say, a body mike are now unnecessary. When I think back to the first experience I had working on miked musicals, I am lost in sheer admiration of the advances in the quality of sound we have nowadays. Sound can now be wonderfully balanced in all kinds of space and with an orchestra. However, there are a few worries and misconceptions I regularly get from performers:

- The microphone is not a great gift for the voice, in fact it can expose flawed technique ruthlessly. Every breath you take is amplified and exposed. Every non-verbal sound is heard. A gulp, a gasp, any vocal tic is read and heard. Anything in your voice or presentation reads. Every sound, even unintentional ones, become important. Your vocal technique, on one level, has to be even better than it is without amplification.
- Most microphones boost you over difficult spaces, music or sound effects. It is not a licence to ease off work. You should be doing technically whatever the space demands vocally and use the microphone to ease the effort or fight the noise. There are some conditions and musical instruments which the human voice can deal with unaided, with others you need the microphone. When miking came into musicals it was because the musical orchestration had enlarged to such a point that the unamplified human voice could no longer cope or compete. Normally, the human voice can rise above string or woodwind instruments, but it can't compete with a huge brass section, percussion or amplified electronic music. In these situations, the actor cannot sit back and not use technique. The mike should bond with your voice to give you an even chance.
- Many sound effects are amplified. To ask the human voice to come in after amplification, after a huge electronically boosted sound, is possible but perhaps unfair. The audience has to adjust very quickly from amplification to a natural sound. Again, you still have to work to enable the balance between your voice and the amplified sound effect to be effective.
- Some modern spaces are acoustically so poor that mikes are used to reinforce all parts of the voice on stage. The actors are

not individually miked but there is general cover. Again, this doesn't mean the actor can relax. You are being aided to combat a dead space, all your voice work should be in place and your full vocal energy activated. Equally important is the notion that you might be receiving help to be audible in space, but you still have to be physically open in order to fill the space. I have seen so many actors fill a space technically, but not with their physical presence, their imagination or their emotional life. You can never get blasé.

- The same principles apply to television or film. Yes, you are being miked, but you still have to communicate and follow through with your voice and speech. You won't need as much power, but you do need to sustain lines and be clear. The mike is not a magician. I have often been called to a film set in order to make some young, inexperienced actor sound clear. Clarity has to be there for the mike to pick it up.

- Generally, the inexperienced actor relaxes on a microphone to such an extent that he forgets to support, articulate and sustain the thoughts and words. Nothing can be done as nothing is there to be captured – even by the most advanced technology. Microphones boost the voice, they don't enhance a technique or cover your shortcomings. In fact, they expose them.

- Remember that when you are miked, a technician is controlling your audibility, not you. This awareness is of paramount concern when you are teching a show. Get your sound levels right at the technical rehearsal. It is unwise to be marking your voice as the level is set. It is always hard to hear or monitor your voice when it's miked; so as the level is set, feel what technical requirements are needed. That is the level of support, the energy of the voice and the sustaining required to fill the theatre and deliver the speech with clarity.

  I recently had to reprimand a musical company at the Royal National Theatre because many had relaxed into the run and assumed the amplification would carry their voices. The leading company members who had worked with amplification before complained to me that they couldn't hear their fellow actors. The actors at fault had gone off voice and were just relying on technology to boost their performance. Your usual monitoring devices – those you use when you are not miked – will have to be readjusted. You will have to feel, not hear, whether you are filling a space.

- Many actors complain about the shock of being wired up on-stage and losing all acting contact with other actors. Amplification alters your relationship with and proximity to other performers in order to avoid feedback. What was a nicely understood scene in the rehearsal room can suddenly become strangely disconnected and distant. You hear each other differently and the scene suddenly distanced could force a delayed reaction from the performer which is all at once out of synch. Build this awareness into early rehearsals.

- The other factor which can bewilder you is the presence of a pack on your body, wires and either a mike in your hairpiece or just below your throat. This can be awful for a dancer or singer, but take comfort, the mikes are getting better and smaller and are no longer distorted by sweat. They used to whistle and hiss as the body heat rose. Also be aware that you do not control whether they are switched on or off. Stories about miked actors going off-stage to the toilet or saying something derogatory about the director abound in theatre.

- Probably the most problematic mike you can use is the hand-held or stand mike. This requires a slight juggling act in terms of focus. You have to breathe to the mike. Place your hand up as though it's a hand mike – breathe to it. That's the breath you need in order to speak. But you have to reach out beyond that in your imagination. If you don't, you will not make contact with the audience. Yet if you breathe beyond the mike you'll blow them all away with the power of your voice. Like everything else, microphone technique takes practice!

- Radio mikes are equally sophisticated, with great technicians balancing you, but consider this. On radio we can't see your face so a whole area of communication is cut down. You must consider a richer, more expressive voice to compensate for this loss of physical presence and you will have to pace more carefully with extra time for the text to filter into the listener's ear. Radio acting demands vocal presence.

Trouble-shooting Problems

Even the most successful and carefully trained actor will have problems with his or her voice from time to time. Actors need their voices and come to know them so well that they will suspect something wrong long before an audience does. Fellow actors or doctors could hear the difference, but not an audience. When an experienced actor complains about her voice, it has to be taken seriously and investigated.

If you have a regular routine of working out and warming up, voice problems will become instantly detected. Analyse where and how the exercises are different. What is not working? The simpler the exercise, the more apparent the hiccup will be. A gentle release on a 'ha' or humming down through the range will reveal any vocal problems on the folds or vocal cords. A simple floor breath exercise – breathing in and out but waiting for the breath between inhalation and exhalation – will often expose any breath holds. Standing for some minutes in the centred, ready state will often tell you of any body tension or misalignments.

These are all checks to clarify any physical problems with the voice. If you are still worried about your voice, run these further checks:

- Try to understand what is going wrong physically. Don't be surprised if you uncover tensions way down the line. The voice is a jigsaw puzzle and the root of a problem could be well removed from its original manifestation and might be one you've never had before or something that results from an injury or recent illness.
- Check your known habits first. But because they're known, you are probably keeping them at bay. Then go into new territory if the habits are not the cause.
- Run the standard checks for tightness in shoulders, jaw, back of tongue, spine, knees, rib-cage, abdominal muscles
- Check your range. Has some of it gone or is it less firm?
- Do you have more mucus than usual?
- In the morning, everything that is wrong will be heightened.

Then think of the cause. As you do these checks, remember that some events in life will only manifest themselves months later in your voice.

- Have you been ill? A bad dose of flu can weaken your support and play havoc with your voice weeks after you've recovered. Diet. Have you changed what you eat? Losing weight can weaken the support and the voice, but if you are eating different food you might be clogging the voice (e.g. dairy foods will create mucus).

- Have you taken up a new sport? A young actor recently worked with me, as his voice was suddenly failing. It turned out that he had started working out with weights which were tightening his shoulders and his throat. The problem was solved by doing extensive release work after a work-out at the gym.
- Are you taking new medication? Penicillin can dry the voice. Any drug will have a knock-on effect and will, in some way, affect your voice.
- Trauma. Obviously this will invade your voice but maybe only months after the event. An actress worked with me recently whose voice had gone completely. Not a sound. Doctors were mystified. Because I knew her personally, I knew that nine months before this happened her mother had died. She had spent months 'coping', then her voice just went. As soon as she could connect the two events the voice began to return.
- Have you been working or living in unusual conditions? If your body is not used to air-conditioning that will immediately dry and impede the voice. An actor's voice failed and he was trying to find the cause. It turned out his house was being reconstructed and he was breathing in plaster dust.
- Have your sleep patterns altered?
- Have you been socializing differently? Noisy parties, heavy drinking, or going out with a heavy smoker?
- I worked with a very good actor whose speech wasn't as easy as he was used to. I know he was hiding something and he eventually admitted having dentures fitted a year before. Of course the trouble started then, but he was too embarrassed to admit this.

The more you use your voice, the quicker you will know when something is up and it will also remain healthier. The voice likes being used. You gain nothing from 'saving it'. It does need rest, however, from prolonged use, like two hours on-stage. For this reason, the more successful the actor, generally, the less vocal trouble-shooting is needed. Success breeds confidence and confidence is a great boost to the voice. When successful actors work on their voices with me, they are extending their work, not repairing it.

It is often different when less successful actors come for work. They might be blaming their lack of confidence or success on their voices. They don't get work, they think, because of their voices. But the voice fails because it never gets worked properly. Unlike many art forms, an actor always has the hope of the big break. Dancers, singers and musicians generally know by a certain age whether they will make it or not. Actors have the example of many who made it late in life. This possibility keeps them plodding on in the business long after they've lost enthusiasm and the will to work at their craft.

To a certain extent, the 'big break' is a myth. Actors who achieve success late in careers are ones who, in some way, have been constantly working. I will always remember some American actors describing a wonderful new British actor whom they had seen in a film. This newcomer had, in their opinion, finally got her 'big break' and was cited as an example of an older actor who made it at last. The newcomer turned out to be the late Dame Peggy Ashcroft! Actors hitting the headlines later in their lives have been working away for years, developing their craft and doing the work.

The Ageing Voice

Voices do age. The extent of ageing will depend on many factors such as physical and mental fitness. When physical support weakens, the voice will age. Posture, general wear and tear from life-style, alcohol, smoke and drugs over many years will begin to take a toll and increase the signs of vocal ageing. Loss of hearing will affect the voice long before it has physically aged.

Most actors who have used their voices properly over many years do not necessarily suffer the effects of an ageing voice. Memory loss and physical weakness retires them long before vocal problems. The huge advantage of years of work behind the voice means that older actors use their voices so economically and efficiently that they fare much better than younger, less experienced actors. Most actors who are working in their eighties are clearer and more vocally flexible than actors fifty years younger. I have occasionally trained an actor starting in theatre in his or her sixties. It is possible to train the voice to a point, although certain areas will probably be less flexible, particularly if the voice hasn't been used in an extended way for years. I remember working with two actors, both in their sixties. One had retired from accountancy and had decided to act. The other had been a builder and handed the business over to his son. The builder was fitter, but his voice was never going to be enormously flexible. The retired accountant had been an amateur actor since he was eighteen, performing in five or six shows a year. His voice was well oiled and actually achieved maximum flexibility.

The Actor's Life-style

An actor's working life can mean that he is using his voice from 10.30 in the morning to 11.30 at night, with only a few short breaks in the work cycle. In this time span he is not just using his voice for conversation but is working in a very extended way, in a large space, speaking an emotionally charged text in an unsympathetic environment (rehearsal rooms and theatres are often dry, which is very destructive for the voice). These conditions would not be tolerated by opera singers, but actors plod on with only the occasional moan.

Directors will often be asking for technically demanding vocal extensions again and again, and to fulfil the director's will, actors use their voices in unnatural ways; we don't normally scream for hours on end, for example.

Actors will probably eat late at night after the show and consequently suffer indigestion which will cause reflux, a common cause of vocal problems.

Performers tend to smoke and drink too much alcohol, coffee, tea and colas (probably to keep themselves energized and to combat nerves). All these things are terrible for the general health of the voice. The non-smoking actors may have to work alongside, or worse, share a dressing-room with a smoker: always a great point of contention among company members. Actors are sociable animals. They like to go out and mix after the show. They feel they have to 'come down' and will also feel the added pressure of socializing to help promote their careers. A lot of business is done at parties. All this socializing takes place in smoky, noisy and dry places, accompanied by the consumption of alcohol: a wonderful cocktail for vocal abuse!

Many actors are frightened of never working after their present job. This inbuilt fear leads them never to admit to illness, or miss a rehearsal or, worse, a show. They don't want to have a reputation for being unreliable and consequently they will work through illness, physical injury, emotional trauma and bereavement without complaint and are then horrified when their voices go.

An actor's voice is her living, her pay cheque. Many actors will focus all their fears and insecurities onto their voices. A dancer worries about her body, a pianist about his hands, an actor her voice. An actor knows a great deal about his or her own voice. They know when something is wrong and will only go to a doctor as a last resort. I know there are wonderful doctors and voice and speech therapists around but I do have to report that many actors mistrust the medical profession where their voice is concerned. They have two major categories of complaint. One is that the doctor doesn't always understand what they have to achieve with their voices and the work they put into it. A voice might be functioning very well for a non-professional user, but that is not good enough for an actor speaking or singing in a large theatre eight times a week. A second concern is that they have worked on their voices over many years and find it difficult to hand them over to practitioners who can't use their own voices as well as they can.

I remember being at a voice conference when an American voice coach and a close colleague made the above point to a hall full of medical authorities on the voice. She nearly created a riot and it took great courage for her to stay on the platform. She had touched a sore point. Two revealing results arose from her comments. As the week proceeded and she and I lectured on actors and their voices, most medical people had no idea how much work and knowledge went into an actor's training – hours, weeks and years of concentrated work. Secondly, she and I sat through lecture after lecture listening to medical voice experts speaking with the help of a microphone and still not being clear or audible!

Daily Prevention of Vocal Problems

Drink water to keep you hydrated. You will need at least a litre a day. The drier the building, the more air-conditioned it is, the greater the intake of water will be required. The sign of a well-hydrated voice is pale urine. The darker the colour, the more problems will arise using the voice. Remember, iced water will cool down a warmed-up voice. Drink water (preferably bottled) at room temperature.

Give up smoking! If you really can't, at least cut down. The evidence is overwhelming: smoking will endanger your voice as well as your life. After stopping, you will have up to two months struggling with a lot of loosening mucus so the voice might initially feel weaker and less clear, but persevere as it will clear after some weeks and you will uncover a new, freer and more flexible voice. Marijuana burns at a very high temperature, which is not useful to the vocal folds. I am not condoning its use, but if you must smoke it do so through water using a hookah. Herb cigarettes are used by many actors to replace the real thing on the stage. Be aware that they also burn at a high temperature so the voice is under threat. Water and steam can balance this effect.

Avoid eating a heavy meal late at night. If you must eat late, avoid red meat, dairy or fatty foods. After drinking alcohol at night, drink a fair quantity of water. Red wine and beer create more mucus than any other alcoholic drinks. Cut down on full-fat dairy products. They can actually clog the voice. Cut down on tea, coffee and cola-type drinks before performing. Herb teas and hot water with lemon can be useful to drink before going on with a cold or sore throat.

Warm up the voice before rehearsal and performance. A few minutes will make all the difference. Steam frees the voice. A hot shower or bath, or even holding your head over a bowl of hot water, will rapidly rehydrate or rejuvenate the voice. Air travel really dehydrates your voice. Apart from that, you are travelling amid a lot of noise so conversations on planes can be abusive to the voice. If you are travelling to perform, drink large quantities of water, keep chat to a minimum and, when you get to your destination, steam the voice. Even a hot shower on arrival will help.

If you sleep in a centrally heated bedroom, have water in the room to keep some moisture in the air.

Acting in smoke, cosmetic dust or pyrotechnics will also dry the voice and it will need some extra hydrating.

Avoid whispering, particularly if you are trying to save your voice. It doesn't help, in fact it traumatizes the voice more. The more you support and stay on your voice in everyday contexts, the healthier it will be.

Some people have a habit of clearing the voice. This is not good. Try to avoid this by keeping the throat more relaxed and swallowing.

Painkillers of all sorts, from booze to pills, are always problematic because pain is one of those warning signs from your body. Take note of any signals. Avoid taking aspirin for colds and sore throats; choose a painkiller without aspirin. Medicines that contain mucus-drying ingredients such as menthol and eucalyptus will dry you.

They are useful to take when you are not performing but can prove another hindrance to the voice if used a couple of hours before the show. All drugs, like cocaine, will eventually erode your voice and to keep up with the abuse you will have to resort to more and more concentrated vocal technique. I do know actors who spend hundreds of pounds a year on voice coaching just to balance the effects of their habits! Remember the adrenalin of a show might mean you don't recognize the problems or damage until the morning.

An increase in mucus is often a warning sign that vocal abuse has taken place. The colour of the mucus is important. An infection will produce mucus coloured from light yellow to green but if the mucus is clear, then it might mean vocal problems.

Lastly, remember that your voice is linked to the whole of your body, emotional life and psyche. Any physical injury could show up somewhere along the line in your voice. Here's a list of injuries that regularly find their way to stop or impede your breath or voice: jaw or dental work; neck or spine injuries; injuries to the shoulders or rib-cage, which will weaken the support; throat infections could get worse.

All these are obvious kinds of injuries that will get into your voice rapidly, often within days. Less obvious ones are: foot, knee or hip injuries; operations around the stomach area; a bad bout of diarrhoea which will weaken the breath support muscles; severe menstrual pain. Any debilitating illness weakens the whole breath system and will create voice difficulties.

Emotional trauma will show up in the voice, particularly if you try to work through it without acknowledging its existence. Even an awareness of emotional pain can troubleshoot the large fall-out. Again, it might not lodge in the voice until some time later.

Warning signs that must never be ignored:

- Pain in the throat, particularly if you haven't a cold or similar infection. Don't insist in pushing through that pain, stop and consider before being a dutiful actor!
- Pain as you speak.
- Pain as you swallow.
- The voice tiring more easily than before.
- A hoarse or scratchy voice that isn't connected to an infection.
- The voice changing pitch rapidly, swooping or staying stuck in one area.
- Taking much longer to warm up and the warm-up being full of discomfort.
- Complete or partial loss of voice.

None of the above necessarily means permanent problems with your voice, but be safe. Go to a doctor or better still insist on seeing a specialist – a laryngologist. You are not being a nuisance, you are protecting your career. Medical equipment is now so developed that anything pathologically wrong with your voice will be, in most instances, detected immediately. Wonderful results can now be obtained in healing a damaged voice, but again be prepared to fight and protect your voice. Never let a surgeon operate without a second opinion. Some of the greatest surgeons I know in this field who understand actors have other, less drastic, solutions.

A spell of silence can do wonders in healing an abused voice. And I mean silence. No whispering, which is very bad for the voice.

How to Go On with a Cold or Weakened Voice

If I know an actor has a bad infection or cold, that there is no real vocal damage and the laryngologist has given me complete assurance that the actor concerned won't hurt his voice, my job is to help the actor get through a performance safely. I am lucky to have good access to doctors and specialists and I would advise any voice coach to look about and get a strong medical team behind her to help assist any actor who is in trouble.

The thought that the voice might not work or be heard in front of an audience is, understandably, terrifying. This terror can produce the wrong instincts. In trying to save it, the actor will often choose not to support the voice – WRONG! Really connect to the support and use it. I often find that sick actors who do this will improve vocally during the show. If there is a chest infection you might find the support makes you cough more, but that's something you will have to deal with.

In any case, get the stage managers to have water in the wings or, better still, on the set, so you can get to a drink if it becomes too awful. Don't go with the instinct that encourages you to push in order to get an ill voice across space. Instead, place the voice above any soreness; normally this will mean a light placing in the head. Use a lot more articulation. In this way you are replacing the work from the throat into the head and the muscles of articulation.

If the theatre has a good sound system, a body mike would be useful. It will take the pressure off you to produce volume. Many actors balk at this idea but I promise it need only be used and switched on by a technician if you suddenly become inaudible or under pressure. One of the major advantages of using a mike like this is that it removes a physiological block and I've often experienced an ill actor being wired up and then performing audibly, without ever having to use the mike.

Another method of releasing pressure on an actor before he has to perform is to have the front-of-house manager tell the audience before curtain-up that the actor may be ill. The audience then knows what's going on and if the actor is making strange sounds they will be forgiving. Audiences love that kind of announcement because it lets them into an acting secret and, in a strange way, knowing that the actor is human, they appreciate the performance even more.

During the performance, apart from using support, placing the voice and using extra articulation, you can help yourself by getting the breath as low as possible, with the jaws and shoulders free, knees unlocked and head well placed. You might have to make a few compromises if you are performing with a strong physical transformation or alter your costume slightly if it is impeding you too much. Pace yourself.

If you sense you can't get the volume or range normal, go for the intensity of the word and focus your voice into the mask of the face.

Don't be too hard on yourself if your work feels below your normal level of dedication. You are ill! Go home, not to the bar, drink water, keep warm and sleep. Avoid taking aspirin for colds and sore throats; choose a painkiller without aspirin.

Index